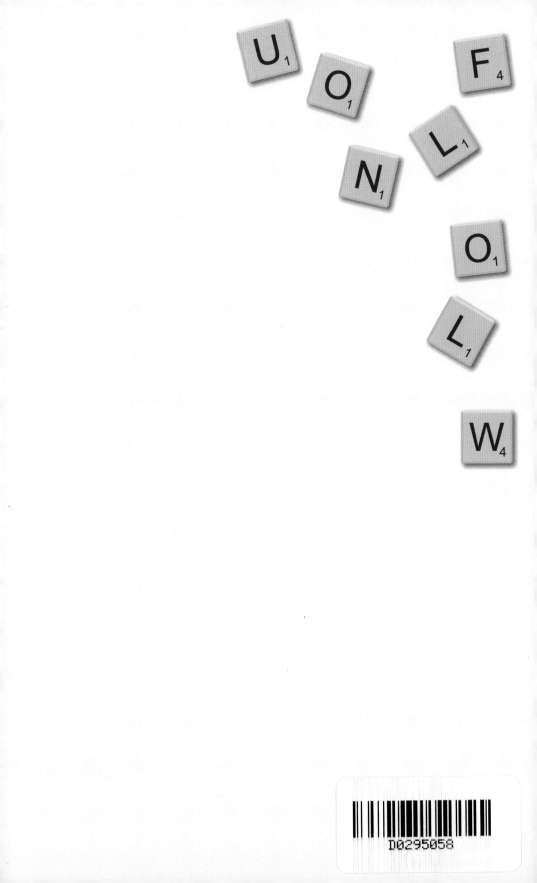

UNFOLLOW

UNFOLLOW:

A Journey from Hatred to Hope,
Leaving the Westboro Baptist Church

Megan Phelps-Roper

riverrun

First published in the United States in 2019 by Farrar, Straus and Giroux
First published in Great Britain in 2019 by

riverrun

an imprint of
Quercus Editions Ltd
Carmelite House
50 Victoria Embankment
London EC4Y 0DZ

An Hachette UK company

A CIP catalogue record for this book is available
from the British Library

HB ISBN 978 1 78747 800 8
TPB ISBN 978 1 78747 799 5
EBOOK ISBN 978 1 78747 798 8

Every effort has been made to contact copyright holders.
However, the publishers will be glad to rectify in future editions
any inadvertent omissions brought to their attention.

10 9 8 7 6 5 4 3 2 1

Printed and bound in Great Britain by Clays Ltd, Elcograf S.p.A.

Papers used by Quercus Editions Ltd are from well-managed forests and other responsible sources.

To my beloved parents, Shirley and Brent, whose tenderness fills my memories. I left the church, but never you—and never will. I am humbled to be your daughter.

Reserving judgments is a matter of infinite hope.
—F. Scott Fitzgerald, *The Great Gatsby*

Contents

UNFOLLOW

1. The Quarrel of the Covenant

If a mother thinks something is important enough to take a public position about, shouldn't she teach her children that value? Where else should children be at the time of public debate? At the local video arcade? I don't think we should pretend that these vital issues don't affect children.
—Shirley Phelps-Roper, letter to the editor, *Topeka Capital Journal*,
August 26, 1991

I didn't understand what was going on, not at first. The signs simply appeared one day and never left, like some undeniable force of nature. I'd guess Topekans experienced their arrival that way, as well. My mother's family had been a well-known and polarizing presence in the city for decades—but in my memory, the picketing is the beginning, and it started at Gage Park.

It sure didn't look like a park to me. There were no swings or slides or jungle gyms—just an open field that separated the place where we parked from the busy intersection of 10th Street and Gage Boulevard. As pastor of the tiny Westboro Baptist Church, my grandfather would drive the big red pickup filled with signs he'd made, and the rest of the church—consisting almost entirely of my aunts, uncles, cousins, parents, grandparents, and siblings—would follow in a caravan of vehicles. I couldn't read the messages Gramps had carefully written since I was still a few months shy of kindergarten, but when I saw photos as a teenager, I was surprised by how small and restrained some were compared to what came later: WATCH YOUR KIDS! GAYS IN RESTRMS.

The adults would pick up as many signs as they could carry, walk them across the field, and lean them against the trunks of the two biggest trees. The rest of us just had to walk by and grab one. During those first few months—June, July, August of 1991—our habit was to hold our signs and walk in a big circle just next to the roadway, cars whizzing by in all four lanes of traffic. The baseball hats my dad made us wear always gave me headaches, but I was glad to have them once I was out there walking in the heavy afternoon heat.

As I got older, I came to learn the story of Gage Park and the events that prompted our first protests. In the summer of 1989, two years before we started picketing, Gramps had been biking through the park with my brother Josh, who wasn't quite five years old at the time. My grandfather's custom was to ride ahead a bit, and then circle back—ride ahead, and circle back. One of the times he did so, he thought he saw two men approaching my brother, apparently attempting to lure him into the wooded area shrouded by bushes at the southwest corner of the park. Alarmed and livid, Gramps got to work. He spoke with one park official who told him, "At any hour of the day or night, male couples may be seen entering and exiting the area." The official also mentioned that he regularly passed along citizen complaints to his superiors—but to no avail. My grandfather soon discovered that sex in the park was a well-documented issue in the local media; sting operations conducted by the Topeka Police Department had resulted in a string of high-profile arrests over the years. A nationally circulated gay and lesbian travel guide listed the park as a "cruisy area"—a place where men could cruise for anonymous sex. Even now, Gage Park is listed in that guide, though a warning was added shortly after Westboro's picketing began: AYOR. *At your own risk.*

Armed with this information, my grandfather took action. He began by detailing his findings in a letter to the mayor, opening with a colorful description of the problem ("A malodorous sore with the scab off is open and running at the extreme southwest corner of Gage Park") and concluding with a question: "Do you think Gage Park's running sore could be permanently fixed? Your consideration is appreciated."

The mayor's response acknowledged that the city of Topeka was "well aware of the situation" at the park, and that they were "in the process of putting together a program to bring the situation to a halt." Nearly two years passed, during which time my grandfather monitored the situation, with no apparent improvement. He continued to write letters to city officials and to appear regularly at city council meetings, insisting that they clean up the park. According to church lore, my grandfather accused city officials of "sitting around like last year's Christmas trees" during one such meeting—at which point the mayor instructed the police to escort my grandfather out of the council chambers.

Convinced that the city would persist in its idleness, Gramps decided that we would take to the streets and demand that it take action.

In hindsight, our protests were bound to elicit an intensely negative reaction—especially because our message went far beyond calls for the cleanup of Gage Park. Gramps was an "Old School Baptist," he said, and was determined to represent the Scriptural position on homosexuality. He leapt immediately into attacks on the gay community as a whole, blaming them for the AIDS epidemic and proclaiming that they deserved the death penalty. The *Topeka Capital Journal* published many Westboro letters, including one signed by one of my aunts comparing the United States to Sodom and Gomorrah, cities destroyed by God "[b]ecause of their sin regarding homosexuality." She declared AIDS to be "a disease for which the homosexual must take the sole blame" and insisted that the blood of straight AIDS victims "should be avenged upon those guilty of introducing and gleefully spreading this deadly disease: the homosexual." Even during an era in which disapproval of LGBT people was more common and socially acceptable, it took only four short sentences for my aunt to make claims scandalous enough to outrage most readers—and our signs managed to do the same with even greater economy. MILITANT GAYS SPREAD AIDS. EXPOSE GAY-AIDS PLOY. GAYS ARE WORTHY OF DEATH (ROM. 1:32) = AIDS. And soon enough, what would become our most infamous message: GOD HATES FAGS.

The community response to our protests would mystify me for years, thanks to an ignorance borne both of youth and of the religious education I was receiving at home. I was five years old when the picketing began, and I didn't understand why anyone would reject our

message, let alone why our protests would draw counterprotesters—
"counters." They came every week in the beginning, and I was scared
of them at first. "Young punks" and "diseased, probably got AIDS,"
Gramps would say. The Bible forbade girls to cut our hair, but some
of their women came out with cropped manes colored bright reds and
blues and purples—"Kool-Aid hair"—and with metal in their faces.
There were boys with mullets, others with half their heads shaved and
the other half covered by long black hair that hung in greasy strands
across ugly faces. Some looked like my dad, tall and skinny in tank
tops and the awfully short running shorts in style at the time, and
some were fat and bearded, combat boots on their feet and flannel
shirts tied around their waists. They'd come out in angry mobs—fifty,
a hundred, more and less—and try to surround our group of about
thirty, starting fistfights with the Westboro dads who made a human
barrier between us and them. Sometimes there were cops and sometimes there were handcuffs and sometimes we were in them—which
wasn't fair, I thought, because we were just trying to protect ourselves
from those "ruffians." I held my breath whenever I walked by them,
so I wouldn't catch whatever it was that was making them such awful
people.

The counters would urge drivers to honk and yell and flip us off,
which they did en masse. *"Hatemongers!" "Nazis!" "Go home!" "Get a
job!" "What the fuck is wrong with you?" "I'm gonna kick the shit outta
you!"* They threw eggs and beer and big plastic Pepsi bottles filled with
urine as they sped off down the road. Drivers and passengers would
sometimes abandon their vehicles in the middle of the street, car doors
hanging wide open, and cross lanes of traffic to come after us on foot.
My cousins and I would scuttle away, back behind Mom or an aunt
who stepped between us and them. From behind my sign, I watched
them approach us to hit and threaten and shove and bellow and spit
and grab for our signs, our bodies, our hair. The police rarely seemed
to help, but my parents kept us safe. Still, I was alarmed and angry.
How dare they, I raged. *That's my mom!* What made them think they
could do this to us? Why weren't the cops stopping them?

But my grandfather had a different perspective on the opposition
and scorn we faced: it was proof that God was with us. He would quote
Jesus, who warned his disciples to expect the hatred of the world: *If the*

world hate you, ye know that it hated me before it hated you. If ye were of the world, the world would love his own: but because ye are not of the world, but I have chosen you out of the world, therefore the world hateth you. "In fact," Gramps would roar during his Sunday sermons, "I'd be supremely afraid if the people of this evil city *were* on our side!" *Woe unto you, when all men shall speak well of you! for so did their fathers to the false prophets.*

Musical combat became an important front in the battle for Gage Park, and this was one that I relished: I was too small to physically defend the church against our opponents, but by God I was gonna make myself heard. While they were chanting things like *Two, four, six, eight, Phelps is always spreading hate*, we would sing hymns or this new song Gramps had written, upbeat and so catchy. It was a parody of Gene Autry's "Back in the Saddle Again," and because the first and final lines had the same melody, we could sing it in a loop without end. The end of one verse was the beginning of the next.

> *Get back in the closet again!*
> *Back where a sin is a sin*
> *Where the filthy faggots dwell*
> *While they're on their way to Hell*
> *Get back in the closet again!*

As time wore on, the counterprotesters' will to battle us on the streets dissipated along with their numbers. We began to find ourselves alone on the sidewalks. Still, Gramps didn't take victory for granted. Rain or shine, Westboro members stood vigil along Gage Boulevard every day without fail. We soon wore a path into the lawn, one of the first marks our picketing made on the city of Topeka—this place where the grass suddenly shifted from green and lush to trampled and dead.

My grandfather's fervor was contagious, and I was proud to stand on the front lines with the church even if I didn't always understand the message. Yet the decline in direct opposition rendered pickets something of a slog for my young self, and boredom became my new enemy. On days when the counters were fewer and less violent, I'd scan the ground beneath my feet for anything interesting as I walked. Once, there was a small brown mass beside the circle, flies buzzing all around it, and I spent nearly the whole picket trying to figure out what it was. A dead squirrel, I finally realized, making out its once-fluffy tail, now flattened and matted with blood. I was glad the picket was almost over—had it been an hour? Two?—and I reported to Dad, who kicked it away so I wouldn't have to watch the carcass decay. We'd be coming back.

From the time we first brought our signs to Gage Park, my mom was my most important interlocutor. She spent a lot of time answering questions from my siblings and me, trying to explain what was going on out there: why we were picketing, why everyone was so angry, what it all meant. She had my older brothers, Sam and Josh, memorizing the last fifteen verses of Romans chapter 1—a task I was spared because of my age, but I still managed to get a lot of it down: *And likewise also the men, leaving the natural use of the woman, burned in their lust one toward another; men with men working that which is unseemly.* The only part of my mother's explanation that really got through to me in the beginning, though, was the overarching theme of it all: that our lives were part of a never-ending struggle of the good guys against the bad. *The quarrel of the covenant.* This was the eternal conflict between the righteous and the wicked, and we would not back down.

———

As it turned out, the vast majority of the righteous had grown up at Westboro and were members of the Phelps family. My father, Brent Roper, was one of the few who didn't fit this profile: He had grown up Episcopalian. He'd been best friends with my mom's youngest brother in high school, and as he came to know my mother's family, he found himself compelled by them. A Tom Petty–loving skateboard stunt-man, he ended up converting and joining Westboro when he was just sixteen. It was a big decision. Though the church's anti-gay protesting was still more than a decade off, its pastor was already a controversial figure: armed with a law degree, righteous indignation, and unwavering antagonism, Gramps had a habit of collecting powerful enemies wherever he went.

My father had seen another side of the family, though. He loved how tight-knit they were, their love and willingness to sacrifice for one another, their dedication to complete fidelity to the Scriptures. Shortly after joining the church, my father took a job at Phelps-Chartered, the family law firm. He would later credit his successful career in human resources to his time working there in his teens and early twenties. The Phelps family taught him diligence, he said—responsibility and a proper work ethic.

He fell in love with my mother, and they married a short four years after he joined the church, when he was twenty and she twenty-six. But only after he'd proved himself worthy to Gramps.

My grandfather demanded that all thirteen of his children *and* their spouses attend law school and continue the family business, but my mom had always had a special position at the firm. She was dearly beloved by her father, and they'd had a unique relationship from the time she was young. She and Gramps began to work closely together when my mom was just fourteen—and of the seven eldest Phelps children, my mom was the only one who would never abandon the church to *enjoy the pleasures of sin for a season.* She urgently took to heart a saying that her father repeated often: "The best ability is *dependability.*" As a result, her parents leaned on her more than any of her brothers and sisters, and she was entrusted with ever greater responsibility: keeping her siblings in line, managing the law office, taking care of the finances, and more. She learned to run a tight ship, to never settle on her lees. There was *always* something more to accomplish, and my mother was dedicated to doing it all.

In order to secure my grandfather's permission to marry my mother, my dad finished high school, worked at the law office while completing a four-year bachelor's degree in just two and a half years, and, as he told it, narrowly beat out my uncle Tim to get the last available spot in Washburn University's law school class that year. Neither my mother's pace nor my father's slowed after they married. "I hope you will have the joy of the promise of Psalm 127," Gramps told my parents at their wedding. *"As arrows are in the hand of a mighty man; so are children of the youth. Happy is the man that hath his quiver full of them: they shall not be ashamed, but they shall speak with the enemies in the gate."* It was expected that there would be many children, and it was also expected that those children would be provided for. Understanding this, my father continued working his way through school—next up, an MBA program—and, almost out of thin air, created for himself a second career as an author writing textbooks about legal software and law office management.

Meanwhile, my mother managed the Phelps law firm and cared for our growing family. Her role in the church was ever-expanding, as well. She gave interviews to reporters, organized cross-country picket trips and the scheduling for the whole congregation: the daily pickets in Topeka, the mowing, the daycare, the weekly church cleanings, the monthly birthday parties—her contributions were without end. The dynamics of my parents' marriage never fit with the paradigm commonly associated with conservative Christianity: that of an authoritarian father dictating to a mealy-mouthed mother who just needed to stay in her place and recognize that her husband always knew better. Wifely subjection was certainly in the Bible, but in practice, my parents operated as a team. My father couldn't have been further from authoritarian—gentle, intelligent, hard-working, so respectful of my mother's thoughts, and so undeniably in love with her—and my mother couldn't have been further from mealy-mouthed. My father never weaponized his husband status to demand my mother's silence or obedience, and their mutual respect was an example for all. My parents had each found a perfect counterpart in the other, and even Gramps—who hadn't wanted to believe *anyone* could be worthy of my mother—was impressed.

By the time my dad finished law school, there were three of us kids: my two older brothers, Sam and Josh, and then me. Over the next sixteen years, eight more children would be born into the Phelps-Roper household. It took me several years to stop shaking my head in bewilderment each time someone would ask "Are you Catholic?" upon learning that I was one of six, seven, eight, nine children. Birth control wasn't something I realized was even possible, let alone widely practiced. I just knew the verses. *Lo, children are an heritage of the Lord: and the fruit of the womb is his reward.*

"The womb business is *God's* business," Mom summarized. "You can't outsmart the Lord!"

The Catholic stance against artificial contraception was a relatively fringe position, but—in a pattern that would extend to virtually every aspect of our lives—Westboro Baptist Church was prepared to take it even further, to the letter of the Scriptures as we understood them.

And when the Lord saw that Leah was hated, he opened her womb: but Rachel was barren. It was for God alone to give or withhold children, and even the "natural family planning" endorsed by Catholics was unacceptable. The single time I heard about an aunt of mine attempting to defy God and "counting the days" to avoid pregnancy, it was in the context of her *mis*counting. She and her husband had been struggling to provide for the six children they had already, but when she'd tried to take matters into her own hands, she'd ended up pregnant with twins. God was teaching her a lesson, my mother said, because my aunt had failed to trust Him. It wasn't for her to decide when or how many children to have, it wasn't for her to have any feeling or opinion on the matter at all, except to be grateful to the Lord for each one.

And oh, was my mama grateful. I remember feeling it most in the music, when she would sing to us, always singing. Before I turned five and had to join in with the rank and file for Saturday morning cleaning marathons, my little sister Bekah and I would dance on matching window seats in the living room, mouthing along as Christopher Cross or Fleetwood Mac blared from the big stereo while the others cleaned. Dad would pick us up and twirl us around, and Mom would sashay over with a dusting rag in one hand and a can of Pledge in the other— that sickly sweet scent of chemical lemons filtering through the whole house—and she'd lean in to kiss our cheeks, serenading us at the top of her voice: "No, I will never be the same without your love / I'll live alone, try so hard to rise above." This was the same era in which I sat just to her left during church, when she belted out the hymns so high and so loud that it hurt my ears. I discovered that to protect myself from the sonic onslaught, I could stick a finger into my left ear, press myself into my mother's side, and listen to her sing from *inside her body*. It was so soothing, the warmth and the vibrations and the feeling of her arm holding me close as I tucked into her. I didn't know then that this special place at her side would always be mine. That as her eldest daughter, I would become to her what she had become to her father—and as that relationship had defined my mother, so this one would define me. *For I was tender and only beloved in the sight of my mother.*

Samuel. Joshua. Megan. Rebekah. Isaiah. Zacharias. Grace. Gabriel. Jonah. Noah. Luke.

Sam. Josh. Meg. Bek. Zay. Zach. Grace. Gabe. Jonah. Noah. Luke.

SamJoshMegBekZayZachGraceGabeJonahNoahLuke.

It would be entirely reasonable to expect that my mother's dedication to *doing it all* might wane with the birth of each additional child, that it would be impossible for her to maintain that commitment to having her children, her legal career, *and* her work for our church. Instead, the opposite was true. As our family swelled with each passing year, so, too, did the church's profile and the added pressure we all faced as a result. I've never known another woman who could have stood up under the strain of the burden my mother carried, not without collapsing under the weight of it. She had an inexhaustible supply of strength, tenacity, and resourcefulness—whose origins, it seemed to me, must surely have been divine.

—

Soon after our initial protests at Gage Park, our war with the city of Topeka began to escalate. Every anti-Westboro effort they made only served to strengthen our resolve, and we answered each one by dramatically expanding the pace and variety of our pickets. Nearly two years in, we now targeted the newspaper (which regularly editorialized against us), the police department (which failed to protect us from the violent criminals who frequently came out to attack and threaten us), the city government (which worked to draft anti-picketing ordinances), many local churches (which joined the counterprotests against us), and any location related to any person who made any public statement against us or for gays.

Even our language had intensified. The word *gay* had disappeared entirely from our signs and vocabulary—a misnomer, Gramps said— and it was replaced by *fag*, a word that literally signified a bundle of sticks used for kindling. "*Fag* is an elegant metaphor!" Gramps insisted. "In the same way a literal *fag* is used to kindle the fires of nature, these metaphorical *fags* fuel the flames of Hell and the fires of God's wrath!" Of course, *fag* also had the added benefit of being scandalous and offensive, which only garnered more attention for our message.

One of the verses that Gramps quoted often included a command from God to *shew my people their transgression*—and as with the rest of the Bible, my grandfather took this literally. For my cousins and me, this resulted in a precocious knowledge of gay sex practices, at least insofar as they were presented by our pastor. Revulsion filled his voice as he spoke of gay people "anally copulating their brains out," and "suckin' around on each other, lickin' around on each other." He started adding stick figure depictions of anal sex to our picket signs, one man bent over in front of another. I could articulate the meanings of "scat," "rimming," and "golden showers" all before my eighth birthday, though I was loath to do so. To publicly accuse gays of these filthy behaviors would leave a girl open to challenge—"How do you know?"—and thus put her in the unenviable position of having to explain that it's in a book called *The Joys of Gay Sex* . . . which, no, she had not read . . . but her grandfather had told her about it . . . during church . . . from the pulpit.

"Golden showers" was a term featured in our parody of *The Twelve Days of Christmas*. On December evenings, I'd don my colorful winter coat, pick up a sign, and belt out the lyrics with gusto alongside my uncles and cousins, illuminated by streetlights or the glow of the marquee announcing *The Nutcracker* at the Topeka Performing Arts Center: "Five golden showers! Preparation H, three bloody rectums, two shaven gerbils, and a vat of K-Y Jelly!" I knew even then that this was transgressive, but there was something so delightful about it, so appealing: this sense that my family had some secret knowledge about the world, that we were not subject to its rules or its judgments. There might be an overabundance of regulations governing life within our own community, but the social niceties of the broader world held no sway over us in the context of the protests. In that respect, we were a law unto ourselves, and all bets were off as long as our words were justified by the Bible. Truth was an absolute defense against any and all claims made against us.

Unfortunately for us, it was not always an adequate defense.

One evening when I was seven, as my siblings and I cleaned up after dinner, there was the wail of a police siren, growing loud as it passed near our house and then fading. And then there was another. And another. My mother frowned. Our house sat just a block east of Gage Boulevard, one of the city's main thoroughfares, so sirens weren't especially unusual. For some reason, these ones were making her uneasy.

"Maybe it's our guys at the Vintage . . ."

The Vintage was a little restaurant advertising "Cocktails" and "Fine Foods" at the east end of a run-down shopping center just a few blocks from our house—targeted by Westboro because one of the managers was a lesbian serving on the Mayor's Gay and Lesbian Task Force. I had desperately wanted to picket the Vintage that Friday night, because my cousin Jael had told me she would be there. She was one of my best friends, but since we now attended different elementary schools and lived on different blocks, the most regular time I had with her was when we were protesting. Jael and I had this great routine whereby we'd grab a sign from the truck—her favorite was FAG GOD = RECTUM while I preferred FAG = AIDS with the skull and crossbones underneath—and then we'd plant ourselves somewhere on the picket line and chat it up for half an hour. She'd bring those little patriotic-looking packages of Bazooka Bubble Gum, and we'd chomp noisily while I taught her the lyrics to songs I'd learned from my big brother Sam ("Baby Got Back," "Santeria," etc.).

At the sound of the third siren, my mother's anxiety shifted to alarm and we took off in the family van. The scene in front of the Vintage was chaos, the small parking lot filled with curious bystand-ers, half a dozen patrol cars with red and blue flashing lights, EMTs, and cops taking statements from my aunts and uncles, and from mean-looking men in sweats. We'd been attacked again, I saw, but worse than usual. Dad and I stayed in the van while Mom jumped out to help. She picked up a sign lying askew on the ground, which I sounded out—ABSTINENCE NOT CONDOMS—but didn't understand. Here, my memory of staring out the van window gets fuzzy, fusing with images I got from photographs and home videos later: my uncle Tim, neck braced and nose bleeding, being treated by EMTs on the running board of a big red fire engine; my skinny cousin Ben, seventeen years old, strapped onto a gurney with a series of black belts, a white brace around his neck and a white strap across his forehead, his left hand outstretched to hold on to our aunt Margie. As Ben was being wheeled away, Margie seemed beside herself with outrage and grief. "*Never!*" she bellowed across the parking lot. "*Never.* We're never—gonna—stop—picketing!"

Sitting at our family Bible reading the next day, my mother explained it all. The "Jew lawyer" who owned the Vintage—the same guy we'd later see in a photo with his hands around my uncle's neck, choking him unconscious—had hired a dozen bouncers from his strip club to come and beat us up for picketing his restaurant. A local priest had witnessed the attack from the bank next door, and wrote a letter to the mayor: "The attackers walked with deliberate speed and apparent determination toward the picketers. Then I saw the signs falling like sunflowers being cut down by cornknifes and bodies being knocked down and into Gage Boulevard." Eight of our people were taken to the hospital that night. Three were teenagers.

As tensions with the city continued to mount in the months following what Gramps called "The Vintage Massacre," my mother helped me piece everything together. She liked for pickets to do double duty as preaching and exercise, so I'd listen to her stories as we walked the picket line from end to end. There was a new prosecutor in our county, my mom told me, a woman who had campaigned on the promise that she would get us off the streets. We were bad for the city, bad for its image, bad for commerce, bad for children, and she represented a community that was as determined to shut us up as we were to be heard.

Ever since this woman had taken office as district attorney, my mother explained, she was doing everything in her power to stop us. It was her encouragement that had the cops arresting us so often now, it was she who charged us with crimes we hadn't committed. And now people were attacking us more frequently because of her refusal to file charges when *we* were victims, like at the Vintage. The prosecutor had gotten search warrants so that sheriff's deputies could beat down the church doors with battering rams and confiscate our property—even though we hadn't done anything wrong and the officers had had to give it all back. They raided the law office, as well, even though the vast majority of Phelps-Chartered's work involved representing individual members of the public—criminal cases, personal injury, family law—and had nothing to do with Westboro. No matter how careful we were to follow the law, the DA could have us arrested, and Mom would have to run downtown and bail our loved ones out of jail again.

The attacks at Topeka protests and the vandalism of our homes grew worse during the term of that prosecutor. I woke up one summer morning and followed my mom into the backyard we shared with the church, only to find that it had been torn apart. There was patio furniture at the bottom of the pool, the seat cushions slashed open and strewn across the yard. The weights my uncle used to benchpress had been dropped and broken into heavy chunks. All of our garden hoses had been sliced open, and a huge gash in our beloved trampoline had rendered it worthless. As a kid, I was most frightened by the lacerated state of the trampoline; anyone who could do harm to such a beautiful object clearly would not hesitate to turn the knife on a person. Later on, someone did take a knife to my cousin's tiny Westie, nearly beheading the poor creature for being on the wrong picketer's property at the wrong time. Little April managed to pull through, but we took this as just another in a long line of violent criminal attacks we faced for lawfully standing on public sidewalks to preach the standards of God. Persecution in the purest sense of the word.

2. The Bounds of Our Habitation

Throughout my childhood, my mother was determined to make my siblings and me understand one idea above all: *We* were not in charge of our lives, but God—and that God ruled via the parents and elders He had set over us. Our duty was singular: to obey them. *Children, obey your parents in all things: for this is well pleasing unto the Lord.* Their power over us was absolute, and we would do well to accept that without question or protest. These were, as the New Testament put it, *the bounds of our habitation.* It was one of my mother's favorite phrases.

In Westboro's theology, obedience was about more than family life. My mother began trying to get this across to us as soon as we were old enough to understand words, and my earliest understanding of it came during a car ride we took together. I was settled in the backseat of our white Toyota Camry, with Bekah buckled into the seat next to me and our mother at the wheel. I think we were headed to or from the family law office, but some parts of the recollection are slippery—sometimes I look over and Bekah is in a car seat, sometimes not, sometimes it's winter, sometimes spring—so I can't be sure. What I do remember is that we were young enough to each have a Barbie doll in our laps, and that Mom was telling us about predestination.

My mother's ardent love for the Scriptures manifested itself in many ways, but it was especially apparent in the joy she took in teaching the Bible for its own sake—not when one of us had disobeyed and needed correction, but while she read and expounded upon the stories to us, taking care to make sure we understood the complexities as well as we could at any given age, going a little deeper each time we returned to the same story. *For precept must be upon precept, precept upon precept; line upon line, line upon line; here a little, and there a little.* She was revealing to us the secret ways in which the world worked, and Bekah and I were full of questions. In the car that day, we were trying for the first time—but certainly not the last—to wrap our young minds around the idea that everything we did, every word, every deed, every blink of an eye, beat of the heart, twitch of a muscle—all had been caused by God, *who worketh all things after the counsel of his own will.* My first response to this assertion was to do what I assume many people do upon discovering predestination: to make a split-second decision and suddenly shift course in an attempt to prove the idea false. With all my strength, I squeezed my fists into tiny balls, fingernails biting into my palms, and then released. Had God seen *that* coming? My eyes widened as I realized that the doctrine of predestination was impossible to thwart; God controlled even those impulsive flailings, even the impulses themselves. ("Unfalsifiability" was not yet a term in my repertoire, and so presented no difficulty for me at the time.)

Mom continued on, telling the story of Jacob and Esau to illustrate predestination. It wasn't the long version of their story from the Old Testament, of Jacob's deceit in securing the blessing of the firstborn and of Esau's vow of murderous revenge. Instead, our mother focused on the most salient part of their tale, found in the book of Romans: their fates. Jacob and Esau had been grandsons of the patriarch Abraham— *twin* grandsons, Mom stressed, as biologically similar as it was possible for two humans to be. "And *yet*! Before those two boys were even *born*, God loved Jacob and hated Esau. They hadn't done anything good or bad to deserve it. They were *still in their mother's womb*!" In the Bible, she told us, God is likened to a heavenly Potter, with humans as clay in His hands to mold as He pleases. *Cannot I do with you as this potter? saith the Lord. Behold, as the clay is in the potter's hand, so are ye in mine hand.* God had elected—chosen—the beloved Jacob for honor, to be welcomed into Heaven for an eternity of bliss. His twin brother, Esau, meanwhile, had been created to be condemned to Hellfire—all through no fault or cause of his own. *For the children being not yet born, neither having done any good or evil, that the purpose of God according to election might stand, not of works . . . As it is written, Jacob have I loved, but Esau have I hated.*

But Jacob and Esau weren't the only ones created with their fates predetermined, Mom continued. Indeed, these twins were the standing symbols of the two types of people living in the world: *the elect,* represented by Jacob, chosen by God for love, mercy, honor, glory; and *the reprobate,* represented by Esau, chosen by God for hatred, cruelty, wrath, destruction. Of all the people who had ever existed or ever would, only a precious few were God's elect. *Narrow is the way, which leadeth unto life, and few there be that find it.* The vast majority, both of the living and of the dead, were created for destruction. *For wide is the gate, and broad is the way, that leadeth to destruction, and many there be which go in thereat.* My mother must have been through this story over and over ad nauseam through the years, but she spoke as if it were the first time, her tone filled with impossible awe—as if she *still* couldn't believe the elegance of this scenario, as if the beauty of this divine truth could come only from the mind of God Himself.

I was puzzled. My mother seemed elated at something that sounded so dreadfully unfair: that God would create these two brothers to give mercy to one and cruelty to the other, when they had done nothing to deserve either. Of course, it wasn't the undeserved kindness that disturbed me—it was the hatred. Why would God make Esau for evil, and then send Esau to Hell for being evil? Wasn't God Himself responsible? It seemed wrong to condemn Esau for doing what God created him to do. When I piped up from the backseat to say so, Mom was only too pleased to go on. I had posed just the objection that the Apostle Paul addresses in his own account of the story: *Thou wilt say then unto me, Why doth {God} yet find fault? For who hath resisted his will?* If we are what God created us to be, how could it be just for Him to punish us?

In modern parlance, Paul's response to this question amounts to something like "Who the Hell are you, a wretched human being, to ask such a question?" That's an answer I would have understood, but my mother quoted the apostle's reply as given in the King James Version: *Nay but, O man, who art thou that repliest against God? Shall the thing formed say to him that formed it, Why hast thou made me thus?* Mom's

eyes met mine in the rearview mirror and I stared blankly. Searching for a way to help Bekah and me make sense of this conundrum,
her eyes lit up as they fell to the dolls in our laps. "It would be like
if those Barbies in your lap stood up and said, '*Why* did you dress me
this way?!'" Mom would always laugh heartily when she described our
reactions later: "Your eyes were as big as saucers, you two girls starin'
down at those Barbies like you were afraid they might actually get up
and start talkin' at you!" For decades, this would be my mother's go-
to illustration for those who dared question why God would design
most of humanity for the express purpose of tormenting them in Hell
for eternity. Our dolls demonstrated how patently ridiculous it was to
presume to ask such a question.

Although I took my mother's point about the Barbies' insolence,
a more pressing question had presented itself as she laughed at our
bug-eyed response to her hypothetical: What about *me*? Was I a Jacob
or an Esau? What about Bekah? What about Sam and Josh? How
could we know? From the driver's seat, Mom somberly explained that
we couldn't. That we wouldn't know for sure until we all stood before God at the Judgment. Her words filled me with dread, calling
forth a mental image of the whole world awaiting judgment at the feet
of God, standing at rapt attention like an army of the damned—and
me, standing among them. What could I do to avoid a ruinous outcome? Predestination, clearly, had not yet sunk into my little skull—of
course, I could do nothing to change my fate if God had chosen me for
Hell—but my mother understood my need for comfort. "It's a good
sign that you're afraid," she said. "It means that you care what God
requires of you." *Come, ye children, hearken unto me: I will teach you the
fear of the Lord.*

Many more years and innumerable Bible studies would pass before
I fully and practically appreciated the meaning of this doctrine—that
a person's goodness was a *symptom* of God's love, the effect of it, and not
the cause—but I soon found predestination an immediate and compelling motivator. Its power came from beauty and from terror, a conflu-
ence of two desires. There was the desire to be like Jacob, to be one of
God's *jewels*, with all the rarity, purity, and virtue that signified. *And
they shall be mine, saith the Lord of hosts, in that day when I make up my
jewels; and I will spare them, as a man spareth his own son that serveth him.*

And then there was the abject fear of being like the despised Esau, *before of old ordained to this condemnation.* We were powerless to alter our destiny, but the surest sign we could have that we were one of God's elect? Our obedience.

I came to love the clarity and simplicity of this idea, how directly the Scriptures connected obedience to goodness. It was even implicated in God's commandment to "love thy neighbor." *Thou shalt not hate thy brother in thine heart: thou shalt in any wise rebuke thy neighbour, and not suffer sin upon him. Thou shalt not avenge, nor bear any grudge against the children of thy people, but thou shalt love thy neighbour as thyself.* The context made it abundantly clear to us that to love our neighbor was to rebuke him, to warn him away from the sins that would result in punishment from God. If we failed to do so, the blood of the wicked would be on our hands. *When I say unto the wicked, Thou shalt surely die; and thou givest him not warning, nor speakest to warn the wicked from his wicked way, to save his life; the same wicked man shall die in his iniquity; but his blood will I require at thine hand.*

We had taken to the streets because we had a solemn duty to obey God and to plead with our neighbors to do the same. It didn't matter that the world hated the message. It didn't matter that it required vast amounts of our time, money, energy, resources. This was what God required of His elect.

Whatever it cost us, we would pay.

———

While our daily protests were an explosion of overt hostility between my family and the city, school was a subtler matter. The decision to send us to public school was due primarily to practical considerations: the adults needed to work in order to support their growing families and the church, which refused all (exceedingly rare) donations from nonmembers. But once it became clear that our protests would continue for years and decades to come, the elders came to a few additional conclusions. First, that our presence in public school classrooms was a testimony against the people of Topeka: though they accused us of being hateful, we were polite, friendly, well-behaved, and accomplished students. *Having your conversation honest among the Gentiles: that, whereas they speak against you as evildoers, they may by your good works, which they shall behold, glorify God in the day of visitation.* Our parents described us as "walking picket signs." They also weren't especially afraid that we would be unduly influenced by our peers or teachers, that we might be persuaded to doubt or question Westboro's teachings. The intensity of our daily religious education at home was a bulwark against such heresies.

Plus, they were in possession of divine truth. They weren't afraid of questions, because they had all the answers.

For my part, school seemed to be an elaborate play where each of the actors—teachers, classmates, parents—pretended not to notice that we were on opposite sides of an epic, spiritual battle between good and evil. It was a tenuous truce that relied heavily on the First Amendment: no matter how much they disagreed with us or how often we picketed their churches, teachers were agents of government and barred from punishing us for our religious activities. But more, it relied on mutual consent to keep up the pretense—our shared willingness not to speak, for instance, of the nine-foot-tall picket sign that called out the citizenry as TOPEKA: A CITY OF WHORES at pickets after school.

It wasn't easy for me to separate my life at the elementary school from the rest of my existence, and I had to learn that skill the hard way. One day in first grade, I tried to deepen my friendship with a classmate, Megan G., by taking her into my confidence during recess. Cupping my hands around my mouth and leaning in close, I whispered into her ear that our music teacher was "a fag" and not to be trusted. When I'd heard this warning from my mother at home, I'd thought of Mrs. Epoch's dark hair and dark eyes and plump figure and began imagining her as the menacing witch from one of the fairy tales Dad sometimes performed for us before bed, *Hansel and Gretel*. Plus, she was Jewish! I thought Megan G. should know to be careful, but she, duly horrified, tattled immediately, and I was hauled into the principal's office, sobbing in shame. My mom took me aside that night to help me understand, and I knew that she was right when she told me about *these people*. "Every single thing you do reflects on this church. These people don't care about you! They wouldn't think *twice* about hurting you in order to hurt the church! More than anyone else, *our* behavior has to be above reproach. School is not the time or the place for this discussion. You're there to learn." Thenceforth, I kept my standard postscript ("PS: God hates fags!") out of notes passed to my cousins and confined to the diary I locked with a tiny metal key.

Despite the knowledge that I couldn't trust my teachers or class-mates with anything but pleasantries, I adored school. My sister Bekah could be relied upon to regularly chase the van down Arnold Street after our mom dropped us off in the morning, begging Mom to take her home, but I could never understand why. There were no chores at school, no crying babies, no laundry, no vacuuming. We only had to *learn*. It was the freest time we had, and became the portal to my favorite place: books. Once I mastered reading, my nose was always stuck in one: under the table at dinner, pushing kids on the swing set out back, or hiding in the stairwell (close at hand but out of sight, so I was less likely to be called on for errands). Mom or Dad or Sam would take us to the Topeka Public Library, and Josh and I would load our-selves down with armfuls. And when the library began a new service that let us request books to be sent to us by mail—for free? "Katie, bar the door," Mom said.

My literary choices were heavily influenced by Josh's penchant for science fiction—R. L. Stine's Goosebumps and Fear Street series, Christopher Pike's *The Last Vampire*, the Animorphs books by K. A. Applegate, and once I hit third grade, anything written by Stephen King. We had wide latitude in our consumption of books, television, film, and music, and for much the same reason that we attended public schools: our parents weren't particularly worried about negative in-fluences slipping into our minds undetected. They'd prepared us too well for that, and our response to depictions of sinful behavior was instinctive. *Whore. Criminal. Adulterer.* When fundamentalists would approach us and tout their decision to rid their homes of television and secular music, our response was chastisement. "How can you preach against the abominable teachings that litter the landscape of this na-tion if you *don't even know what they are?*" my mom would admonish. I cherished the time I spent peering into alternate realities, and each day I'd race through my schoolwork so that I could escape into them: worlds where I had no responsibilities and lives that bore no resem-blance whatsoever to my own.

In truth, school itself became an escape for me—an escape from Mom and the frequent eruptions of her caustic temper. This was a fact that I acknowledged to myself uneasily, with a deep awareness of how foolish, how melodramatic I was being. I had a good life, I was always told. The *best* life, one filled with people who loved God and hated evil and would teach me the truth about the world, unlike my misfortunate classmates. Still, I couldn't deny the relief I felt when we'd finally pile into the van at the end of the often-nightmarish period between waking and school. It was nearly impossible to get through those two hours without a meltdown of some kind, without at least one of us at the other end of Mom's razor tongue or even the big paddle—a three-foot-long, one-and-a-half-inch dowel rod she'd started using on me in second grade, when I'd spent fifteen seconds admiring a cousin's gingerbread house after school instead of coming straight to the van (my delay forced her to hold up traffic on the narrow street in front of the school). The expectation of total obedience may have been the same in every Westboro family, but no one exacted it as vigorously, tenaciously, or *continuously* as my mother. I harbored few desires stronger than the one for her approval, but her standards seemed always to be shifting, tightening like a noose until I felt choked with the futility of my own rage.

I wasn't the only one. Just sixteen months apart, little Bekah and I were sworn enemies all through grade school, engaging in sisterly combat at every opportunity. On one particularly explosive morning when I was eight or nine, she and I got two beatings each—for fighting, and for insufficient progress on our piano lessons—and they were bad. They were the sort that left big red welts, the kind that would bloom into bruises of blue and purple and black and finally yellow as I examined them before my bath each night. *The blueness of a wound cleanseth away evil. Chasten thy son while there is hope, and let not thy soul spare for his crying.* After the beatings that morning, I was the first to make my way to the van for school, relieved to be getting out of the house and away from the immediate danger, but my sister was furious. Bekah was a matchstick of a girl, yet what she lacked in size she made up for in the force of her temper—and that day it was directed at our mom.

When Bekah slammed the van door behind her, waiting for Mom to climb in and take us to school, her pixie face was a bright red splotch. She clenched her jaw, teeth grinding, and erupted: "I'm going to tell my teacher about this! FUCK. HER!" She let out a wild, word-less scream with all the rage her runty self could muster. Mom came out the door and down the steps a moment later.

I wanted Bekah to tell. I was petrified Bekah would tell. I en-visioned a black and white police car pulling up to our driveway to take us away from Mom and Dad, and my heart surged, clutching for them. No one made hot chocolate like Mom, who was always standing over the stove singing and stirring a pot full of it when we came back from sledding the big hill at Quinton Heights. And no one could do bedtime like Dad, pretending to be a helicopter as he cradled us in his arms, *vroom-vroom*ing us one at a time from the living room, up the stairs, around the big banister, and down the hall to our rooms for bedtime stories that always ended in tickle fests.

And then I imagined the cops themselves in our driveway—the same cops we serenaded with accusations of "corpulent coward!," the same cops who let those big oafs punch and choke us on the picket line. I knew what I had to do. We only made it a few blocks on the way to school before I told Mom of Bekah's threat, even though I was terrified of what Mom would do to her for it.

"DO YOU REALLY THINK THE LORD IS GOING TO LET YOU SABOTAGE US?"

My face flushed hot and I felt sick as I watched the van pull away from the school with Bekah still in it. I wouldn't have wished Mom's unbridled fury on anyone, not even my sister-nemesis—but I had to protect us. *These people were evil.* No one outside of Westboro cared about us. They were always and only after the church. Everything always came back to that.

———

Westboro Baptist Church sat on a quiet street lined with trees and ranch-style homes, many of which belonged to my aunts, uncles, and cousins. An eight-foot-tall stockade fence ran around the block's pe-rimeter, enclosing our common backyard and cutting inward to ex-clude the two houses that didn't belong to church members. The whole setup had led many a contemptuous reporter to call our block a "compound"—implying some sort of spooky, David Koresh–style cult scenario—but my mother always cut them off when they spoke in such terms. The fence was originally built when the pool was put in, she'd tell them, back in the seventies. "You're talkin' to a bunch of lawyers," she would chide, "and that pool is called an 'attractive nuisance' in the law. If that fence weren't there, and some child wandered over off the street and fell in, we would be liable for that. It's that simple." People were always acting like we were crazy, like there must be some sort of nefarious scheme being hatched and meticulously cultivated behind our fences at every moment, but "we're just *people*!" Mom would insist.

Unless you counted the various plots hatched by quarreling children, the block had never been a place for nefarious schemes. It was a place for *us*—for pool parties and trampoline jumping and tennis playing in the summer, and for football and snowball fights and sledding down the little hill behind our garage in the winter. It's where I'd sit on the white porch swing with the big canopy, rocking gently with a paperback and a baby sibling propped in the crook of my left arm, the perfect excuse to sit and read for as long as it took Mom to realize that the baby had fallen asleep and tell me to come inside and put him down so I could help clean the kitchen or do the laundry, of which there was no end. It's where Dad had taught us how to ride bikes and play croquet when we were kids. He and the uncles had even built us a BigToy when I was about three, with a rope bridge, scratchy wooden monkey bars that always gave me splinters, and, at the end of the big blue slide, a sandbox we'd once forgotten Isaiah in when he was a toddler. Mom had driven a van full of us noisy kids all the way to the family law office before we realized he wasn't in his car seat—and then sped home only to find him busily digging away with his plastic shovel, safe and blessedly unaware of any drama.

More and more as the years had passed, I'd come to see our block in just that way: safe, secure, shielded from anything bad that could possibly happen. A refuge. Here there were no counterprotesters to steal our picket signs, no angry passersby to drive their cars at us, no jackboot cops to threaten arrest, and no one around to yell at us except our relatives. Here there was just *same*: heat and sticky humidity, the scent of newly mown grass, the insistent buzzing of cicadas, and kids biking around the track I'd been walking laps on since my legs were too stubby to keep up with Mom and her power-walking sisters. The familiarity of the scene could be like a sedative, and there were times when I'd be hurrying out our back door and just stop in my tracks, staring out into that wide-open space, stalled by the sense of comfort and calm that washed over me.

I felt that calm on the Sunday of my baptism, too.

Among the many mainstream religious traditions condemned by Westboro Baptist Church, infant baptism was a particular iniquity. Without any hint of hyperbole my grandfather likened it to burning the child alive in sacrifice to a pagan god. Only believers could be baptized in our church, following the examples of the adults baptized in the New Testament. The Ethiopian eunuch professed his belief before he was baptized, as infants cannot. The masses baptized by John the Baptist confessed their sins, as infants cannot. Even Jesus Christ Himself was baptized as an adult. Baptism, then, was not a rite of passage at Westboro. It would only take place if a believer felt called to ask for it, if they believed that they were one of God's elect—a Jacob, and not an Esau. They would have to show evidence of an "orderly walk," obedience to the standards held by the church, and active, eager participation in the work of the church. A candidate for baptism must speak with every member of the church, and may only be baptized if all members respond with silence when the question is posed: *Can any forbid water?*

When I turned thirteen and asked to be baptized, no one forbade me. My mother would be the first to tell you that I could be as willful and goofy as any thirteen-year-old girl, but she kept me on a tight leash, and I was learning. Earnest and enthusiastic about our beliefs, I zealously pursued the Bible knowledge needed to "defend them against all comers," as Gramps instructed. Eight years on the picket line had convinced me that there was nothing in the world of greater significance than this battle for the cause of God and truth, and I was ready to dedicate the rest of my life in service of it. I'd had a brief crisis of conscience that spring, when I'd been involved in the seventh-grade musical, and when I came out of it, I knew it was time to seek baptism. School had become a parallel culture to the one I inhabited at home, one that I had long since adapted to. I knew my classmates saw me as some sort of weird hybrid of a person: a friendly girl who enjoyed helping others with homework on the one hand, but a hateful religious fanatic who believed everyone was going to Hell on the other. I had

friendly acquaintances, and, for the most part, we all compartmental-
ized my conduct during class from my existence outside of it. I rarely
saw my peers outside of school, but in spending extracurricular time
with them each day—sitting around joking about mean teachers, listening to music, doing homework together—I began to wonder: Were
my classmates really as bad as I'd been taught?

The question lingered in the back of my mind for a time, but I
batted it away as soon as I consciously acknowledged it. There were
only two kinds of people in the world, and my classmates belonged
firmly in the Esau category. They didn't seem to know or care about the
Bible. Their parents were divorced and remarried. And some of them
were as good as committing fornication already, what with all the hand-
holding and kissing they were doing in the hallways. They might be
friendly to me, but these "friends" of mine were enemies of God—and
therefore must be my enemies, as well. *Do not I hate them, O Lord, that
hate thee? and am not I grieved with those that rise up against thee? I hate them
with perfect hatred: I count them mine enemies.*

During the winter, baptisms were done in the baptismal font in
the church sanctuary—essentially a large blue bathtub near the pulpit,
typically hidden from view by peach-colored curtains. Summer baptisms took place in the in-ground pool. It was about fifty feet long and
located just outside Westboro's rear entrance. On the afternoon I was
baptized, the congregation filed out into that communal space in the
blinding noonday sun, and I joined them a moment later, after changing into a white T-shirt and cutoff jeans. In silence, we all clustered
around the shallow end, waiting for my grandfather to emerge. Three
black stripes were painted the length of the pool to identify lanes for
lap swims, and when Gramps walked out in a red windbreaker suit
and old Nikes, I followed him as he waded to the stripe in the center.
When I was a child, he would stand in just this spot, lift me out of the
water as if it cost him no effort at all, and toss me several feet for a big
splash, to the place where the bottom of the pool slopes down to the
deep end. And then Bekah. And then Josh. My cousins. Over and over
we swam back to him, one after another after another.

Now he stood to my left and motioned for me to use both of my
hands to take hold of his left wrist. He was nearly seventy now, with
slight tremors in his hands. He began with a passage of Scripture:

Know ye not, that so many of us as were baptized into Jesus Christ were baptized into His death? Therefore we are buried with him by baptism into death; that like as Christ was raised up from the dead by the glory of the Father, even so we also should walk in newness of life. He spoke of my profession of faith, and that I'd given evidence of being one of God's elect. "I baptize you, my sister . . ." he declared, but his conclusion was lost to me as he covered my nose and mouth with a white cloth, supported my shoulders with his right hand, and pressed me down into the water.

———

Five years later, on the morning of my high school graduation, my brother disappeared. Saturdays were as welcome in my house as they are anywhere, and that one—sunny, warm, breezy—seemed like the perfect start to summer.

Still in pajamas, I was the first of the sisters to slip into the kitchen, which was brightly lit and full of activity. Several of my younger brothers were seated on bar stools around the island, chattering, munching happily, and swiping bits from each other's plates. At two, Luke was the youngest, and his face was deceptively cherubic: he was the one most likely to do the swiping and least likely to tolerate such insolence from anyone else. Mom was standing over the stove making breakfast—pancakes, maybe, or scrambled eggs—and singing a seventies pop song I'd only ever heard in her soprano. I heard the huge smile in her voice before I saw it, and when she turned, her eyes caught mine and then she was singing the love song to *me*, with exaggerated feeling and theatrics at full voice. I couldn't help but laugh to see her in such high spirits, because this was one of the places my mom seemed perfectly in her element.

"Where is Josh?" she called over the din. "It's getting late! Would one of you boys run down and wake him up?" My brothers tumbled over themselves to race down to Josh's basement bedroom. Moments later, they were thundering back up the stairs, Jonah leading the pack.

"He's not there! It's all gone!" Jonah was seven and a little confused, but not worried. I wasn't, either; bizarre declarations were par for the course in a family with eight brothers. My brow furrowed a little, and I looked to Mom, whose mouth was ajar.

"Would you—"

"I'll go look," I said, and headed for the stairs with three little brothers trailing. There were fourteen steps down, and with each one, more of the stripped basement came into view. The television was gone, and so was Josh's beloved Xbox. The bookcase, too. No clothes or random knickknacks strewn about. It had been years since I could see this much of the blue carpet, and I wondered briefly if he'd cleared the place out for the carpet cleaners. Rounding the corner, I was reassured to see that the dresser was still there and the bed neatly made. He was probably just in the shower. The boys flung open the flimsy double doors of his closet, and time slowed down.

The shelves and racks were completely bare.

One of the boys suddenly thrust a white envelope he'd found into my face. "Go show it to Mom," I said, waving him on. They all took off.

I checked the bathroom, just in case.

———

"Mom and Dad, I didn't think I would ever be saying this . . ."

The letter was one page, single-spaced, Times New Roman font, size twelve, dated May 21, 2004. The day before. He must have left in the middle of the night. I knew that meant he was a coward, just like two uncles of ours who had left the family long before either of us was born. "Slunk away in the dark" is how it was usually put. It wasn't often that Mom spoke of her four absentee siblings, but when she did, it was with an edge of disdain. She didn't seem *hurt* by their loss, precisely, instead vacillating between a strident good-riddance attitude, an outraged how-dare-they sense of betrayal, and a but-for-the-grace-of-God-there-go-I pity. The stories I was told were copious, and they painted clear portraits of the defectors: Kathy, vain and whorish; Nate, a thief and criminally rebellious; Mark, an entitled manipulator; Dot, an idolatrous witch. As such, their reasons for leaving the church could never be valid—just paltry attempts to mask the fact that they were wretched creatures controlled by their lusts, dastardly, selfish, unable to hack it in the rough and tumble of the Wars of the Lord. The implication of these tales had always been abundantly clear: these deserters were not like us, and we were better off without them.

We all knew this, but my mother had never been the sort of parent to let a lesson—or anything, really—go unsaid. Still standing over the stove, she was only quiet for a moment after she read through the letter. All four little boys were clustered around her, hushed now, waiting to be told what was going on, where Josh's stuff had gone. Her tone was sober, and there was finality and resignation in it: *"They went out from us, but they were not of us."* She was quoting the Bible, I could tell, but this wasn't a verse we'd focused on before—not in my memory— and I was as mystified as the boys.

I couldn't pay attention anymore, though. My thoughts were racing. My nineteen-year-old brother had gone apostate. We'd been together since my birth precisely seventeen months after his, but I'd never see him again. I'd never speak to him again. He hadn't said goodbye. Why did he leave? Where did he go? What was our family without him? I tried to imagine our house without his near-constant recitation of esoteric movie quotes, and failed. I tried to imagine our family "Sock War" game without him pelting me with pairs of striped kneesocks, and failed. I tried to imagine never again standing on the picket line discussing the philosophical questions raised by Stephen King novels, and failed. I knew that none of this was important, that his departure was the only thing that mattered. That he was just like Mark and Nate now, and that I should feel about Josh what Mom felt about her departed siblings. I didn't, though. I couldn't conjure an image of Josh that made him like our degenerate uncles, couldn't exchange this new picture of him with the one I'd had just the day before, just that morning: my big brother, the one who taught me the cheats and secrets to *Super Mario Brothers 3* on Nintendo, my verbal sparring partner and fellow bibliophile, lover of mashed potatoes and abuser of ketchup. It was impossible to reconcile these two narratives.

"Can I . . . ?"

I reached for the letter, and Mom passed it over. I read through it once, and then again, hoping repetition would reveal why he'd done this drastic thing. He had a wide array of complaints—rejections of everything from the church's picketing ministry to the way our parents ran our household—but at first, none of his grievances made any sense at all. I paused briefly and reconsidered: I could appreciate some of his grumblings, but none of them was a reason to leave the only known place in the world where God meets with His people. So what if babysitting our little brothers could be a miserable, thankless job? So what if he hadn't been allowed to get an apartment? I'd been appalled that he'd even asked, frankly. He was only nineteen! We were supposed to be at home, taking care of things there.

There was one part, though, that I simply couldn't fathom.

"We picket these people and they hate us for it and I have had enough of it."

I shook my head as my eyes traced that line again and again. I knew there were some difficult parts of the life we'd been living, but being reviled wasn't one of them. The fact that people hated us was cause for great happiness. Jesus Himself said so: *Blessed are ye, when men shall revile you, and persecute you, and shall say all manner of evil against you falsely, for my sake. Rejoice, and be exceeding glad: for great is your reward in heaven: for so persecuted they the prophets which were before you.* Gramps always said from the pulpit that "rejoice" meant "leap for joy."

Dismayed, I set the letter down on the counter. Maybe Josh really was a coward.

Mom made an announcement on the intercom, and speakers built into walls all over the house rang with her voice calling the family to the living room. I made my way there, and stared at Josh's vacant seat while we waited for the stragglers. Since I had been a child, this was the place where we'd convened as a family at least once a day to read the Bible, talk through family matters, and discuss the church's interpretation of current events. This was how my parents kept our household of twelve—*eleven*, I mentally corrected myself (Sam having moved out a few years earlier)—on the same page, united, working toward common goals. The couches were hunter green with tiny flowers printed on them, and they were arranged in one big rectangle, an invitation and a signal that each of us should be participating in these discussions.

My parents were sitting at their end of the rectangle, and when everyone was in place, Mom began with the passage she had quoted earlier from First John. *"They went out from us, but they were not of us; for if they had been of us, they would no doubt have continued with us: but they went out, that they might be made manifest that they were not all of us.* Don't you see, children? Josh was here, but he was never *of* us. We have a promise right here—that if he *were* of us, he would have continued here with us. '*No doubt*'! But he did not. He's come to years, and he's decided that he is *not* going to serve God in truth. Flip over to Hebrews 10."

The older ones of us opened our Bibles to the book of Hebrews. We'd memorized chapter ten during a recent summer, including a particularly terrifying meditation on the fate of those who leave the faith. It was full of the promised vengeance of God, of *judgment and fiery indignation*, and a grave warning: *It is a fearful thing to fall into the hands of the living God.* The chapter ends thusly:

But we are not of them who draw back unto perdition; but of them that believe to the saving of the soul.

We are not of them. Long ago, I had dedicated my life to serving God and His people, and I would not be like Josh and draw back. I would not follow him to destruction.

They are not of us. I comforted myself with these words, searching for every distinction I could find, for any shred of evidence that would distinguish me from my Judas of a brother. Josh was wicked, a coward. He wanted the praise of the world, he'd said so himself. He had denied Jesus, *trodden underfoot the son of God.* No, I was not like Josh. My heart was fixed.

I will never leave this place.

———

A steady stream of visitors poured into our house throughout the day, church members coming to affirm our righteousness and my brother's wickedness. Their bitter demonization of him began almost instantly, so quickly that I had to fight hard against my instinct to defend him. On the picket line that afternoon, I listened as my cousins referred to Josh as a "punk" and a "little bitch" and a dozen other insulting names. We were planted on the sidewalk in front of the Kansas Expocentre, picketing my graduation ceremony before I headed inside to get my diploma—and though it was still a little strange when my two separate worlds collided, the context of the protest barely registered. My brother was gone, and it was disquieting to think of how my loved ones would have spoken of him just the day before, the same tender, loving words they were now using to describe those of us who remained. I furrowed my brow and stayed quiet. I trusted their judgment far more than my own.

The following day, our family vacation to Colorado went on in Josh's absence. The nine-hour drive would be filled with tears both going and coming—even from my dad, the only time I can ever remember seeing him cry. But from the moment we returned to Topeka one week later, our tears were no longer acceptable. "We're gonna make the Lord mad at us if we keep this up," my mother warned sharply when she came upon me in tears the day after we got home. "This is from the Lord. We *must* be thankful and praise Him for *all* things, not just what seems good to us. We *have* to be in charge of our spirits. You hear me?"

My mother's words were shades of a sign that would come many years later—GOD HATES YOUR FEELINGS—and correlated perfectly with a passage she called upon often: *Casting down imaginations . . . and bringing into captivity every thought to the obedience of Christ.* We were to bring *every thought* into control and obedience to God, and our mom was going to help us get there.

With great effort I stifled my tears for Josh, but I couldn't stop thinking about him. For years, Josh and I had been comrades in discontent, united by the bitterness we felt at the way our mother often treated us—her wavering between incredible kindness and unjustified cruelty. She could be so very abrasive, provoked into a fit of rage by the smallest infractions: a flash of anger across our face, an edge in our voice, any sign of hesitation or displeasure at what was being required of us. These were unmistakable signs of rebellion that she simply could not abide, and her lack of patience for our wayward emotions was one of the great hallmarks of our upbringing. But over time, I'd come to see things differently, in a way that Josh had never seemed to. I understood our mother's hardness to be a painful necessity, not unlike our picketing: an expression of love manifesting as a harsh warning against sinful behavior. That was her duty as a mother.

It was a hard-won perspective, one that I had arrived at only after years of battling with my mom and with myself—but all the while, Josh's heart had apparently been drawn further and further away. *Take heed, brethren, lest there be in any of you an evil heart of unbelief, in departing from the living God.* He was an Esau, our enemy, doomed to eternal destruction. I felt so sorry for him, and so grateful to have been spared. As Josh and I had walked through the years of our teenage rebellion, he had missed the lesson that had become so clear to me: that happiness came only through submission—to the people and the circumstances and the limits that God had set for my life. *The bounds of my habitation.*

With that realization had come a peace with my mom that I had never thought possible. Just a few weeks before we lost Josh, she and I had walked in lockstep one afternoon, arm in arm like the close confidantes we had become. We were picking up Gabe and Jonah from the elementary school—the same one I had escaped to as a child. The spring sun was so warm on my face and the world was green and coming to life again, and I felt such a surge of joy and gratitude for my place in it that I started to cry. "Oh, what is it, sweet pea?" Mom asked, rubbing my arm soothingly with her free hand.

"I'm just so content," I sobbed, clinging to her. "So happy and so grateful and *so content.* I don't ever want that to change. I'm so afraid that it will. I don't ever want the Lord to be mad at me for being ungrateful for my lot. I want to always love this life."

My mother shushed me reassuringly. "The Lord has blessed you with so many wonderful talents, and you use them to serve Him. But more importantly, He's given you a heart to know Him, and to love Him, and to love and serve His people. All we can do is trust Him and keep doing what He's put in front of us to do."

I pushed my sunglasses up and brushed the tears away.

"I love you, little girl."

3. The Wars of the Lord

Three days after nineteen hijackers crashed four commercial aircraft into the World Trade Center towers, the Pentagon, and a field in rural Pennsylvania, a lamentation sounded forth from Westboro Baptist Church pastor Fred Phelps. It was not a mournful cry for the thousands who had been murdered. It did not echo the grieving prayers sent up by thousands more whose loved ones had perished in wreckage and rubble. It did not reverberate with the near-universal horror that overtook the world, nor with anguish at the unspeakable atrocities that human beings are capable of visiting upon one another. To my grandfather, such sentimentalities were entirely beside the point—and therein lay his grief. For three days straight, the American media juggernaut had been a continual dirge, wholly devoted to the "caterwauling" of preachers, pundits, and politicians alike. Of all the "backslidden, hypocritical" preachers and "self-aggrandizing" politicians whose words were filling the airwaves, my grandfather insisted that not a single one was speaking a word of truth as far as the Word of God was concerned. And the truth was that in the council halls of eternity, God Himself had issued the command, sending those airplanes like missiles through time and space, casting down these symbols of American strength and vitality in punishment for her great sins: homosexuality, adultery, fornication, idolatry, rebellion.

There was no sound among the congregation as our pastor spoke.

Not a cough or a sneeze, not even from the babies—just a somber still-ness as we contemplated the exhortations of this holy preacher, referred to as *a star in the right hand of God* in the book of Revelation. Regard-less of how unpopular or unpalatable his message, we trusted him to preach it with complete faithfulness to the Scriptures, without ambi-guity and without timidity, as he'd done for more than fifty years. He didn't have the praise of the world, and he didn't seek it. His work was unpaid as a matter of principle. My grandfather would have no finan-cial conflicts of interest, no incentive to abridge the Bible the way he so frequently accused others of doing. That my grandfather kept himself from such sordid concerns was another layer of assurance of his dedica-tion to preaching the unvarnished Word of God.

I never saw the confidence we had in our pastor as being rooted in the familial relationship he shared with about eighty percent of us, though this was generally presumed by outsiders to be the case. It was a galling thought—as if we, unique among human beings, would be forever possessed of our childhood credulity. As if all our faculties of reason, perception, and will could be entirely overruled by blood rela-tion. It seemed that the goal of this assertion was to render us blind followers of an angry patriarch—because if we could be dismissed as such, it meant that no one need fear the wrath of the God we preached. In truth, the familial nature of Westboro's ministry tended to make us, his children and grandchildren, *more* skeptical of our pastor, not less. As hecklers and journalists so frequently pointed to it as evidence of the lemming-like nature of our following, his status as "Gramps" became a pit out of which my grandfather had to climb. The burden of proof weighed the more heavily on him as a result, and he delighted in meeting that burden, utilizing every tool at his disposal to dem-onstrate the errors of the masses, their failures of logic, law, history, Scripture, righteousness.

My grandfather continued his sermon, which was—like all his sermons—laden with Bible quotes and references to expositors and theologians, evidence to support his frequent assertion that "I do not make this stuff up!" He never appealed to his own authority. Today's sermon was a freewheeling condemnation of "fag America," delivered in an old-time fire-and-brimstone polemic. But he wasn't speaking only or even primarily to those of us seated in the austere sanctuary—

1960s-era wood-veneer paneling, pews to seat about a hundred, devoid of iconography except a few new picket signs propped on easels flanking the pulpit (THANK GOD FOR SEPT. 11), and carpet a friend would later describe as "shockingly mauve." This special sermon would be uploaded to GodHatesFags.com, an address to the nation intended to make the power brokers of the world stand up and take notice. He contrasted America's maudlin response to the carnage of September 11 to England's godly call for repentance in 1666, when the Great Fire blazed through London leaving immense destruction in its wake. He pointed to the old Puritan preachers who had seen the hand of God in that conflagration, proclaiming that the Almighty was punishing the inhabitants of London for their sins—and that England was doomed if they failed to heed God's warning and repent.

As a fifteen-year-old, I was familiar with some of the Scriptural support for this theology, but it had failed to crystallize in my mind the way it did sitting in my pew that day. My formative years were an endless stream of opportunities to learn the church's culture emphasizing the celebration and mockery of tragedy and death, and I had fully assimilated into that culture by the time 9/11 rolled around. Any misgivings I might have had were long since snuffed out by the verses demonstrating the example of our God, who had declared, *Because I have called, and ye refused; I have stretched out my hand, and no man regarded; I also will laugh at your calamity; I will mock when your fear cometh.* And then there was the passage in the book of Psalms: *The righteous shall rejoice when he seeth the vengeance: he shall wash his feet in the blood of the wicked.* By age eleven, I was standing on the picket line exultantly repeating the words I'd heard from Gramps: "Two whores in a week!" I fancied myself cutely counterculture to be reveling in the deaths of two widely beloved women, though I had little knowledge of either Mother Teresa or Diana, Princess of Wales. No matter. When their deaths came just a few days apart, I knew all I needed: that the one was Catholic, and the other an adulteress. Elton John rewrote his song "Candle in the Wind" in tribute to Lady Diana, and less than twenty-four hours after he performed it at her funeral service, I was singing along to a chilling parody written by my mom and my aunt:

Goodbye, royal whore
Though you never spoke the truth
You know and hear it now
As do all of this world's youth
You crashed into the stone wall
As you played your whorish games
They set you on a pedestal
And bow down to your name

But it seems to me you lived your life
Like a harlot full of sin
God cut you off
Now the flames set in
And you know we told you, though you're
A throne away
Your name will die out long before
The pain will ever sway

Similar scenes played out following every death that caught my grandfather's attention, everyone from Matthew Shepard ("His lying fag friends can't help him now!") to Mr. Rogers ("Sissy Pied Piper From Hell"). Day after day, month after month, year after year, I took in the gleeful reactions that Gramps modeled until they became mine. On the morning of 9/11, there was only a split second between a classmate's frantic announcement of the attacks and my genuine excitement and glee at the demise of "those evil people." I knew my lines. When the mayor of New York announced, "We will rebuild," my memory called up the verse: *We will return and build the desolate places; thus saith the Lord of hosts, They shall build, but I will throw down.* When "United We Stand" became the national rallying cry, the simplest retort came from the book of Proverbs: *Though hand join in hand, the wicked shall not be unpunished.* And when other Christians insisted that God was not responsible for the calamity that had befallen the American people, many were the passages we would quote to confound their claims: *shall there be evil in a city, and the Lord hath not done it?* And again, God insists, *See now that I, even I, am he, and there is no god with me: I kill, and I make alive; I wound, and I heal: neither is there any that can deliver out of*

my hand. And the Apostle Paul reminds the Ephesians, *For this ye know,*
that no whoremonger, nor unclean person, nor covetous man, who is an idolater,
hath any inheritance in the kingdom of Christ and of God. Let no man deceive
you with vain words: for because of these things cometh the wrath of God upon
the children of disobedience. This last passage implies that some would
deny a causal connection between the sins of men and the wrath of
God—and declares that such denials are but *vain words* intended to
deceive.

Clearly, the whole world was deceived—but *we* weren't. How lucky
we were to have the favor of God.

What stirred me most during my grandfather's sermon that September day wasn't just the oft-repeated refrains from the Bible; it was
the historical context he had given these events. He had invoked "the
Puritans of old England," and the wheels turning in my mind almost
audibly screeched to a halt. There had been people outside of the Bible
who actually *believed* what we believed? It struck me as unlikely if not
impossible, my surprise betraying how acutely myopic was my perspective at the time. As I experienced it, the modern world had always
been deeply inhospitable to our beliefs, and it was easy to feel as if
Westboro were an island existing outside of time, the one true connection to a righteous past—the lone bastion of truth in this "insane
orgy of fag lies," as Gramps was wont to say. He never needed to come
right out and declare that our church was the only way to Heaven, not
explicitly; that kind of sweeping assertion isn't so easy to substantiate,
and certainly would have invited much more suspicion and scrutiny
from my highly analytical family.

Instead, my grandfather studied other churches extensively, teaching us all the ways they were full of error and sin. Methodists? Works
righteousness. Catholics? Idolaters. Lutherans? Lukewarm idolaters. He
referred to them as "social clubs" with little interest in knowing or
doing what God required of them. In the era of megachurches and
multimillionaire preachers of the prosperity gospel like Joel Osteen,
he found the perfect foil: *perverse disputings of men of corrupt minds, and*
destitute of the truth, supposing that gain is godliness. To us, such pastors
were motivated by money, smoothing away the hard corners and sharp
edges of Bible truths, sculpting them into enticing figurines to package and sell to ever larger congregations that sought not truth but

comfort: *which say to the prophets, Prophesy not unto us right things, speak unto us smooth things, prophesy deceits.*

Divorce and remarriage had become a national pastime since the institution of no-fault divorce laws in the 1970s, and now "the pews of these churches—these whorehouses, these dog kennels!—are littered with divorced and remarried people! The Lord Jesus Christ calls them adulterers!" And indeed He had: *Whosoever putteth away his wife, and marrieth another, committeth adultery: and whosoever marrieth her that is put away from her husband committeth adultery.* Voice dripping with disdain, my grandfather railed against "Christians" so often in his weekly sermons that I spent my elementary school years believing the term to be synonymous with "evil" and denying that it applied to me. In the end, we drew the obvious conclusion from his attacks on other faiths—fortified by direct Bible quotes that we carefully memorized: that Westboro was the only safe haven from the wrath of God, both in this life and in the world to come.

But the Puritans had believed—or so Gramps declared. When the special 9/11 sermon came to a close, I walked home across our common backyard, flipped open the lid of my laptop, and brought up Google, searching for evidence of Gramps's assertion about the destruction of London. Had the Puritans really believed as we did? Did their contemporaries believe them to be the crazy, hateful zealots that ours considered us? It didn't take long for me to light upon the words of James Janeway, a popular Puritan minister and writer. To a city ravaged first by the Great Plague and just after by the Great Fire, Janeway wrote:

> The Great and Dreadful God hath been pleading with poor England in these last Years [. . .], and written Divine Displeasure in Letters of Blood. The Righteous Judge began his Circuit the last Year in London, and in that one City above one hundred thousand received the Sentence of Death from his just Tribunal. He hath not yet ended his dismal Circuit, but he rideth still [. . .], pleading his Cause with us in a lamentable Fire, which in a few Days space, hath turned one of the most glorious Cities in the World to Ashes. The Voice of the Sword was not heard; the Language of the Plague was not understood; wherefore the dreadful Jehovah speaks louder and louder

still [. . .]. O stupid Creatures that we are, when shall we hear
the Rod and him that appointed it!

I read on, astounded. Here it was, yet more proof—*objective* proof—
that Gramps wasn't just a hateful man fabricating these doctrines to
bolster his preexisting prejudices, as the case was often made. Janeway
was even quoting the same verses that my grandfather had. I would
soon come to learn that this wasn't the only Westboro doctrine deeply
rooted in major branches of Christian theological tradition. My mother
had so carefully used Barbies and Bible verses to explain the concept of
predestination to my sister Bekah and me, but centuries before Westboro existed, this view was espoused by Christians the world over. It
was popularized by the reformed theologian John Calvin and summarized by the acronym TULIP, which my grandfather put on a sign
that hung behind his pulpit for years:

Total Depravity: All humans are, by nature, slaves to sin and
incapable of choosing to follow God.
Unconditional Election: God has chosen who will be saved
based solely on His mercy, not their merit.
Limited Atonement: God could have chosen to save all men,
but sent Jesus to die only for His elect.
Irresistible Grace: Those chosen by God have no power to resist His call to salvation.
Perseverance of the Saints: God's elect will persevere to the end
and be saved.

These beliefs had long since fallen out of favor with the wider
Christian community, and we understood their "evolution"—belief
in free will, in universal salvation, in the idea that God loves all of
mankind—to be apostasy and betrayal of the plain words of Scripture.
The foolish shall not stand in thy sight: thou hatest all workers of iniquity.
But all of this history, the venerable past of so many of our core doctrines,
lent our pastor a substantial new credibility to my mind—and at age
fifteen, I found myself newly humbled by his knowledge and understanding. I had always believed him to be intelligent and guided by
God, but youthful condescension had led me to underestimate him.

He was an old man, had trouble understanding technology, frequently slept with the news blaring all night long, and generally smelled of a potent mix of tea tree oil and the cloves of raw garlic he began consuming in copious quantities after watching a segment about its health benefits on one of the television morning shows. Jesus said, *No prophet is accepted in his own country*, and that rang true to me; it's easier to accept a human as divinely ordained when you're not intimately familiar with the mundanity of their daily life and the eccentricities of their personality. Church members also actively denied that my grandfather's history mattered at all, except insofar as it reflected the path on which God had led him; because God had predestined all things, nothing about our pastor's life or decisions could be attributed to him or his influence as an individual. For a long time, both this perspective and the quotidian realities I witnessed caused me to largely dismiss the complex history of a complicated man—a history that multiplied questions like a hydra, each answer producing twice as many curiosities as the one it sought to address.

———

Instead of replacing her surname with his, my mother combined the two when she married my father in 1983. It would be the name they gave to their eleven children: Phelps-Roper. "We wanted you kids to have the Phelps name. That name means something around here. It's part of your legacy." When my mother made this comment, I presumed she meant the legacy of the picketing; it's what we were known for, and what was getting us ever more attention in the press. Later, though, when I heard her telling one of my siblings the same story, I realized the obvious: that if the picketing didn't begin until after her sixth child was born, there must have been another part of this legacy. What had it been? "Oh, honey," my mom said, "long before this city hated us for picketing, they hated us for defending the rights of black people."

As the stories were told to me, my grandparents moved to Topeka with their young son in the spring of 1954, when the city was at the heart of a nationwide civil rights battle. Their arrival coincided with the publication of the United States Supreme Court's decision in the landmark case *Brown v. Board of Education of Topeka*. The Court had ruled against the city, overturning the previous "separate but equal" standard and banning racial segregation in state-run schools, which Topeka had fought all the way to the highest court in the land in order to maintain. Born in 1929, Gramps had grown up in Meridian, Mississippi, in the deep South—a place where first slavery and then segregation had had roots sunk deep. "He saw the way those black people were treated," my mother told me, "and by the mercy of God, he knew it was wrong." She quoted to me and my siblings the same verses that her father had quoted to her and her siblings: *One law shall be to him that is homeborn, and unto the stranger that sojourneth among you*, because God *hath made of one blood all nations of men for to dwell on all the face of the earth.* In the eyes of the law, all must be equal.

But the ministry brought my family to Topeka, not the civil rights movement. In spite of his father's best efforts to prepare him for a career in the military, my grandfather had become a preacher instead. He grew up a quiet, studious child in a highly respected family, and was a high achiever. He graduated high school at sixteen, sixth in his class, an Eagle Scout, Golden Gloves boxer, recipient of an American Legion Citizenship Award, class commencement speaker, and the best-drilled member of the Mississippi Junior State Guard. His father worked hard to help him secure a principal appointment to the United States Military Academy at West Point, but because candidates must be at least seventeen years old, my grandfather had to wait several months before he would be able to matriculate. During those months, he attended a tent revival meeting at a local Methodist church in Meridian and "got saved." Gramps described that event as "a genuine religious experience" and "an unction or impulse on the heart," referencing the verse that declares that *ye have an unction from the Holy One, and ye know all things.* The sermon my grandfather heard that day was the parable of the wedding feast, in which Jesus likens the kingdom of heaven to a certain king who makes a feast for the marriage of his son, and sends his servants to bid the invitees to come: *But they made light of it, and went their ways, one to his farm, another to his merchandise: And the remnant took his servants, and entreated them spitefully, and slew them. But when the king heard thereof, he was wroth: and he sent forth his armies, and destroyed those murderers, and burned up their city.* The parable continues, but this part was frightfully compelling to my grandfather, the fate of the men who were bidden to the feast and the pitiful excuses they gave for their refusal to come—their work. Their livelihood. He would not be one of those wretched men to spurn Heaven itself, but one of the servants who would call the world to the feast. All the dreams he and his father had shared, all the plans they'd made, all the work they'd done to get my grandfather into West Point became irrelevant in the face of God Himself calling my grandfather to become a preacher. His father was furious, but Gramps's decision was made.

Between his high school graduation in 1946 and the summer of 1951, my grandfather never seemed to stay in one place for very long, enrolling variously at Bob Jones University, the famed evangelical school then located in Cleveland, Tennessee; at Prairie Bible Institute in Three Hills, Alberta, Canada; and at John Muir College in Pasadena, California, where he earned an associate's degree in engineering in 1951. He left Bob Jones because of their racial discrimination in excluding black students from the university, but not before embarking on a mission assignment during summer break in 1947. He traveled to Vernal, Utah, where he worked as a seventeen-year-old missionary to the Ute Indians, and on September 8, 1947, he was baptized and ordained to the ministry by the pastor of the First Baptist Church there, both of them wading into a cold mountain stream so the pastor could fully immerse my grandfather beneath the running water—the true Baptist way.

His first taste of notoriety came when my grandfather was profiled in *Time* magazine in June 1951. He kept a framed print of the story on the wall of his office for as long as I can remember, and I read it often over the years, laughing at the image it painted of my twenty-one-year-old Gramps, unmistakable and utterly unchanged by the decades that had passed: stern-faced and pleading, holding an open Bible in one hand and gesticulating with the other.

Five-year-old John Muir College at Pasadena (enrollment: 2,000) has no more than the average quota of campus sin. But to Fred Phelps, 21, a tall (6 ft. 3 in.), craggy-faced engineering student from Meridian, Miss., John Muir is a weed-grown vineyard. Day after day this spring he has called upon his fellow students to repent. His method: to walk up to groups of boys and girls munching their lunchtime sandwiches in the quadrangle, ask "May I say a few words?" and launch into a talk. Fred Phelps's talks drew crowds of up to 100. Over and over he denounced the "sins committed on campus by students and teachers . . . promiscuous petting . . . evil language . . . profanity . . . cheating . . . teachers' filthy jokes in classrooms . . . pandering to the lusts of the flesh." Such strictures sent Dr. Archie Turrell, principal of John Muir, and most of his faculty into a slow burn.

Every single move was classic Gramps. School officials ordered him to stop his on-campus ministry, both because they felt attacked and because he was in possible violation of California's state education code, which forbade the teaching of religion on public school campuses. In response to their demands, he simply took it across the road, off campus, and kept at it. But Principal Turrell pursued him there, too: "He accosted me in very stern language, and told me that he would call the law. So I told him I had no fears. If the police arrested me I would preach to them in jail." After police forced his growing audience to disperse and "invited" him into a police car to drive him away from the scene, the school suspended him—but he was back preaching from the lawn of a friendly neighbor the next week, now with "something of the attraction of a martyr." And then this little gem: "Students were delighted with the story that Phelps had been ordered to consult the school psychologist, a middle-aged lady, and that he had turned the tables on her by 'psychoanalyzing' her."

Each time I read the profile, I couldn't help but laugh in fond recognition of the whole picture, familiar though it had happened long before even my mother existed. He wasn't focused on the gay community in those days—LGBT rights hadn't yet become a cultural touchstone—but this was unmistakably my grandfather: defiant, tenacious, and ultimately triumphant, calling out sin wherever he found it, fighting the powers that be to do what he believed was right, no matter what forces they brought to bear on him. Something of a martyr. Something of a hero.

Oh, how perfectly it seemed to capture my Gramps.

—

Five months after the profile was published, my grandfather was preaching in the chapel of the Arizona Bible Institute in Phoenix. He was introduced as "the young man from the *Time* magazine article," and a considerable crowd had gathered to hear him speak—among them my grandmother, a twenty-six-year-old postgraduate music student who was working for the professor who'd invited him, Mr. Woods. She watched from the back of the room as he paced back and forth on the platform, guessing he must be thirty years old to be behaving so seriously. "It was the way he always got when he had to preach," she told me later. "He'd get so sober it was scary. That's the way he was." I didn't need to ask what she meant, because it was something that had never wavered. It was impossible to hear him speak from the pulpit without being overtaken by an almost paralyzing sense of gravity; these were matters of eternal import, and it was your never-dying soul that hung precariously in the balance. "He laid it on us for about ten or fifteen minutes. I mean, he didn't hardly breathe . . . It was just shocking, it got everybody's attention." Mrs. Woods slipped in the back during my grandfather's presentation and told her, "I want you to pay attention to that young man, and be nice to him." Mrs. Woods was an Italian lady, and she was matchmaking, Gran chuckled later. But at the time, her only thought was, What *young man?* It didn't occur to her that Mrs. Woods was referring to the man onstage.

They both remembered that she had an apple in her hand when he first saw her, shortly after they'd left the chapel. Biting into the apple, she practically ran right into him coming around a corner. "Are you Margie, ma'am?" he asked in his Southern drawl, and launched into another talk about how Mrs. Woods had told him all about her, how highly she thought of her. Gran was a transplant from rural Missouri, and the praise embarrassed her Midwestern sensibilities.

They saw each other several more times in the next few weeks. First at one of the school's street meetings in downtown Phoenix, when Gran was on her way to sing at a wedding. Then Gramps gave her a ride to get her driver's license. After that there was the New Year's Eve party, where he said he first really noticed her, sitting at the piano with her back to the keys, singing along with all the others in an aqua-colored dress, looking radiant. When it came time for my grandfather to preach every night for two weeks at a church in nearby Glendale, she'd catch the bus to see him, and he'd drive her home afterward, taking circuitous routes so they could talk a bit more—about the Bible, mostly. "He didn't go very long without talking about some verse . . . He just had Bible verses rolling out of him." This part of the story took me aback when I first heard it; such behavior would certainly be characterized as *the appearance of evil* in the strict operation Gramps was running at Westboro. A boy and a girl in a car together alone, without a chaperone? For shame. When my grandmother would get home, she'd dissect the whole evening with Mrs. Woods, who told her, "Well, he's gonna ask you to marry him when this is over." The last church meeting was a Saturday afternoon, just before Gramps was set to head back to Mississippi for more preaching. He told her he had something for her in the glove compartment, and did she want to see what it was? She opened it up and found the ring. Many years later, when my sisters and I asked her what she thought in that moment, she said, "I didn't have anybody—and Mrs. Woods was all excited about it. She thought it was wonderful. She was my dearest friend. I never had a friend like her. And she—and I thought that'd be just fine. That it would probably work out okay. That's all I thought.

"I guess I was kinda scared. I mean, what was happening—I didn't know if I wanted to or not. Well, it's a funny feeling: you gotta make a decision, and you don't feel like you're prepared to make a decision. Well, I couldn't think of any reason why not.

"I had no idea."

———

My grandfather's proposal was in January, and he returned to Arizona in time for the wedding on May 15, 1952. Less than a year later, their first child was born—a son named Fred Jr. My grandfather continued his work as a traveling preacher during the first two years of their marriage, leaving his wife and young boy at home. I never learned why they chose to leave the Southwest, but leave they did, in search of a place to settle down. Their first stop: Topeka, Kansas. Gramps took it as a sign from God that the trio had arrived in Topeka on the day that the decision in the *Brown* case was published—a sign that he should stay in Kansas's capital city and work for the righteous cause of the civil rights movement. He found a steady ministerial position, too: the East Side Baptist Church was looking for a preacher to lead a new church on the other side of town—Westboro Baptist Church. In those early days, my grandfather's fire-and-brimstone sermons were pretty typical of the era—but his preaching would grow ever more radical over the years, eventually causing East Side to cut ties with Westboro. The church's reputation as being a proponent of hate wouldn't develop until the launch of the picketing campaign at Gage Park, but for East Side, the breaking point came many years earlier. My grandfather's growing certainty in the righteousness of his every belief made him unwilling to yield to another perspective on any matter.

My grandmother was seven months pregnant by the time they moved to Topeka in 1954—their second child in as many years, establishing a pattern that would continue for several more. Between 1953 and 1965, the only year without a birth was 1960. There were thirteen in all, with the youngest an outlier, born in 1968 when Gran was nearing her forty-third birthday. Fred Jr., Mark, Katherine, Margie, Shirley, Nathan, Jonathan, Rebekah, Elizabeth, Timothy, Dortha, Rachel, and Abigail. Eight girls and five boys. In addition to his ministry work, my grandfather sold insurance, vacuum cleaners, and baby strollers to support his ever-growing family. He also attended Washburn University School of Law, and by the time he graduated in 1964, he had been both editor of the law journal and captain of the moot court team.

In my teens and twenties, I would listen as my mother recounted the stories of her father's decades of civil rights work—not just to my siblings and me, but to journalists, to students at universities and high schools across the country, even to international law enforcement executives attending the FBI National Academy at Quantico. It was a privilege to be her assistant and travel companion, to be present to hear interlocutors push for details I hadn't thought to ask for. My mother would describe the early years of her father's legal career, how one of his first cases out of law school had been to represent a group of black students from the University of Kansas who'd been arrested for staging a sit-in—among them Pro Football Hall of Fame legend Gale Sayers, a celebrated running back who joined the National Football League in 1965 as a first round draft pick for the Chicago Bears. She praised

her father's work ethic, the brilliance with which he'd represented his
clients, how distinct and effective his courtroom strategy had been,
and how intimidated opposing attorneys were to face him. She waxed
lyrical about the importance of the work he did—work that came at
enormous personal cost to my grandfather and his young family. At
a time when Topeka was still "a Jim Crow town" where "nobody was
effectuating civil rights," a city that wasn't about to take school inte-
gration and black equality without putting up a fight to maintain the
old banners of white supremacy, the Phelps family suffered. "People
would call on the phone, screaming 'nigger lover!' and carrying on,
death threats and so forth. Over and over, we had our buildings shot
up, cars shot up . . ." Uncle Tim, my mom's youngest brother and a
shy redheaded kid at the time, had been beaten up more than once at
school and as he'd walked home.

None of it moved my grandfather, not the violence or threats of
violence, not the backlash, not the unrelenting opposition from the
legal community. None of it moved him an inch off his mark. In his
view, racism was the great sin of society during that part of his life,
and I imagine he quoted the same verses to steel himself in the face of
that opposition as he did later, during our fight against LGBT rights:
*Behold, I have made thy face strong against their faces, and thy forehead
strong against their foreheads. As an adamant harder than flint have I made
thy forehead: fear them not, neither be dismayed at their looks.* Not only did
he continue that work himself for more than two decades, but he required that my mother and her siblings join him, each one as soon as
they were able—and whether they liked it or not. By the late 1980s,
he had received the Omaha Mayor's Special Recognition Award, an
award from the Greater Kansas City Chapter of Blacks in Government,
and another from the Bonner Springs chapter of the NAACP for his
"undauntedness" and his "steely determination for justice during his
tenure as a civil rights attorney."

My father first got a camcorder back in 1988 so he could film home
movies: our bedtime stories, the cookie-making operations he'd lead
in Mom's absence, and enthusiastic renditions of "I'm a Little Teapot"
and Winnie-the-Pooh Sing-Alongs. Among the very earliest of that
footage is a speech my grandfather gave on April 4, 1988, at an event
sponsored by the Kansas Committee to Free Southern Africa. Orga-

nized to oppose apartheid in South Africa, the event took place at a local black church and featured remarks by a county commissioner, the president of the Topeka Public Schools board of education, the state treasurer, Topeka's deputy mayor, a state representative, and the Kansas Attorney General. When Gramps approached the podium, he brought with him a copy of the *United States Reports*, Volume 60, containing the opinion passed down by the U.S. Supreme Court in the infamous *Dred Scott* case, which held that Americans of African descent, whether free or slave, were not American citizens and as such could not claim rights guaranteed to citizens. My grandfather spoke eloquently against the "de facto bondage" of blacks in South Africa, and of the moral outrage of the white supremacy espoused in the *Dred Scott* decision. He quoted the opinion at some length, which described blacks as "so far inferior that they had no rights which the white man was bound to respect." Full of righteous indignation, my grandfather's voice reached its crescendo as he read the Court's assertion that "the negro might justly and lawfully be reduced to slavery *for his benefit*." He could hardly contain his shame and disgust for the black-robed justices who'd written such words. "*Eighty-four years* after Lord Mansfield, with the stroke of his pen, set all the blacks in England free, we're over here like some stone-age barbarians writin' our cockeyed Supreme Court opinions about black people—you oughta know this!"

Decades later, CNN would interview leaders in the black community who'd known my grandfather during his days as a civil rights attorney:

Jack Alexander, a Topeka native and civil rights activist, says the *Brown* decision opened the door for discrimination suits. Phelps would take cases in the 1960s that other lawyers, black and white, wouldn't touch, he says. "Back in that era, most black attorneys were busy trying to make a living," says Alexander, who became the first black elected in the city of Topeka, as a member of the Topeka City Commission. "They couldn't take those cases on the chance they wouldn't get paid. But Fred was taking those cases." Phelps was so successful that he became the first lawyer blacks would call when they thought they were being discriminated against, says the NAACP's [Rev. Ben] Scott.

The more details I learned of the first wave of my grandfather's war on the city of Topeka, the more my heart swelled with pride for him and for our family. This was our legacy. In spite of all the vicious words spoken against us, there could be no question as to the twin evils of racial discrimination and white supremacy. There could be no question that my family had been on the noble side of that dispute. History had proved us right. That Topekans would hate us for it seemed like dispositive evidence of just how morally bankrupt our city truly was.

———

This glowing portrait of my family, courageously taking up arms in the battle against evil, was first called into question by my unwitting adversaries online. I was thirteen when the Internet first became part of my daily life, and one of my favorite things to do around this time was to argue Bible doctrines with strangers in the chat room on GodHatesFags.com—at least until I'd be unceremoniously kicked offline by our temperamental dial-up connection. The *Topeka Capital Journal* website was another frequent destination, as it maintained now-defunct message boards where I could pose as an objective observer and mount anonymous defenses of Westboro.

I learned early to ignore the casual insults they tossed around— "hateful," "evil," "monsters," "stupid"—for the simple fact that I knew my family. Not only did these descriptors fail to capture the essence of the people I knew and loved, they were *diametrically opposed* to it. Nearly all of the adults in my orbit were college graduates, many with postgraduate degrees in law, business, and public administration. Whether they chose to pursue work in health care, corrections, or information technology, their careers flourished. They were natural comedians, clever and creative, and I'd often laugh myself to tears listening to outrageous stories they'd spin and parodies they'd write. My daily existence was a living testimony against the slanders hurled at my family, and made it easy to dismiss the accusers as liars who could not be trusted in any context.

Shortly after I emerged on the message boards at thirteen, references to my grandfather's expulsion from the courts began to crop up. He hadn't stopped practicing law because he'd retired, my opponents said; he'd been disbarred. I knew it to be true, but I'd always heard his disbarment dismissed as an unjustified punishment, because "these people hated us." I paid the accusers no mind at first, but it made me uneasy: disbarment wasn't a matter of unsubstantiated opinion, but a verifiable fact. They started to lay out the case that cost my grand-father his license in 1979: that he had flown into a rage when a court reporter failed to have a transcript ready for him in time; that he had sued her in a frivolous lawsuit demanding $22,000 in damages; and that he had abused her on the witness stand, badgering her for days on end. When they began quoting from the disbarment proceedings, I couldn't ignore it any longer: "The seriousness of the present case . . . leads this court to the conclusion that [Fred Phelps] has little regard for the ethics of his profession." I needed to find out the facts so that I could learn how to respond to these allegations—something more than "everyone just hates us." I went to my mother in her capacity as the keeper of our collective history, an informal role she played in the church because of her punctilious mind, unparalleled memory, and uniquely close relationship with Gramps. *She* would have the answer for me.

Gramps had been disbarred, my mother told me, but it was in retaliation for his civil rights work—not for any actual transgression on his part. "Those people hated us for that work. The courts hated us, the businesses hated us, all because we won those big verdicts. We were holdin' their feet to the fire in those discrimination cases, and they weren't gonna get a free pass on *any* of their misdeeds. They could hardly be civil to us, they hated us so badly." Yes, I pressed, but what about the court reporter? "Hon, do you think your Gramps is crazy? It wasn't just because that woman was 'late with a transcript.' It was a strategic move on her part, delaying that transcript. It was an essential piece of evidence in a case, and her deliberate refusal to produce it on time was to ensure that we missed the deadline to file. There are *all kinds* of ways for people to screw you over in the courts with techni-calities like that, and that's exactly what she was doin'." My mother explained that it wasn't just our word against the court's, either. Mon-roe Friedman, one of the nation's leading experts in legal ethics, had written a dissertation in support of my grandfather, summarized in the *Wichita Eagle-Beacon* in 1983:

> In a long dissertation filed in federal court in support of Phelps, Monroe Friedman, law professor and former dean of Hofstra University Law School, said, "It was as clear to me as could be that the kind of conduct that Fred Phelps was accused of is commonplace among the bar, that it is proper conduct, and that it would never be subjected to a disciplinary attack unless there was some other motive."
>
> Friedman said the motive is the nature of Phelps' clientele.
>
> "It has become professionally dangerous for a lawyer to be involved in representing poor people and in representing unpopular clients and unpopular cases," he said.

Still, my mother wasn't finished. She pointed out that perhaps the clearest indicator of all that her father's disbarment had been a sham was the fact that the *federal* court had refused to disbar him. "Normally, if you've got some ethics violation and the state court disbars you for it, the federal court just rubber-stamps it, and kicks you out of their courts, too. They wouldn't do that to Gramps. They said he hadn't done anything worthy of disbarment, and he kept practicing in the federal courts for another ten years."

My mother didn't ask where I'd discovered the accusations I'd presented to her, likely assuming they'd come from our daily pickets—eight years in and still going strong. I didn't volunteer their source, either. I was afraid she'd tell me not to waste time arguing with Topeka's riffraff on the Internet, and I didn't want to stop. I thought engaging with people was important, that it was a perfect opportunity to "maintain and defend pure Gospel truth," like my grandfather was always encouraging us to do. He preached extensively about the believer's duty to *be able by sound doctrine both to exhort and to convince the gainsayers.* "Convince means confute!" he would say. "It means to overwhelm them with sound arguments, logic, and evidence, to prove the folly of their position." I knew I would need to practice if I wanted to join Gramps in declaring with the Apostle Paul, *I am set for the defence of the gospel.*

—

Hunched over the keys of the living room computer, I continued to pore over the message boards whenever I had a spare moment. The accusations kept coming. One impugned my grandfather's motives in battling racism, saying his goals were not moral but financial, that he only represented blacks because he could make money off of them: exploitation of the black cause masquerading as noble sacrifice. "I made a lot of money," my grandfather told the *Capital Journal*, "I have to admit that." I couldn't accept this view. I'd heard Gramps preach against racism with the same venom he employed against gays, and it was clear that he saw his civil rights work in the same way he saw our daily picketing—as a moral imperative. I noted a similar accusation people made about our protesting, too, the insistence that the true heart of Westboro was an elaborate scheme to make money. We would provoke onlookers into assaulting us on the picket line, they proffered, and then we would sue both our attackers and the police for failing to protect us. Such a scenario never played out even a single time, but that never stopped people from believing it was true. It struck me that this desire to exchange a financial motive for an ideological one was a convenient evasion of a distressing truth: it was easier to dismiss our stated intentions than to acknowledge that people who were otherwise bright and well-intentioned could believe and behave as we did as members of Westboro.

I didn't want to bring too many of these Internet accusations to my mother, so I reasoned with myself about whether the money my grandfather had earned devalued his civil rights work. Didn't my grandparents have thirteen children to support? Was it wrong for him to try to make a good living for them? And hadn't he represented many people who couldn't pay him at all? If he hadn't made money on the cases he won, he couldn't have afforded to represent those who didn't have money. Was justice only for the rich? *Defend the poor and fatherless: do justice to the afflicted and needy. Deliver the poor and needy: rid them out of the hand of the wicked.* This allegation, too, was a nonstarter for me.

But there was another that nearly proved ruinous.

Rumors of extreme child abuse had filtered in and out of my awareness for almost as many years as I had memories. Their source: the two uncles whom I had never met, Mark and Nate. I knew to find them odious and repugnant from the way my mother and her siblings spoke of them, even when ostensibly paying them a compliment. "Those two boys were very smart, probably smarter than many of us who're still here—but they thought they were smarter than God." My aunt's voice was loaded with derision. "They're just rebels, and that's all there is to it." The dismissal was final, the door to discussion firmly shut.

Except it wasn't. The rumors resurfaced time and again, and had even been printed in a series of articles the *Capital Journal* had published about my grandfather in 1994: "Hate for the Love of God." Reporters Steve Fry and Joe Taschler had done extensive research into my grandfather's past, looking up childhood friends and neighbors, interviewing classmates, and chronicling the evolution of the man who had laid siege to the city of Topeka with more than three years of daily protesting against all who crossed him. They had also found his estranged sons, then living in California. Mark and Nate described brutal violence: beatings that lasted for hours as my grandfather yelled and cursed them, the heavy leather straps and a mattock handle he used, bloodcurdling screams, bruises on top of bruises that would split open their skin. The eerie joy he took at their pain, grinning at the wounds he had caused. There were so many examples, so many specifics.

Publicly, my mom and her siblings always vehemently denied the stories told by their estranged brothers: no, they had not been abused—only spanked. Disciplined. Their brothers were just angry because they hated God. Because they wanted to fornicate and commit adultery and live as they pleased. Those two boys were throwing a public hissy fit because they didn't want to obey their father *or* the Lord, and they didn't want anyone to interfere with their disobedience. Incredulity would creep into the voices of reporters as they somberly repeated my uncles' allegations for comment: Was my mother *really* going to suggest that every one of her brothers' stories was entirely exaggerated? Was she going to deny that there had been any abuse at all?

She was, indeed. Her siblings would deny it, as well, though they avoided addressing it whenever possible. They'd laugh out loud at the reporter's queries and ask rhetorical questions intended to shame him for his lack of insight: Would *nine* of the thirteen Phelps children have remained at Westboro if they'd been subjected to savage abuse? How

was it that the *loyal* children were all so well-educated and profes-
sionally accomplished—meanwhile, Nathan had dropped out of school
and was driving a cab for a living? My grandfather also dismissed their
charges, telling the *Capital Journal*, "Hardly a word of truth to that
stuff. Those boys didn't want to stay in this church. It was too hard.
They took up with girls they liked, and the last thing them girls was
gonna do was come into this church. These boys wanted to enjoy the
pleasures of sin for a season. I can't blame them. I just feel sorry for
them that they're not bound for the promised land."

At home, other details painted a more complicated picture. My
mother and her siblings dodged the word "abuse," and always maintained that Mark and Nathan were liars—but even at thirteen, I
recognized the obfuscation. I knew my uncles could be "liars" (technically, weren't we all liars?), and still be telling the truth on this question. My grandfather had nearly always been gentle and sweet to me,
and I would forever strive to earn his approval. I found such joy in
being his go-to tech assistant, my phone number written on a Post-it
and taped to his computer screen. At his slightest erroneous mouse
click, I'd take off running through the backyard, in the church's west
door, up the stairs, and into his office. Once, when I was demonstrating the correct keystrokes to save his work, he showed me the icon
he clicked—"that little button," he called it—to accomplish the same
thing. We looked at the icon together for a second, and I said, "It's
actually an old floppy disc." Gramps laughed. "That sounds like what I
feel! An old, floppy, disc." We cracked up, and as always, he gave me
a hug and a kiss on the cheek to see me out. "I think I'll take that as
my new nickname!" he declared. For the work I did for the ministry,
for my aptitude in memorizing and defending church doctrines, and for
my increasingly loud and zealous voice for Westboro in the media,
I had my grandfather's approval, and he liberally showed me his love
and praise. "I just love all that good work you do, sug'. I love it, I love it,
I love it! You learned how to put together a sentence like that from
your ol' Gramps, didn'tcha? Ha!" That little twinkle in his eye when
he'd tease us, and then toss his head back and chuckle . . .

But growing up, I was also a bit afraid of him, of what would
happen if I stepped out of line. The few times I gave him occasion to
be dissatisfied with me—as when I failed to play a hymn at the correct

tempo the single time I was accompanist at our Sunday church
service—he berated me without pity, his harsh temper provoked at the
slightest displeasure. The fear I had was also passed down by my parents' generation, by the way they spoke of anything that might upset
or disappoint my grandfather: in hushed tones with intense strategiz-
ing about the best way to reveal a problem to him. It was not uncom-
mon to hear, "Stay clear, Daddy's throwing one of his fits again!"

And then there was my mother. Sometimes she seemed exhausted
just thinking about the years growing up with her father. The Phelps
children spent long days at school, followed by hours of selling boxes
of candy on the streets of Topeka, Kansas City, Wichita, to support
the family and the church, followed by a daily ten-mile run. My grandfather had found the running program on the back of a Wheaties box
and forced all his children to join him in following it—even the ones
in elementary school. When he decided they would start training for
marathons, their Saturday mileage increased to twenty-six. "His motto
has always been, 'If a little's good, a lot's better.' No moderation, always
to the extreme," my mother told me more than once. When they ran
the Heart of America marathon in Columbia, Missouri, my uncle Tim
was the youngest to compete. He'd turned seven just a few weeks before the race. It took him seven hours to finish. *Runner's World* thought
it was a great story and published it in their November 1970 issue,
which hung proudly on the wall of the church office next to the *Time*
profile. "We were too young to be doin' that—sellin' candy and run-
nin' like that," my mom would say. "Too damn young. He shouldn't
have had us out there like that, and that's all there is to it. Nothin' to
do about it now, though."

It was in the past. Gramps didn't do that anymore.

Such was the essence of the position my mother took when I came
to her one day in tears of outrage and despair: my sleuthing on the message boards had led me to a book. It had been referenced a few dozen
times before my curiosity got the better of me. I knew it was full of
lies, per my parents. They explained that even the *Capital Journal*—
certainly no friend of ours—had refused to print what they referred to
as an "agenda-driven" manuscript. The ex-intern who'd authored the
book had been fired by the newspaper "as a result of our inability to
place any reliance on his judgment and his work product. His actions

as an employee here were unprofessional and ethically questionable." I clicked the link and began to read.

An hour later, wailing with an anguish the likes of which I'd never known, I stormed out of the living room and into my mother's office. She jumped out of her chair and rushed over. "Is it true?!" I demanded, hardly able to force my mouth to form words around the sobs, doubling over as I folded myself into her arms. This was not a tone I ever took with my mother, but I had no control. I had not asked her about all the accusations I'd found on those message boards. I needed to ask her about this.

"Is what true?! Is what true?!"

"Gran!" I squalled. The writer's detailing of my grandfather's child abuse had made me gasp as I read, yet I'd managed to hold on to the lifeline that this was not a trustworthy account. But when I read of my six-foot-three Gramps going after my tiny, gentle Gran decades earlier—punching her, beating her with heavy implements, dislocating her shoulder by throwing her down the stairs, and *cutting her hair to the scalp* because she wasn't sufficiently in subjection to him—I instantly came apart. This was a reality I could not bear to consider. It contradicted everything I knew about my faith and my family, everything I needed to believe. That we were righteous. That we were loving. That we were the good guys.

The truth was that my grandfather's remarkable lack of self-restraint couldn't help but extend to his discipline. And despite all the practice I had in denying it, *I knew it.* I had known only echoes of Gramps's rage through my mother, but the intensity of even those echoes had been a frequent source of terror for my siblings and me— the way it transformed the features of my mother, twisting them into something sharp and menacing and filled with violence. I pushed away the memories of my five-year-old self, the nightmares that ensued when I failed to learn the week's piano lesson. *Withhold not correction from the child: for if thou beatest him with the rod, he shall not die. Thou shalt beat him with the rod, and shalt deliver his soul from hell.* I'd cry out hysterically with each stroke of the wooden paddle until she finally stopped, but when I'd return to the piano bench a blubbering wreck, Mom wouldn't leave me to work. Instead she'd slam the paddle down on the piano top and sit down next to me. *"Go,"* she would snarl, though I was shaking and could hardly see the music through tears. *Chasten thy son while there is hope, and let not thy soul spare for his crying.* There was no way to concentrate with her beside me, and yet she would sit for the next hour, yelling, jabbing the beat into my shoulder, yanking me up for another spanking every few minutes, the force of the blows rising with her ire. More discordant notes would ring out when she smacked the tops of my hands, smashing my little fingers into the keys. *He that spareth his rod hateth his son: but he that loveth him chasteneth him betimes.*

My mother rarely mentioned her father's abuse directly, but it was apparent nonetheless. It was in her tone when she spoke of her father "always going too far. His policy was to beat first and ask questions later." It was in her despair when she would recall being *"at—his— mercy!"* It was in the way she responded to the howls of her children as she disciplined us: "These kids don't *know* how good they have it!" Her outrage at our distress made it clear that whatever she was doing to us wasn't even in the same league as what her father had done to her and her siblings. The Bible required strict discipline, but in her mind, she was delivering a more moderate version to my siblings and me. My mother didn't tell me until I was twenty-five—almost surely because of the way I responded to the discovery of this book at thirteen—that her father had done permanent injury to her. She would have chronic pain for the rest of her life.

"Stop it, stop it!" she pleaded, holding on to me. "No, it's not true! And even if it were, you don't think he's doing that stuff today, do ya?!"

"No," I admitted. I needed to let myself be comforted. I needed her to convince me that it wasn't true.

"And if it *were* true, d'you think it'd be right to keep beatin' a guy up for old sins?" Of course it wasn't. We believed in repentance and forgiveness. If a person changed, their past had no bearing on the present. *For I will be merciful to their unrighteousness, and their sins and their iniquities will I remember no more.* "I don't want you reading that stuff anymore! There's no value in it! Go shut that down, and don't be goin' back to it." I was only too relieved to let her direct me away from these thoughts, because pressing at the edge of my consciousness was an uncomfortable parallel: between my grandfather's physical brutality on the one hand, and the way our church responded to the suffering of outsiders on the other. Our joy at their demise. Our delight at their destruction. I took my leave of this line of thought and accepted the shield of my mother's instruction, because I needed to believe that our ministry had not been influenced by the pathologies of a human being. I needed to see that Westboro's monopoly on truth would continue to stand. I needed to know that the past had no bearing on the present.

I could never bring myself to ask my mother about one of my earliest memories of her. In my child mind, I'm alone in the living room, playing with blocks on the floor. Suddenly I'm looking up across the room at Mom and her twenty-something sister Dortha—Dottie, we called her—by the half wall with the wooden columns to the ceiling. They're screaming at each other, and Mom grabs Dottie by the hair and yanks hard. She grabs Dottie's arm and digs long fingernails into her flesh. I know it hurts, because she does it to me when I misbehave. Four little crescent moons. This is the beginning.

This was how you taught obedience. Until fear of God replaced fear of pain, this was how you learned obedience.

Come, ye children, hearken unto me: I will teach you the fear of the Lord.

My grandfather lost his license to practice law in federal court in February 1989. My mother could give me a detailed explanation of the state court disbarment from ten years earlier, complete with objective legal experts to support her conclusions, but I never understood how she rationalized the "nine-judge complaint" that came close to decimating the Phelps-Chartered law firm—nothing beyond "These people were always coming after us. They hated us." She dismissed the charges filed against seven of the firm's attorneys as "our annual Disbarment Rites of Spring," as she and her siblings had begun to call them: trumped-up charges filed with the goal of shutting down our family's civil rights work. In the disciplinary complaint, nine senior federal judges charged that my grandfather, my mother, and five of my aunts and uncles had made false accusations against them, and that they all deserved to be disbarred. A prolonged investigation ensued, one that found that Phelps-Chartered lawyers had violated the Code of Professional Responsibility. More than three years after the complaint was filed, my grandfather surrendered his license in exchange for the federal judges allowing my mother, aunts, and uncles to continue practicing in the

federal courts. Nearly a decade later, my Gramps would commemorate
the death of one of those nine judges in his Sunday sermon—a celebration of the murder-suicide in which the judge and his wife were both
found dead, his courthouse revolver on the bed between them. *And
shall not God avenge his own elect, which cry day and night unto him? I tell
you that he will avenge them speedily.*

Many years later, I would email to ask my aunt Dottie about the
disciplinary complaint that finally ended my grandfather's legal career.
I hadn't seen her since the incident I'd witnessed in my living room
at age four, my only childhood memory of her being the moment she
chose to leave Westboro forever. I wasn't sure I could trust her. Reading her account of those days, the first thing that leapt out at me was
the timeline—a connection I had missed all my life. Gramps had surrendered his law license in the spring of 1989, the end of his decades
of successful and acclaimed civil rights work. At nearly sixty years old,
he was suddenly and unwillingly facing an enormous vacuum in his
life—and just a few months later, the biking incident at Gage Park
with my brother Josh and the two men emerging from the bushes.

The end of one crusade leading directly into the beginning of
another.

Dottie also asserted that her father's removal from the federal court
was justified, recounting a scene of deliberate lies and fabrication of
evidence that I found difficult to imagine. As I pondered her assertions
for a moment, trying to determine whether my family was capable of
such things, an uncomfortable memory surfaced.

In my twenties, my mother and her siblings agreed to be interviewed once more on the subject of their father's abuse, but only
because it would get Westboro a platform on the Oprah Winfrey
Network, a show hosted by Rosie O'Donnell. My uncle Nate had been
interviewed, and the producers wanted to give us an opportunity to
respond to his claims. Stomach twisting, I watched the interview the
day it was published, expecting my family to cleverly evade the grisly
accusations, to tell selective truths, to employ misdirection. These
were all deceptive tactics, I knew, but I was consoled by the fact that
they weren't outright lies. The truth was important to me—it was our
defense against the never-ending attacks that came at us every day—
and I anxiously wondered what Nate was going to say and just how

my family would be able to respond honestly without hurting the church.

The answer was that they couldn't. There sat my mother, four aunts, and two uncles—all in their forties and fifties by this point—giggling at the reporter's grim questions, all pretending they had no idea what Nathan could possibly be referring to. "I don't even know what a barber strap is!" said one incredulously. "Does he have a picture or something, so that we might know what he's talking about?" another derided. "Nate always had an overactive imagination." The smugness and condescension stunned me. The footage went on for nearly twenty minutes, and it was painful to watch. "There wasn't any physical abuse, just *forget* that!" "They used to call it spanking!" As if it were all just a confusion of terms.

"Did you feel emotionally abused as a child?" the producer asked quietly. They erupted in laughter.

"Do you mean by Nathan?"

They went on at length about Nathan's shortcomings as a child—"disruptive, destructive, distressing"—and I sat there mouth agape at the double standard. My family would never stop harping on the sins of Nathan's youth, but would lay none of the responsibility at the feet of their father. Nate was to be held forever accountable for not conforming, for not just learning to fear and obey the way that they had all learned to. My mom and her siblings were holding *Nate* to account for the chaotic state of their childhood home—but they never would with Gramps.

Because Gramps had stayed. And Nate had left.

A vexing thought began to take hold. As members of Westboro, we behaved as if everyone in all the world were accountable to us, as if they all were steadfastly bound to obey our preaching—because we were the only ones who knew the *true* meaning of God's Word. Presidents and kings, judges and governors, Princess Diana and Mother Teresa—all were subject to our understanding and our judgment. And all the while, we ourselves were accountable to no one outside our fences. *But he that is spiritual judgeth all things, yet he himself is judged of no man. For who hath known the mind of the Lord, that he may instruct him? But we have the mind of Christ.* Who would have the audacity to contradict the mind of Christ?

Nathan had dared to question the judgment of the church, and he had faced our collective wrath as a result. The facts were in Nate's story, but we said he was fabricating it all in order to make a name for himself off of the church. "But go ahead and write some books and whatnot," one of my uncles scoffed. "We don't really care." We dismissed Nathan as being driven by the same pecuniary motive people falsely assigned to us, and for partly the same reason: to avoid facing an uncomfortable truth, a blurring of the line between the good guys and the bad. So we called the truth a lie and rewrote history—as though it were in our power to dictate reality so long as it was in the church's judgment and interest. So long as we all held the line, no one could prevail against us.

We were the Jacobs. We were always under Satan's attack. We had to protect ourselves.

I was beginning to see that our first loyalty was not to the truth but to the church. That for us, the church *was* the truth, and disloyalty was the only sin unforgivable. This was the true Westboro legacy.

I walked away from the video and pushed the troubling thoughts away, knowing without thinking that Nate would go away at the end of this news cycle and something else would take his place. I wouldn't have to think about it anymore. I instinctively held on to the hope that had carried me through all the storms we'd weathered at Westboro.

As long as I stayed and did what I was told—as long as I believed—everything would turn out okay.

4. The Tongue Is a Fire

"Talking to her is like taking a drink from a fire hydrant!" my mother exclaimed with a slight shake of the head. She leaned down to take the paintbrushes from my grubby hands, and for a moment her blue eyes were level with mine—now wide with mischief imagining what it might be like to take a drink from a fire hydrant. "You're so much like her." She grinned and kissed my cheek.

I only had a fistful of years under my paint smock back then, but already—and to my greatest delight and honor—the comparisons to my aunt Margie came swift and steady: big hair, big voice, big personality. "Big personality" was sometimes code for "big drama," but I didn't know that yet. I adored Margie, and from the way my mother, grandmother, and the rest of my aunts spoke of her, I knew this resemblance to be a very good thing. "She has such beautiful, beautiful hair," said one. "She is so sharp, just smart as a whip," said another. "You sure do talk a lot," said most of them. I couldn't seem to stop myself, though it didn't often occur to me to try. Mostly the words tumbling around inside my head mirrored the unruly curls that sat atop it: copious and uncontained, inevitably springing loose from every paltry attempt at confinement.

It fell to my poor mother to shoulder the yeoman's share of the burden this created. She tried to help me build something inside myself, a sort of internal levee system to keep my mental machinations from flooding every adult conversation in the vicinity—not to mention the rare moments of peace that so seldom found purchase in our household of five children and counting. Although it wasn't a particular strength of hers, either, my mother worked diligently to teach me the art of holding my tongue, of knowing when to speak—and as with every challenge she faced, her tools of choice were found in the Bible, 1611 King James Authorized Version only. *"The tongue is a fire, a world of iniquity,"* she would quote. *"But the tongue can no man tame; it is an unruly evil, full of deadly poison."*

These verses only served to confuse me for a number of years. I wondered what was so "deadly" about my constant complaints about my four-year-old sister's horrid behavior toward me. I couldn't see how my never-ending interrogations surrounding the puzzling characters we encountered on the picket line—"Karl the Fat Fag"—could ever be considered "iniquity." No matter how much effort my mother invested in the construction of this system, my incipient levees failed miserably, washed away by the endless streams of syllables that surged from brain to open mouth with the force of a great deluge. I wouldn't have had the vocabulary or self-awareness to convey it at the time, but at the root of all my words was a pathological imperative that has never left me, one that continues to override the usual etiquette of distant, restrained discourse with strangers. I was animated by a set of twin desires that I now understand will never be satisfied: the need to understand, and to be understood.

I grew up considering myself exceptionally fortunate to be surrounded by people who could help me on both of these counts. Conversations with elementary school classmates taught me young that the Westboro way of life was not common—not just our daily protesting, but the fact that nine siblings had settled down in the immediate vicinity of their parents' home, forming an exclusive, tight-knit community. I pitied the poor chumps who were their parents' only child and the ones with cousins flung halfway across the country—meanwhile, I had dozens living nearby. My aunts and uncles were my teachers, and my cousins my confidants. Who needed school friends when I had family? There was always someone to talk with. I never had to be alone.

My parents carefully avoided favoritism in our home, but I found myself unable to do the same when it came to my aunts. They took turns cycling in and out of the top spot for various reasons. Rachel was beautiful just like her biblical counterpart, and she shared sticks of mint gum in little foil packets. She'd call me Mickey and find fun ways to teach me new skills—like how to make change while collecting Happy Meals in the drive-through at McDonald's. Lizz would let me sit in her pew during church sometimes, taking my hand firmly in hers whenever I'd get fidgety; she'd use the pad of her thumb to rub soothing little circles on the back of my hand, so that the move never felt like a punishment. Becky had the most boisterous laugh, and before she got married, she'd come over to watch my siblings and me during the pickets when the weather was too cold for us to attend. We'd play Farkle and crack up each time we'd accidentally-on-purpose call it "Fartle" instead. Abi was the baby of my mother's family, funny and crass. We'd take turns massaging each other's shoulders, and she'd remind me of how much I loved to have my hair washed as a baby. How it was the one thing that never failed to calm me down.

Margie, though, would always be particularly special to me. She'd been named for my grandmother, and I for the two of them, though I never used the name outside of official documents. *A good name is rather to be chosen than great riches*, goes the Proverb, and I had one. Nothing pleased me more than when Margie would drop by and scoop me up to run errands with her—to the bank, the post office, the grocery store, I took any and every chance I could have to be near her. All the comparisons from my loved ones might have influenced me, but I recognized a kindred spirit in her. She'd come in like a whirlwind, a bundle of energy enthusing about one topic or another, whatever she happened to be turning over in her mind in that moment. An epiphany! A revelation! An unexpected turn of events in a case she was working! Can you walk with her while she talks? There's so much to do, not a moment to spare! Gran would jokingly ponder the absurdity that if Margie was able to *speak* her thoughts as rapidly as she did, how much faster must her mind be *thinking* them, unencumbered by the mechanical burden of forming sounds? I say without conceit that this, too, was a problem I recognized. It was a constant source of frustration that I could never make my mouth move fast enough to keep up with my thoughts— even when I was speaking at a pace that made my words unintelligible even to my own ears. (I'm sure it was a still greater source of frustration to my mother. "Would ya *slow down*, Meg?!")

Where my mom was Westboro's logistical powerhouse, Margie was our legal one. They had fallen into these positions in the most natural way possible—not by vote or by fiat, but simply by doing the work. Their roles were dictated partly, even principally, by their place in the family lineup: following the common pattern, the heaviest responsibilities tended to fall to the older Phelps siblings. When the second and third children abandoned the church as young adults, Margie and my mother were left to pick up the slack. Their individual personalities played into the equation, too, of course. My grandfather required much of his children and he held them to the highest of standards, even when society at large would have considered them either too young or too old to be commanded in such a fashion. Other children might have chafed at his rigid requirements, but my mother seemed to have a perpetual sense of urgency about meeting them. Her deep aversion to disappointing her father, her aptitude at pacifying him, and her willingness to use any means necessary to get her younger siblings on board with the program—including physical force, not unlike what my grandfather had modeled—these were the attributes that helped to mold my mother into a combination of something like a political whip and his girl Friday.

This is not to say that she was unaffected by her father's severe treatment of their family. She told me one day, laughing but abashed, that she and her siblings used to refer to their father as "T.B." in the notes they left for one another at the law firm: "The Beast." Still, the accounts I heard over the years from and about my mom left me with the knowledge that any such quiet dissent was about as far as she went in pushing back against his demands. Many years would pass before I felt the least bit unsettled by the striking correlation between her view of her father and her view of God. "You wanna sum up the whole Bible in just three words?" she would ask. "'Obey, obey, obey!'" It was an approach of appeasement: if only you could work hard enough to placate the strict demands of an exacting taskmaster, his wrath would turn away from you. *Let us hear the conclusion of the whole matter: Fear God, and keep his commandments: for this is the whole duty of man. For God shall bring every work into judgment, with every secret thing, whether it be good, or whether it be evil.* Gramps was not God, but Westboro members were inclined to conflate the moral judgments of the two—in practice, if not in theory—because in spite of his faults, my grandfather had been chosen by God to lead us. Who were we to question His choice?

By virtue of my grandfather's onerous temperament and our family's battles with the Kansas legal community, my mother had grown up in what she called a "pressure cooker"—the same phrase she would later use to describe our life working in Westboro's "War Room," as the office we shared had been dubbed. The unrelenting pressure through the decades only fed her sense of urgency, and it seemed to have had the effect of making her the embodiment of every cliché about diamonds similarly pressured: hard, abrasive, brilliant. My mother had an eye for identifying the roots of problems and their solutions, and she was almost ruthless in her pursuit of both—even when this meant mowing down our loved ones in the process. Tender as her gentle teaching and sweet encouragement could be, her bitter reproaches at the slightest displeasure would bring me to my knees in a heap of desperate sobs on my bedroom floor, face pressed to the floor and tears sliding down my forehead as I prayed to the Lord for mercy, for Him to please just fix whatever was defective in me to have vexed my mother so.

In those moments of sorrowful prayer in my bedroom—despite all my efforts, why could I not just *do things right*? What was *wrong with me?*—I was consumed by terror, frantic at the thought that I had been like Esau all along. The man who *found no place of repentance, though he sought it carefully with tears.* At each of my mother's censures I stood on the edge of a precipice, feeling as if I were only a light breeze away from being pitched headlong into the *waste howling wilderness* of the world, forever cut off from God and His people—and then, finally, awakening to the torments of Hell. Among Westboro members, such was the power of my mother's judgment. The loyal servant had assumed the role of the new taskmaster.

Margie was often the counterpoint to my mother's abrasiveness. Her finesse was evidence that she understood people in a way that my mother never seemed to. One afternoon when Margie was picking me up from middle school, she told me a story that I would remember and attempt to emulate for years. At a meeting with her team at the state Department of Corrections, there'd been a discussion surrounding a thorny question. Margie had figured out the answer, but instead of saying so directly, she alluded to ideas that would lead the others in the right direction, giving them the space to work it out and come to a conclusion for themselves. She described her decision to hold back as having two effects: her colleagues had the satisfaction of learning and meaningful accomplishment, and they were more invested in implementing the solution because they had come to it for themselves.

Had Margie's coworkers been under Westboro's authority, I knew my mother would have seen them as prideful for being at all swayed by their feelings; after all, they should be invested in the right answer for its own sake, not because *they* found it. What vainglorious fools they must be! She would have done her best to stamp out that pride forthwith: "You think you've got somethin' goin' on? You think you know somethin'? This is *not about you!*" Pride was a destructive force in any human being, and it needed to be eradicated at all costs. *Every one that is proud in heart is an abomination to the Lord.* But Margie had taken her employees into account—their personalities, how her conduct would affect them—and in her consideration I saw true humility, rather than just the absence of pride. There was a peace in my aunt's manner that appeared so much more desirable to my eye than the hard lines and harsh tones my mother so often took. I aspired to many of my mother's qualities—strength, diligence, zeal—but my aunt was a powerful introduction to the idea that these features did not require militancy to survive. That strength abides as fully in restraint as it does in aggression. That the tongue, that *world of iniquity* of which my mother had so strenuously warned me, could be used in altogether better ways.

By long forbearing is a prince persuaded, and a soft tongue breaketh the bone.

———

Although the idea of taking a gentler approach resonated with me relatively young, many years would pass before it had opportunity to bloom. "Mildly" was not the way I had learned to speak to outsiders. There would be no mincing of words on the picket line, no euphemisms, no delicacy, no circumlocution. Westboro's provocations would land us in litigation more than once—including, ultimately, a federal case that reached the United States Supreme Court and had the potential to bankrupt the church many times over—but not even this could convince us to change our ways. Even as the church became more radical and adopted ever-harsher prayers wishing death upon a growing list of enemies, I understood the refusal to recalibrate. One of the first verses I memorized was a command from God to the prophet Isaiah: *Cry aloud, spare not, lift up thy voice like a trumpet, and shew my people their transgression, and the house of Jacob their sins.* This had been the charge at my grandfather's ordination at seventeen, and he quoted it ceaselessly—often in conjunction with another phrase he would bellow from the pulpit on Sunday mornings: "WE WERE NOT SENT HERE TO PARLEY!" Ours was a position of strength, our foundation Jesus Christ Himself. Compromise was betrayal. The thoughts of mere humans were irrelevant. In this battle, we would not be the ones to yield.

For all her sophistication and emotional intelligence, not even Margie was above conforming to our antagonism on the picket line and was often cruder than most. When I was nineteen, I stood with my aunt and my Gran on a street corner outside a Seattle hotel hosting an international gay and lesbian leadership conference. With her then-eighty-one-year-old mother standing a few feet away, my aunt waxed vulgar, applying the knowledge Gramps had imparted to us about "scat"—the consumption of feces for sexual pleasure—to an anecdote about an imaginary new drink at Starbucks. "Just go and get yourself a Fececcino!" she brayed, mocking the conference-goers in a tone of prissy faux-refinement. "Add a dollop of feces into your coffee, and then prance in here to discuss your *leadership*!" The stark contrast between the way Margie behaved on and off the picket line was jarring even to me, but I was of the mind that the obscene nature of my aunt's words said nothing about her and everything about gays: that they were disgusting and abominable whether she kept quiet about their manifestly abhorrent sex acts or not. I supposed she felt the same.

Our antics at Westboro protests were vulnerable to criticism for any number of reasons, but their remarkable efficacy at garnering attention could never be gainsaid. This was by design, of course; a major piece of the attraction of our un-church-like methods was the thunderous voice it gave us on the streets and in the media. Both our picketing and the media coverage were finite and local in the very beginning, but

my grandfather swiftly found ways to colonize the burgeoning power
of the twenty-four-hour news cycle for his own purposes. Westboro
members began traveling across the country, from gay pride marches
in D.C. to the Castro district in San Francisco. Our vehement attacks
on public and private figures nationwide were carried by fax machines,
and later the Internet, to newsrooms across the country and around
the world. Westboro's relationship with the media became symbiotic
almost instantly: they gave attention to our message, and we helped
them sell newspapers and generate clicks.

In our estimation, Westboro's chief objective by far was fidelity to
the Scriptures. Apart from that, however, we gauged success primarily
by the amount of media attention we received—a fact which garnered
no shortage of accusations that we were feigning our faith for the sake
of notoriety. People often took our constant employment of shock tactics as cynical and purely attention-seeking behavior, but this was a
fundamental misunderstanding of our purpose and the dynamics of
the picket line. "Some say you're just doing this for attention," one television reporter accused Gramps during an interview I sat in on. My
grandfather looked at her like she was uncommonly dense and said
slowly, "Well, you're doggone right. How can I preach to 'em if I don't
have their attention?"

Not only did we firmly believe in the truth and goodness of all
our message and methods—including what others wrote off as "shock
tactics"—we also recognized that we were living in a sound-bite generation with endless demands on its attention. "You've got to speak
to people where they are!" my mother insisted. We had a message to
preach, and we were going to use every tool in our arsenal to get the
job done: sexually explicit signs and insults, parodies and pop culture
references, sarcasm and sass. Margie was especially good at writing
clever lyrics for our parodies of pop songs, which inspired me to try my
hand at them, as well. When we published the recordings of my Lady
Gaga parodies on Twitter—*Russian roulette is what you're playin', silly
clod / But every chamber's loaded when you're playin' with your God*—her
devoted and active fan base whipped themselves into a frenzy, turning
our songs into an international news story. No matter how fierce the
hostility to our message became, we delivered it with a Cheshire grin:
"You're going to Hell. Have a nice day!" It was important that people

understood that our protests were not done in service of any personal hatred, but of the truth of God.

Our belief in predestination prevented us from using conversion numbers as a measure of our success—fortuitous, considering how paltry they were—because whether a person had the faith to believe the truth of our doctrines was in God's hands alone. In light of this, our goal was not to convert, but rather to preach to as many people as possible using all the means that God had put at our disposal. He would take care of the rest. *And he said unto them, Go ye into all the world, and preach the gospel to every creature. He that believeth and is baptized shall be saved; but he that believeth not shall be damned.* On the cusp of the twenty-first century, at the dawn of the Internet age, we saw ourselves as the recipients of a divine gift unlike any given to the faithful preachers of yore: a global communications system which we would swarm like a conquering army to spread the Word of God unchecked. *Selah.*

"You think the Internet was created by God for these pornographers?" Gramps snorted. "The heck you say. He created it for *us*. For *our* preaching."

———

At first it was a trickle, but then they came in droves. Small-town papers and local TV news segments gave way to Michael Moore's *The Awful Truth* and ABC's *20/20*—the former featuring an enormous pink motor home announcing BUGGERY ON BOARD! that Moore had dubbed the Sodomobile. CNN. Fox News. MSNBC. The BBC produced two hour-long documentaries about Westboro that identified us as "The Most Hated Family in America." We were thrilled to see that our message was beginning to seep into the international conscience, our neon signs and provocative slogans becoming iconic and instantly recognizable. HBO's award-winning television drama *True Blood* was a pop-culture phenomenon from its inception through its conclusion in 2014, and for seven seasons, "God Hates Fangs" flashed through its opening credits—a play on Westboro's infamous rallying cry, "God Hates Fags." As Westboro's profile continued to rise, the Phelps-Roper home became a revolving door of journalists and documentary filmmakers from across the United States, the U.K., Australia, Japan, Italy, France, Germany, and more. A few weeks after my grandfather attacked the Swedish royal family following the sentencing of an anti-gay preacher there ("The King looks like an anal-copulator, and his grinning kids look slutty & gay!"), two journalists from Stockholm knocked on our kitchen door unannounced. "Hello!" I smiled at the two gentlemen unfazed. "Can I help you?"

Our campaign against Sweden only intensified when we discovered that the royal court was looking into possible legal action against us under their hate crimes law. With this sort of attention, how could we let go? We added GodHatesSweden.com to our growing list of Internet domains and attacked the country's leader, Carl XVI Gustaf: "The popinjay King of Sweden—a moral titmouse in the plumage of a peacock, who lives lavishly with his kids on Sweden's largest social security check—is King of Fags." My grandfather spun out news releases, and we unleashed the power of our fax machines, sending the missives to every government-related number we could unearth. "The Swedish Royal Court has confirmed that it has been receiving abusive faxes from the fanatical Westboro Baptist Church sect." (#LedesFrom1991) The technology was antiquated even in 2007, and we found it hysterical that our ol' Gramps could literally cut and paste together the elements of a press release, "send it out on that little machine," and stir up the highest levels of the Swedish government.

The campaign wouldn't be complete without protests, of course. Our policy was not to leave the country and the protection of the First Amendment, but we were undeterred by our inability to travel to picket in Sweden. Instead, we targeted the country through its D.C. embassy and consulates in Chicago, Omaha, Minneapolis, and Portland; the local performance of a Swedish chamber orchestra; a Kansas alcohol distributor whose wares included Absolut Vodka; and a Topeka hardware store that sold Swedish vacuum cleaners. Even *we* laughed at the dubious connection between the vacuum retailer and a man sentenced to jail for an anti-gay sermon preached halfway around the world, but we were determined to make those Swedes hear the truth about their Sodomite sin—and just as important, to make them feel their impotence, the futility of their resistance to our message. This was God's Word, and we were His servants. They had no power to stop us. *No weapon that is formed against thee shall prosper; and every tongue that shall rise against thee in judgment thou shalt condemn. This is the heritage of the servants of the Lord.*

Thanks to my mother's position in the church, our family was right in the middle of the torrent of activity surrounding Westboro. A few years after the start of our picketing ministry, my grandparents had grown tired of answering the phone calls they received on the church line. Prank calls and death threats came in all day long, but it was just as likely to be a journalist or live radio show. My mother did her best to be good to her parents, visiting often, sending one of us kids down to the church with dinner most nights, and executing the plans that she, my grandfather, and the other elders cooked up. So when my grandparents complained to her about their weariness of the phones, my mother wasn't going to let her aging parents linger under that burden for a moment longer than necessary. Although she already worked what were effectively three full-time jobs, she was willing to take on another without objection. She had the church phone line forwarded to our home, and suddenly we were the ones on the receiving end of the abuse and media requests. The battle lines had been redrawn, and the picket line had come into our house.

"Hello?" I picked up the phone just after 8 A.M. one day in sixth grade.

"Hey, is there an adult we can talk to?" I told the man there was not; my mother was taking my siblings to school and I was home sick. He asked my age, and I told him eleven. "Okay, let's talk to you, you're on the air! What do you think about Ellen DeGeneres?" He snickered to his cohost like he'd told a clever joke. I rolled my eyes. Ellen had recently come out, and Gramps had put her photo on a sign after blackening out one of her teeth and drawing pockmarks all over her face.

"She's a filthy dyke, and she's going to Hell for eternity," I said calmly, and then quoted the best clobber verse against gays from Leviticus: *Thou shalt not lie with mankind, as with womankind: it is abomination.* I thought for a second, and then added, "Plus, she's not funny *at all.*" I hadn't seen any of Ellen's comedy or television, but it never hurt to toss in an insult like that for good measure. Margie, Gramps, and my mom gave the most articulate, powerful interviews, and I'd been listening to them long enough to know that switching things up to amp up the shock value was good strategy. I reported the call to my mom when she returned home, basking in her laugh as I recounted my repartee with the radio hosts. Cleverly articulating Westboro's message would become one of the most reliable ways to earn affirmation from my mother and grandfather, and I cherished every opportunity to do so. Plus, it was fun!

All Westboro members had to be prepared to engage reporters and passersby on the picket line, but with the forwarding of the calls, my mother became the church's de facto spokesperson. That she worked from home gave her the flexibility to field calls during the workday when almost no one else was consistently and readily available, and her willingness to take on that job meant that Westboro was in the news more than ever before. One-sided conversations with members of the media would ring through our house at all hours of the day and night, our mother celebrating the hundreds of thousands of fatalities in the 2004 tsunami—the Swedish ones in particular—and cataloguing for an Australian radio station all the reasons that Heath Ledger deserved eternal torment. More than one host referred to my mother's sassy, funny, take-no-prisoners attitude as "radio gold." Margie was the go-to backup when my mother simply couldn't spare the time, and they would even tag-team occasionally—one of my favorite things to watch. Each of the women was formidable in her own right, but together, they were indomitable.

I'd begun to formally work for my mother at fourteen—the same age at which she had begun to work for her father—and I both loved and resented that my place was ever at her elbow. I followed her example, finding great joy in cultivating skills for the purpose of "being a good soldier in this man's army," as she put it. I memorized phone and credit card numbers so I could rattle them off for my mom at a moment's notice. I managed the contacts on her phone and the music on her iPod. I designed and maintained spreadsheets to track litigation and tax expenses, and wrote and edited Westboro press releases. I learned accounting to audit the law firm accounts, and Spanish to give interviews to Univision and translate the FAQ on our church website—all before the end of my first year of college. And yet, it often seemed that none of that mattered. My mother could be just *impossible* to please, and at times I worried that I could never actually grow up under her constant gaze and micromanagement of every detail of my existence.

But when it worked, and all the more as I grew older and learned to accept these constraints, I would cry in gratitude to God for designing this little piece of the world for me, and me for it. My heart swelled when I heard what my mother had begun to call me. "Megan is my right hand," she would say. Each day I had the privilege of being saturated in our doctrines and these questions of eternal significance. I often likened my mother to the hub of a wheel: all roads led to her as she went about orchestrating the day-to-day operations of the church. It became my greatest treasure to support the work of this virtuous woman, to be given a front-row seat for the drama that was forever unfolding before the Church of the Lord Jesus Christ. These were *the wars of the Lord,* and they would be remembered from everlasting to everlasting.

The peace I felt in my role was thanks in no small measure to Margie. Given our similar personalities, she sympathized with how difficult it could get for me at home. She, too, was put off by my mother's particular, carping nature—and so when things went south with Mom, it was Margie to whom I turned for succor. Nothing ever got me back on track faster than the gentle entreaties of my beloved aunt. She sent me a message one day just before my twenty-fourth birthday, and I printed it out and kept it in the top drawer of my desk as a daily reminder. I could hardly read my mother's emails of correction for the dreadful cacophony they sounded in my mind, full of misplaced accusations of deliberate sabotage and the rage of ALL CAPS. Margie was the epitome of kindness. Of reasonableness. Her email read in part:

Hello little Megan whom I love.

You have been near and dear to me since you were born, and you are one of my most favorite people in all the world. More important, I am convinced God has done a work on your heart, and you desire to serve Him.

Like all of us, you have specific struggles in the flesh. It is a piece of rebellion, and it comes out the most with your mother. I know you know this, and you work at it. But you hang on to a piece of pride that is a danger spot for you. You wrap around the axle about how she says it or when she says it or what she says it about, and rationalize that you don't understand why.

I know you know that your mother loves you dearly and

watches for your soul. I am so thankful that you are comfortable speaking your mind and heart to me, and never want that to go away. But it would be such a disservice to you if I didn't tell you from a few steps back that your ever-so-intense God-given-talented sweet self, you kick against the prick of your mother's words of instruction and direction. She is the boss of you, Megan, and always will be. If you can't submit yourself to her, you can't submit yourself to this body, plain and simple. Sometimes some humble, quiet submission is the order of the hour. And you must work at seeing that and getting to that spot.

You have such a spirit of joy and rejoicing and exuberance about serving God, but when you get in that little corner of rebellion with your mom, you are like a completely different person. You are tense, tight, hard, and preoccupied. It's Satan messing with you, little love. And you must resist him, and you have the promise of your Creator that he *will* flee.

Obedience and submission are such sweet comfort to our soul, and such a strong antidote against the enemy we face daily called our flesh. I love you, Megan, and I hope most fervently that these words are right and help your soul.

A soft answer turneth away wrath: but grievous words stir up anger.

———

In the middle of our second decade of daily protests, change came to Westboro. To say that we had already cultivated an atmosphere of unbelievable hostility would be an understatement of epic proportions—and yet I was blind to it for many years, rationalizing it for many more. Whether it came to me from Margie or my mother, my uncle Tim at a picket or Gramps from the pulpit, there was always a well-articulated justification for each extreme measure we took. By my late teens, I had begun to describe Westboro as "aggressively defensive": we were only *responding* to the malice that had been unfairly heaped upon us. We had not started this fight, but America, "Land of the Sodomite Damned." Steeped in a church culture that demanded we disregard, dismiss, and disdain "unacceptable" feelings of every kind—both within the church itself and among the community without—we became desensitized to the reality of the havoc we were wreaking on the lives of our targets. The only pain that mattered was ours.

Fourteen years after we began at Gage Park, this injurious spirit prompted an expansion of our preaching. Our country had declared war on God by granting its imprimatur to the sins of fornication, divorce, remarriage, homosexuality, and the "God loves everyone" lie—and in punishment for those sins, God had dragged America into two wars, the casualties of which were being mourned and their lives celebrated on the news almost daily. In response, we would develop a new campaign that would bring the masses face-to-face with an aspect of our ministry that had previously been reserved for well-known figures and locals who had wronged us: our sinister celebrations of death via protests at funerals. The impact of this shift was seismic, culminating in a five-year battle that would land Westboro before the nine justices of the nation's highest court—and in the beginning, I was filled with consternation.

"Mom!" I urged, "Can you please slow down a little?"

It was the summer of 2005, and the War Room was overrun by children of all ages. Westboro kids from around the neighborhood had gathered here the way they did most mornings when school was out, waiting to collect their assignments. The older ones of us would stain the fences or mow the lawns or fill up holes in the yard with topsoil, while the younger ones might pick up trash, pull weeds, or chop vegetables from the garden. When my mom's almost-celestial salsa was ready, the kids would take the fruits of their labor home with them in mason jars. My mother coordinated the program like a day camp for the righteous, another task she had assumed when she realized how pointless and unedifying it was for children to be idle at home, watching television and playing video games while their parents were off at work. Instead she would lead us in an hour or two of maintenance work in the morning, pickets before lunch, and then we'd regroup in the Phelps-Roper basement. The big room was mostly used for church gatherings, like the parties we'd throw to celebrate all the birthdays that fell during that month. In the summer, we would rearrange the tables for a group Bible study my mother would lead, with Margie and other Westboro members pinch-hitting on occasion.

But on this July morning, *I* needed my mother's attention. She had just announced that our family would travel to Omaha, Nebraska, in the next day or two: we were going to protest the funeral of a soldier who had been killed in Iraq. At my grandfather's behest, Westboro had begun this crusade just a few weeks before, and I had struggled to make sense of the logic behind it.

"What is it, hon?" my mother pulled in close to hear me over the chattering kids.

"I've been listening to Gramps and everyone, but I just don't get it. I need to understand why we're doing this. If someone comes up to me and asks me why we're picketing soldiers' funerals, I'm not going to have an answer!" At nineteen, I was disturbed by the fact that I couldn't articulate the Scriptural support for our new position. I'd been picketing for fourteen years by that point. I had memorized countless Bible verses and was always working on more. One of my grandfather's favorite refrains was that "The key to memorization is attention; and the key to attention is interest." His implication was that the only cause of a failure to memorize was a failure to care—and I cared. I could answer the toughest questions slung at me whether they came from a gentle stranger or an angry reporter with a microphone and a huge camera stuck in my face. *Be ready always to give an answer to every man that asketh you a reason of the hope that is in you with meekness and fear.*

"Well, we better go talk about it. This is an important subject, and it's gonna keep coming up. And if you've got this question, I'm sure these other kids do, too."

A while later, my siblings and I were seated in our usual places around the living room, Bibles open and ready to listen. "Okay, children," our mother began, "we are going to connect the dots here!" And that's what she proceeded to do for the next half hour.

The dots, my mother explained, were (A) sin, and (B) punishment. These two were inextricably connected, and the former was the proximate cause of the latter. (This was the actual vocabulary my mother used when she spoke to us; as an admirer of beautiful words, I found it a sincere joy.) Moses had once given the children of Israel an ultimatum: *Behold, I set before you this day a blessing and a curse; A blessing, if ye obey the commandments of the Lord your God . . . And a curse, if ye will not obey the commandments of the Lord your God.*

So far, so good. This had been part of our reasoning for protesting all along: warning the world that their sin would bring the curses of God upon them.

"I think we understand that part," I told my mother. "But why soldiers' funerals specifically?"

"Well, can we all agree that a dead child is a curse from God, and not a blessing?" she asked. We all nodded. She'd begun to use the word "child" to describe the dying soldiers, because a significant portion of them were exceedingly young. Many were around my age and even younger.

"Okay, now flip over to Hosea chapter nine," my mother instructed. I read along with her and began to memorize: *They have deeply corrupted themselves . . . therefore {God} will remember their iniquity, he will visit their sins. Though they bring up their children, yet will {he} bereave them, that there shall not be a man left.*

"America has deeply corrupted themselves! Adultery, fornication, fags, and so forth. They *worship* those sins, and now the Lord is visiting them for it—and one of the weapons in His arsenal is killing their soldiers in battle!"

They chose new gods; then was war in the gates.

For there fell down many slain, because the war was of God.

If thou wilt not hearken unto the voice of the Lord, he shall cause thee to be smitten before thine enemies.

I wrote the verses down. I would repeat them again and again until they stuck.

"And there is one more piece to this picture, children," my mother continued. "Most of these military deaths are being executed by I-E-Ds. 'Improvised—explosive—devices.' It means homemade bombs. Do you remember that this evil nation *bombed* this church with an IED ten years ago? Back then, people didn't even know what an IED *was*. And now *everyone* knows! That, children, is the vengeance of God. It is the *picture* of that verse that talks about their violence coming back on their own heads. Can somebody look that up?" It only took me a few seconds to find it.

His mischief shall return upon his own head, and his violent dealing shall come down upon his own pate.

Vengeance is mine; I will repay, saith the Lord.

The righteous shall rejoice when he seeth the vengeance: he shall wash his feet in the blood of the wicked.

This last piece of the puzzle was not so compelling to me. Although I understood and believed the verses about God's avenging of His people, my mother and grandfather seemed to vastly overstate the magnitude of the bomb incident each time it came up. I was nine years old when a few college students set off a pipe bomb in our driveway, blowing small holes in the fence and in our van. The blast was strong enough to shake off heavy wall hangings just over the bassinet of my new brother, Gabe, four days old and sleeping in my parents' bedroom just over the driveway. It had been unnerving to be sure, and perhaps I'd just grown accustomed to glossing over such incidents—but to claim that *this* was the cause of the suffering of the entire United States military felt exaggerated and uncomfortably arrogant. I thought it was better to focus on the main cause—that protesting soldiers' funerals was about America's disobedience to God, showing the causal connection between the nation's sins and its military deaths. I suspected others felt the same, because Mom and Gramps were the only ones I ever heard making the argument about the pipe bomb.

"I understand now," I told my mother. "What time do we leave for Omaha on Saturday?"

———

The military pickets quickly took over our schedule. Within ten weeks of the first funeral, Westboro had dispatched nearly two dozen groups of protesters, everywhere from Caldwell, Idaho, to Marblehead, Massachusetts. Hundreds more would come in the years that followed. We gathered a team of aunts and cousins, designing an entire apparatus whereby we could keep abreast of the protest opportunities. Given the last-minute, fast-unfolding nature of the events—the bodies would need to be buried quickly—we would have to be prepared to act in an instant. We decided that one of my aunts would monitor the deaths announced on the Department of Defense website, and assign individual soldiers to church volunteers on a rotating basis. These volunteers would then search the media for information about the soldiers as well as their funeral announcements. As soon as they had the time and place of a funeral in hand, they would call my mother or me and we'd swiftly resolve the question: Would we be able to make the trip to picket this funeral?

The result depended almost entirely on logistics. Was the funeral occurring in a place we could reach by car in ten hours or less? If so, the answer was generally yes. Were the tickets to fly there prohibitively expensive? If so, the answer was usually no. Was the funeral yesterday? Clearly, this picket was not meant to be—but we would need to be more vigilant if we didn't want these opportunities to elude us. If a given trip seemed possible, my mother would send a message to church members and ask who, if anyone, could go. Our decisions were based on the same constraints that govern the lives of every other red-blooded American: work and school obligations, the availability of vacation time, how much travel we had already scheduled ourselves for, and money. Other than parents for their minor children, we each paid our own way. (Although on one occasion, an older cousin of mine used his work bonus to distribute birthday gift certificates granting the recipient up to $200 toward a picketing plane ticket. Elation!) If at least three people could attend, my mother and I would immediately begin assembling the necessary elements for the trip: plane tickets, hotel and rental car reservations, driving directions, and all of the biographical information published about the soldier in the media. The travelers would need to know just what sort of sinfulness the deceased had been up to in the event that anyone were to ask why we were picketing *this* soldier specifically. If Mom wasn't sure, she tended to go with the catchall: "You mean it isn't enough that he was fighting for a nation that has institutionalized sin and made God their number one enemy?"

The outpouring of fury and grief at these protests startled me in the beginning. We stood near the church in Omaha and lifted up our new signs—THANK GOD FOR IEDS, THANK GOD FOR DEAD SOLDIERS—but the scene was devoid of our usual protest antics. We did not sing parodies. We did not dance atop the American flag. We did not call across the narrow street to the soldiers standing just outside the church's entrance. They watched us with bitter contempt, and I couldn't recall seeing anything quite like it in all my years on the picket line. The family arrived in a limousine, stepped out, turned. Though there were police officers stationed between us and them, the close quarters felt like a tinderbox. Both sides afraid to speak, both sides afraid to make any quick movements lest the precarious peace erupt into all-out war.

It was only a matter of time before it did.

As a result of our new campaign and the attention and hostility it generated, violence against Westboro spiked again—including arson this time, the most aggressive act perpetrated against the church. Investigators never found whoever was responsible for setting the church garage on fire in the wee hours one August morning, but the fire department arrived to put out the flames within minutes—tipped off by a woman in a nearby drive-through. An electrician arrived the next morning to get the power running again, but as he surveyed the damage, he seemed disturbed. When my mother asked why, he pointed to the narrow space—just four feet—between the charred edge of the damage and the electrical wiring. "If that fire had lasted any longer, the whole block would have gone up." I'd been shaken watching the blaze and billowing smoke in my pajamas at 1 A.M., but my feelings turned to outrage and defiance with the electrician's words. Anyone who thought they could scare us out of serving the Lord didn't know Westboro *or* God.

Although the arsonists had failed in their attempt to destroy the church with fire, a team of attorneys were determined to use the courts to do the same. Less than a year after our first military funeral protest, a twenty-year-old Marine was killed in a Humvee accident in Iraq. His name appeared on the DoD website, instantly becoming grist for the Westboro funeral mill. The query seeking picketers went forth, the plane tickets were purchased, and the news releases were faxed to media outlets all over the state of Maryland. My grandfather had a way of distilling a message down to its essence, and thus he did in the news release announcing our protest at the funeral of Lance Corporal Matthew Snyder: "They turned America over to fags; they're coming home in body bags."

Late on the evening that my mother returned from that funeral picket in Maryland, we sat at our adjacent desks in the still house. My siblings had gone off to their rooms to settle into bed, and Mom and I were winding down, as well. I got up and walked a few paces to stand behind her chair, put my hands on her shoulders, and squeezed gently. She was exhausted. Her head slumped forward while I worked on her neck and shoulders, and after a moment, she spoke softly. She had wept in the car on the way to the funeral, she told me. As she drove, one of her travel mates had read aloud the news stories published about the young soldier. "The father called his son 'the love of my life.'" My mother's voice took on that quality of desperate urgency again, of lamentation. "I am a *mother*. I have *eleven children*. I *get* that." She shook her head. "It is just *so sorrowful* what these people have done to their children. Does he not understand that his sins have brought the wrath of God down upon his head? Upon his *son's* head? Somebody has to *tell* them!"

I was taken aback to hear that she had cried. This was not the sort of spirit we displayed at funeral pickets. After Omaha, they had gotten progressively more antagonistic, and we now exultantly sang parodies of military anthems in those tense, close quarters: "Then it's IEDs / Your army's on its knees / Count off the body parts all gone, two! three!" I had begun to feel hesitant in those circumstances. Family and friends of the fallen were passing by a hundred feet away, and it was impossible not to see their heaviness. Breaching that grief-stricken silence so that we could bellow our defiance made me feel—unwillingly, involuntarily—like a terrible person. I would talk myself out of it, buttressing our position with Bible verses to justify the behavior—but my mother's tears gave me permission to feel the empathy I'd been afraid to acknowledge. I was relieved to know that it wasn't wrong to do so.

Less than three months later, my mother got a phone call from a reporter. Our whole family was returning from another funeral picket in Illinois, and we were on the final stretch of the seven-hour drive home. "Lawsuit?" my mother asked. The reporter wanted to know if we had a response to the civil lawsuit that was being filed against us for protesting the funeral of a Marine in Maryland—the allegations were defamation, invasion of privacy, and intentional infliction of emotional distress. It was after hours on Friday evening, but the woman had seen a copy of the complaint that would be filed in federal court come Monday morning. My mother first pressed for details, and then answered with characteristic brazenness: we had the protection of the First Amendment and the foundation of Jesus Christ. No one was going to stop us.

As soon as my mother disconnected the call, the cogs of the

Westboro war machine kicked into high gear. She phoned Margie and Gramps, and a plan was hatched. If those men were going to file a lawsuit on Monday, we were going to respond with a press conference on Tuesday. After the case was filed, I emailed and faxed out the press release Margie had drafted to national media outlets: "So long as the families, military, media, veterans groups, and community-at-large, use funerals or memorial services of dead soldiers as platforms for political patriotic pep rallies, we will continue to picket those pep rallies. If they put the flags down and go home, we'll go home. Not before then."

The trick was that our press conference would be at Arlington National Cemetery, where Mom, Margie, and I would simultaneously protest another soldier's funeral. This was not a move I would have thought to make, but all three of them—my grandfather, my aunt, and my mother—had an uncanny knack for finding ways to heighten the drama for the cameras. Addressing journalists was always a bit nerve-racking, but I knew I wouldn't have to worry about it much with my mom and Margie on the scene.

———

Before the lawsuit had even been filed, its effect on the church was far-reaching, momentous, instantaneous.

My parents, siblings, and I filed out of the van that Friday evening, into the house, and down to the church. There would be a meeting to strategize about our response. Gramps sat near the pulpit, wary and weary, and we took our pews near the front. True to his extreme nature, my grandfather began hyperbolizing about worst-case scenarios, appearing to grow more sick with fear and paranoia by the minute. Did the court have jurisdiction to force us to stand trial in Maryland? What if they won? Wouldn't other families begin to sue us in other courts and jurisdictions? What if they made us litigate these funeral pickets all over the country? What if they bankrupted us all? What were we going to do about all this? Most of us waited in silence as my parents, Margie, and the rest of my aunt- and uncle-attorneys weighed in on these questions. They tried to answer him calmly and reasonably, to assuage his rising panic, but the longer the meeting went on, the more they began to mirror his dread.

My grandfather fixed his stare on a nearby wall for a moment, and then spoke matter-of-factly into the strained silence. "The Lord could just kill them, you know."

And thus we began to pray for the Lord to kill the father of the Marine and his accomplices.

Someone googled the names of the lawyers who were filing the complaint—former JAG officers—and for the first time in all my life, we slid down off our pews and prostrated ourselves on the floor of the church sanctuary. The men took turns making elaborate prayers to God to kill these men that very weekend, before they had the opportunity to attack the Lord's church in this way. We were the representatives of the Most High God, and we prayed He would show Himself strong on our behalf. Our requests were made in the spirit of King David's imprecatory prayers—prayers of cursing, invocations of the wrath of God. When David was being pursued by his enemy, he prayed that the Lord would

> Let his days be few; and let another take his office.
> Let his children be fatherless, and his wife a widow.
> Let his children be continually vagabonds, and beg.
> Let there be none to extend mercy unto him: neither let there be any to favour his fatherless children.

Our enemies did not die over the weekend, but this pervasive doctrinal shift would affect the church for years to come, pushing us ever more to the extreme. As with Westboro's decision to shift our focus to military funeral pickets, our new imprecatory prayers caused me significant consternation—but I had trouble discerning its root. King David had plainly made these prayers about *his* enemies, and God had called David *a man after mine own heart*. Even Jesus Himself had promised vengeance to His people: *And shall not God avenge his own elect, which cry day and night unto him? I tell you that he will avenge them speedily*. Clearly, our imprecatory prayers were consistent with Scripture.

But if that was true, why did they unsettle me so?

This was not a line of questioning that I could pursue. I was in the habit of suppressing thoughts that conflicted with the Bible as my family understood it, and by the time I was twenty, that tendency was nearly as second nature as breathing. My feelings were irrelevant. I would sacrifice them on the altar of submission to the church, because that was my first and foremost duty in this life. As Margie had told me in the email that sat in my top drawer: "Sometimes you have to step away from being the one with all the analysis and all the answers, and just submit."

It is disconcerting—shamefully, unimaginably so—to look back and accept that my fellow church members and I were collectively engaging in the most egregious display of logical blindness that I have ever witnessed. I cannot account for my failure to recognize that our new imprecatory prayers were entirely and fundamentally at odds with our long-standing, oft-professed desire to *love thy neighbor*, that they were perfect contradictions of Jesus's command to *love your enemies*. Both positions had been derived from the Scriptures—but how could we have sincerely held such deeply incompatible views for so many years? It should have been inconceivable in a group of Westboro's size and intelligence. Still, the partition between the piece of my mind that confessed love for my neighbors and the piece that asked God to *dash the young men to pieces* was vast, opaque, and impenetrable. That brief spark of nagging discomfort was snuffed out, and I carried on.

A deceived heart hath turned him aside, that he cannot deliver his soul, nor say, Is there not a lie in my right hand?

———

I had decided to follow my mom and Margie to law school as a kindergartner, but the *Snyder* lawsuit was the first Westboro case I was able to follow up-close. I'd been too young to understand the broader context and the legal significance of the ones that came before, even though my mother had never been hesitant to teach me about them. And then as I got older, I became skeptical of my mother's portrayals of the cases, anyway. Margie had an inclination to steel-man her opponent's arguments—depicting them in the best possible light, and then expertly dismantling them to their foundations, brick by crumbling brick—but my mother tended to straw-man. She presented facts in such a way that our side came out as a paragon of virtue, and our opponents as the nadir of evil. Her analysis was just too intense and one-sided to be objective, and it became important for me to read the records for myself. My mother would always encourage me to do so. She seemed to sense that I'd begun to view her as a bit of an unreliable narrator, but she was confident that examining the primary source material would lead me to the same conclusions she had come to.

As the case progressed, one point became abundantly clear: the Maryland funeral at the heart of this conflict was beset by *the worst possible* set of facts for the men who had filed the suit. We had protested well over a hundred funerals by the time this lawsuit was filed, and there were times when only narrow spaces had separated us from our targets. We'd stood in clear view of the funeral entrances where our chilling melodies had shattered the silence, echoing off church facades and into the unwilling ears of the mourners, their sorrow at the mercy of our joy:

> *God sinks your battle ships, you little wimps*
> *Throw out your lifelines, boys*
> *Your time has come to die, die, die, die*

There had been no such scene at the Snyder funeral. Police had "stuck us off in the north forty!" as my mother exclaimed. They had used orange snow fencing to corral her and six other picketers into a small area located more than a thousand feet from the church, on public land, and there was no one around to see them but members of the media and law enforcement officers. The picket was over before the funeral began, and the funeral procession had even been routed so that it didn't pass by Westboro picketers at all. A professional videographer would shoot footage showing that a hill prevented funeral-goers from seeing Westboro's neon signs from the procession route, though the deceased's father testified that he'd seen "the tops of them." We took it as a signal of divine favor that *this* was the funeral we'd been sued for. God was going to use this lawsuit as a preaching tool, and He was going to lead us to victory such that no other family would dare to take us on over this issue again.

At Westboro, it was all hands on deck. Everyone with any skill would have a part to play. My mother and Margie would be at the helm with their familiar split focus of logistics and law; the other lawyers would help Margie with research and strategy; and the young adults would do the menial but important work of transcribing news stories to use as evidence. We were a well-oiled machine, always shifting to make sure that every need was met. Did a mother have to work late? Another would make sure her children got to the evening pickets in Topeka on time. Had Margie finished writing a brief? Her siblings were standing by to edit. Did anyone seem pressed beyond measure? *Bear ye one another's burdens, and so fulfil the law of Christ.*

The Maryland case was a dream for a wannabe lawyer like me. At the time, I was pursuing a degree in business at Washburn University, a small public institution that had been the destination for nearly all Westboro members' post-secondary education ever since Gramps had graduated from its law school. My time at Washburn didn't fit the typical experience of college as a time of questioning and independence. The university was located less than two miles from my home, and we had protested there at least weekly from the early days of our picketing ministry—an unlikely place for a Westboro member to find, or even to seek, intellectual freedom. I loved that the university system allowed me to focus on classes and subjects I found most interesting, and it was an improvement over high school in other ways, as well. I was only required to be on campus for classes and had almost no interaction with fellow students outside of that—which made things a lot easier for me. Westboro's beliefs and public protests had always been such a huge part of my identity, and ever more so as I got older. Having to keep that mostly separated from my life at school—largely ignoring the very most important part of me—hadn't been easy. In college, I didn't have to work nearly as hard to maintain that separation. I already had far more distance from my peers, and I also felt less inhibited about using any relevant university assignments as an opportunity to detail and expound on Westboro's activities—to address how I *really* saw the world.

I couldn't wait to get to law school, but in the meantime, I relished learning the nuts and bolts of the *Snyder* case. The number and scope of legal issues seemed to multiply with each passing day, but one of the central questions was whether a state's tort law—claims of civil wrongs—could be used to punish speakers whose words and actions would otherwise be protected by the First Amendment. The father of the fallen Marine claimed that Westboro's words had caused severe emotional injury and deterioration in his health, ruined the memory of his son, and turned the funeral into "a media circus." Could Westboro be found responsible for those damages? Could we be held liable for "intruding upon the seclusion" of the Marine's family—even though we had been standing on public land that was far from the funeral and unseen by its attendees? And even if they *had* seen our signs, was their grief or offense enough to render our words punishable under the law?

In the legal arguments Margie would eventually make, the answer to these questions was a resounding "No." She argued that even if the court considered the Snyder family to be private figures, Westboro's speech could not give rise to a cause of action. Because the Marine's father had repeatedly made public comments about the war in Iraq and published private details about the family, "a church or anybody has the right to answer that public comment." In protesting the young man's funeral, church members had only stated their religious opinions on matters of public interest, which falls under "the umbrella of protection under the First Amendment that this Court has established firmly."

Or as Gramps put it succinctly: "If these cockeyed lawyers can use tort law to do an end run around the First Amendment, then there *is* no freedom of speech in this country!"

———

During the years of the Maryland case, my mother would often send me over to Margie's office to assist her with anything she might need. It gave me the sense of being on loan from one boss to another, but the feeling was a joyful one. There was no higher calling than to be useful to the church, and I cherished the time with my darling aunt as fiercely as I had when I was a little girl running errands with her around Topeka. Now, though, our travels would have us marching toward the nation's capital.

Westboro had lost at the trial court, and a Baltimore jury issued a stunning $10.9 million verdict against us for protesting the young marine's funeral. The world had cheered at the idea that this judgment signaled the end of the church—that after two decades of violence and threats, unlawful police actions and impotent legal shenanigans of all kinds, America had finally, *finally* found a way to defeat Westboro and end our picketing forever. On its face, our loss seemed devastating and insurmountable—but still, the church adopted the sort of position we always took: one of exultation. We were utterly amazed at what the Lord was doing to our enemies. In allowing them to prevail at the trial court, He was lulling them into a false sense of hope. For two years, they reveled in their victory, throwing it in our faces, certain of their triumph. What fools! Did they not yet understand that God was with us? We knew that He would turn our apparent defeat into a victory— and their initial, illusory success would only cause them to rage all the more.

And thus it was. Margie filed our appeal, and the appellate court ultimately reversed the trial court's decision. They set aside the multimillion-dollar judgment, declaring that Westboro's speech was, indeed, protected by the First Amendment. No matter who was offended by our religious opinion, Maryland's tort law could not be used to circumvent our right to free speech.

Now *Snyder v. Phelps* would come before the United States Supreme Court. The stakes were high, and the stage the most prestigious we'd ever had. We continued to ramp up our efforts with a constant stream of nationwide protests and endless interviews requested by major media outlets from around the world. We were racing to the finish line.

It was September 2010, and Margie and I were making our way to meet with folks from the Thomas Jefferson Center in Charlottesville, Virginia, where Margie would rehearse the tough cross-examination she expected from Justice Scalia and his colleagues. The oral arguments were just a few weeks out, and she was preparing for the most daunting challenge she'd ever confronted as a lawyer, the pinnacle of her legal career. On that Saturday in September, though, one that belonged more to summer than to fall, it was evident that her thoughts weren't on the case. Instead, as Margie and I walked through an idyllic university community, empty of students and full of autumn leaves in brilliant hues, she put her arm through mine and started to cry.

"This is it," she said quietly. "This is where I'd be. If the Lord hadn't saved me . . . I imagine I'd be a professor . . . living in a place like this, one of these houses . . ." She trailed off, and we both walked together like that for a time, contemplating the choices we would have made if we'd had any choice at all. Margie's words were echoes of a lament I'd been hearing from teachers and journalists for years: that a family as impressive as the Phelpses were wasting our lives and talents tormenting people on the streets. How startling it was to hear it in Margie's voice, my mind stirring with the beginnings of a subtle realization: that even among the staunchest of us, the sacrifices we made in order to be at Westboro—our insistent rejection of the world outside—weren't quite as simple and inevitable as they had always seemed.

———

Gathered on the marble plaza in front of the U.S. Supreme Court, the throng of reporters appeared stunned, and I laughed aloud at their bewilderment. Before them stood over a dozen Westboro members with my mom and Margie at the fore, all of us brimming with adrenaline and positively giddy. Just behind us shone all the imposing grandeur of the Court's edifice: broad steps leading up to a portico of Corinthian columns and a white marble façade proclaiming "Equal Justice Under Law," evoking Greece's Parthenon just as it was designed to. Oral arguments in *Snyder v. Phelps* had wrapped moments earlier, and I looked over Margie's shoulder at the assembled mass of cameras and microphones as she and my mother fielded questions from the Supreme Court press corps. Margie had shown deference to the justices and respect for the Court's pomp and pageantry while we were inside the courtroom itself, but we were back outside now. *Our* turf. When a journalist made the mistake of asking whether Westboro members ever considered the Snyder family's feelings, the whole group of us spontaneously burst into song, as one:

> *Cryin' 'bout your feeeeeelings*
> *For your sin, no shame!*
> *You're goin' straight to Hell on your crazy train!*

Dozens of cameras chronicled the incongruity of the scene: the lawyer who had just calmly and cogently expounded First Amendment doctrine to the justices of the nation's highest court, now leading a band of misfits in serenading America's leading media outlets with a parody of "Crazy Train" by the British heavy metal vocalist

Ozzy Osbourne—in three-part harmony. The footage went viral, and we delighted in the fact that NBC's camera angle had allowed it to capture one extra piece of the picture: me, standing just behind my mom and Margie, lifting my hand for a high five and laughing with a cousin who promptly indulged me. "That's our answer about feelings," Margie told the crowd of dismayed reporters as we stood giggling just over her shoulder. "Stop worshipping your feelings, and start obeying God!"

The Osbournes issued a statement the following day, "disgusted and appalled that WBC would use Ozzy's music to represent such hateful and despicable beliefs."

It was perfect.

We knew that the Court wouldn't deliver its opinion for several months, and after a long year of litigation involving courts in Nebraska and Missouri, too, I expected something of a lull in the interim. Instead, the six months following oral arguments were among the most intense the church had ever seen. The explosions of media coverage wherever we roamed, the growing mobs of angry counter-protesters, the teams of journalists who continued to arrive on our doorstep—all of it was proof that God was with us, *strengthening our hands for this good work*, and causing our efforts to prosper. I loved every second of it. My place as my mother's right hand came with high standards and high costs, but I paid them happily, growing more devoted to our cause with each passing day. The world held no allure for me. How could it? I was squarely in the middle of a sea of activity that was being attended to by the angels of God, *ministering spirits sent forth to minister for them who shall be heirs of salvation*. That was us: "heirs of salvation."

Living in my parents' home as a single, childless woman with a college degree and a flexible work schedule, I had the freedom and financial wherewithal to journey far and wide to propagate the church's message. A few days after we returned home from D.C., I traveled to New York to picket gays and Jews. A week later, to Idaho and Washington State to protest schools. Ten days after, to Michigan for Muslims and more Jews. And then off to a Jewish convention in New Orleans, where God led us to a serendipitous post-picket encounter with former Israeli prime minister Ehud Barak and his security detail, pausing a few feet away to listen carefully to our somber parody of the Israeli national anthem: *Wrath will soon pour on you for your awful sin / Your great affliction, it will soon begin.* The next week, a soldier's funeral in Maryland. A high school in Ohio. A Philadelphia television studio for a debate between my mother and Senator Arlen Specter. New York to be on the *Mike Gallagher Show* in lieu of protesting the funerals of the victims of the Tucson shooting that killed a nine-year-old girl and injured U.S. Representative Gabby Giffords. The funeral of a sledding accident victim in Oklahoma. The Super Bowl in Texas. The Grammys. The Oscars. Interviews in Spanish with a television crew from Barcelona. The Sundance Film Festival, where the director Kevin Smith—my longtime Twitter nemesis—counterprotested us following the premiere of his Westboro-inspired film *Red State.* (I'd gotten Smith's attention back in 2009, when comedians Michael Ian Black and Rainn Wilson—and their millions of followers—came after me for tweets I'd posted in celebration of World AIDS Day: "Thank God for AIDS! You won't repent of your rebellion that brought His wrath on you in this incurable scourge, so expect more & worse!" I was twenty-three, and this was some of the earliest success I'd found on Twitter. When the kerfuffle reached Smith, who was best known for his films *Clerks* and *Dogma*, he launched what would become a years-long Twitter campaign to #SaveMegan, in which he regularly encouraged his millions of followers to inundate me with messages persuading me of the errors of Westboro's ways. GOD HATES PHELPS, his picket sign at Sundance read, EXCEPT MEGHAN—GOD THINKS MEGHAN'S HOT. I forgave him the mockery and misspelling of my name. It was good press.)

I traveled with my mother and Margie as guest speakers invited to university classes, to a college media convention in a Times Square hotel, and to the FBI National Academy at Quantico, whose primary purpose seemed to be a thinly veiled experiment in psychoanalysis—an attempt to understand the perspectives of extremists. Each of these was a fascinating engagement with communities that had long despised us. My laptop accompanied me everywhere, and I'd connect it to classroom projection systems so I could show the class in real time that the Bible really *did* say what we claimed it did. Everywhere we ventured, it seemed, the city would explode in outrage. *The tongue is a fire. These that have turned the world upside down are come hither also.* The events of those six months brought more sustained attention, exposure, and legitimacy to the church and our message than ever before, and a spirit of triumphalism and invulnerability took hold of Westboro. I found myself completely in its thrall, blind to the peril until it was too late.

5. The Lust of the Flesh

The only thing he ever lied to me about was his age. Since we were living in the golden era of catfishing, it occurred to me that this was nothing short of a true miracle. I wasn't even sure it counted as a lie, either, since the number he gave me without context ("Age 38.") *was* his age when we first met. It was February 2011, and my church's website, GodHatesFags.com, had just been taken over by the hacker collective known as Anonymous, which replaced our Gospel preaching with a mocking message. The takeover happened live on a popular web show during a joint interview with the hacker and my mother—defiant even in the face of ostensible defeat—and the video spread rapidly, garnering half a million views in twelve hours and featured on YouTube's home page. We responded predictably, my aunt Margie penning a provocative press release that I immediately posted to Twitter along with our challenge to Anonymous: "Bring it, cowards." Westboro and Anonymous are each notorious in their own right, and with the added spectacle of a mid-interview hack, the story was irresistible. The drama was reported by major news outlets across the country—which is how my name and photo ended up in the RSS feed of a man living in a tiny town in eastern South Dakota.

The first tweet he sent me must have been crude, because my response included a warning to "get your head outta the gutter."

His message was lost to me almost instantly, though, one among a deluge. With the advice and consent of my mother, I had become Westboro's voice on Twitter eighteen months earlier, and had found great success at getting attention for our message. For years, my proximity to my mother had thrust me into the logistical work that powered Westboro's picketing engine. Combined with my boundless energy and enthusiasm for our beliefs, that proximity had also given me a high-profile public voice that others of my peers lacked. Reporters would come to interview my mother as our de facto spokesperson, and then turn to me with questions about the perspective of the Phelps grandchildren—the first Westboro generation to have grown up on the picket line. I believed our doctrines to be the very definition of goodness and righteousness—not tedious or burdensome—and I loved them with all the fervor my mother had been modeling since I was a child. *For this is the love of God, that we keep his commandments: and his commandments are not grievous.* Though I was always afraid I wasn't sufficiently articulate to speak for the church, I never let that stop me from stepping up to the plate—and the more I spoke, the more I learned how to speak. I was ever eager to fulfill my duty *both to exhort and to convince the gainsayers* with sound doctrine, and that trend had continued into the social media age.

Thanks to our rising profile after the oral arguments, I was now receiving sometimes hundreds of tweets a day and posting dozens more of my own. Although we protested at Twitter's San Francisco headquarters, I'd come to love the platform dearly: a place for me to spread our message in a way that didn't require the distorting lens of a journalist who just couldn't seem to *get* it, no matter how much effort I spent trying to explain. I discovered I was far more effective at pleading our cause directly to the people on Twitter, absent the influence of Bible-ignorant hacks who wielded professional cameras and microphones. After two decades on the picket line, I was twenty-five years old and a skilled defender of Westboro and its many controversial doctrines. This random guy was just an anonymous face in the crowd asking the same questions I'd answered hundreds of thousands of times before. "'God hates fags' not 'I hate fags,'" I clarified for him. "We love them more than anyone."

MEGAN AMRAM (@meganamram): cool name

MEGAN PHELPS-ROPER (@meganphelps): Thanks! Sometimes your parents give you a cool name, sometimes you go to fiery eternal torment for hating God & teaching sin. =(

Less than two weeks after the Anonymous attack, the Supreme Court published its opinion in *Snyder v. Phelps*, and the media circus surrounding the church ramped up a hundredfold. God had worked in the hearts of the justices, and we had prevailed against our adversaries. Had the *Snyder* lawsuit succeeded, we knew that the much-vaunted American right to freedom of speech would have become little more than window dressing: if one person can label another's opinions on public issues "offensive" and then sue the speaker for millions of dollars in damages, what protection does the First Amendment offer? By that logic, a member of the KKK could sue a black protester for protesting a Klan meeting while promoting the "offensive" belief that racism is a societal evil. The *Snyder* lawsuit *had* to fail, because, as Chief Justice John Roberts wrote for the majority:

> Westboro believes that America is morally flawed; many Americans might feel the same about Westboro. Westboro's funeral picketing is certainly hurtful and its contribution to public discourse may be negligible. But Westboro addressed matters of public import on public property, in a peaceful manner, in full compliance with the guidance of local officials. The speech was indeed planned to coincide with Matthew Snyder's funeral, but did not itself disrupt that funeral, and Westboro's choice to conduct its picketing at that time and place did not alter the nature of its speech.
>
> Speech is powerful. It can stir people to action, move them to tears of both joy and sorrow, and—as it did here—inflict great pain. On the facts before us, we cannot react to that pain by punishing the speaker. As a Nation we have chosen a different course—to protect even hurtful speech on public issues to ensure that we do not stifle public debate. That choice requires that we shield Westboro from tort liability for its picketing in this case.

Emboldened by our success, we announced that we would *quadruple* our protests of soldiers' funerals. In the days and weeks that followed, I was more active on social media than ever before or since, so thankful to be one of God's representatives on earth and utterly exultant that He had put a megaphone to the mouth of our tiny church. I used Twitter to bait celebrities with anti-gay messages, to publicly celebrate Japan's Fukushima nuclear disaster, and to debate the merits of the *Snyder* case with anyone who would listen. Whether I was cooking dinner, sitting on an airplane, or standing at a protest holding two signs in one hand and my iPhone in the other, I spent every spare moment I could find answering thousands of users, whether they were curious, angry, confused, or mocking.

> BRETT MICHAEL DYKES (@thecajunboy): Lil Wayne is making abstinence education videos now, apparently . . .
>
> MEGAN PHELPS-ROPER (@meganphelps): With 1 in 4 U.S. girls aged 14–19 having an STD, abstinence is *clearly* the problem, @thecajunboy. Pssst: #GodHatesFornication!
>
> BMD: Go fuck yourself.
>
> MPR: Why yes—it HAS been too long since WBC's been to [your area]! Picket ideas? You know who to tweet. ;) #Obey

And in the midst of it all, him. Over the weeks, I started to notice his name and photo each time they appeared among the flood of messages I was receiving, though neither gave me any hint as to who he could be. His name was "FormerlyKnownAs," his profile picture that iconic image of Robert Redford as Jay Gatsby, leaning against the yellow convertible; I studiously ignored the spike in my heart rate and the dopamine rush I experienced whenever I saw them. So many of those who messaged me were enraged—understandably so, given that we were disposed to celebrating the deaths of children and blaming their parents for the tragedies that took them—and while he was certainly perplexed by our doctrines, anger had no part in his response after that first tweet. Instead he lurked, his infrequent questions belying the fact that he was reading each and every word I posted. His careful attention was intimidating and intoxicating, and all the more so as a figure of him started to form in my mind:

exceptionally witty, quietly dignified, deeply curious, and above all, respectful and kind. The thoughts he shared were never what I anticipated: reverent praise of my grammar, critiques of the font used on our picket signs, and literary and film recommendations as diverse as Marilynne Robinson's Pulitzer Prize–winning novel *Gilead* and the comedy blockbuster *The Hangover*. Apart from his typical questions about the church, he was all over the board and never where I expected.

I relished confounding his expectations, too. Like many others, he'd arrived at my Twitter under the impression that my church was filled with hillbillies and rednecks, an assumption I was only too happy to dispel. Upon my trumpeting of our Supreme Court victory, he learned that my family is full of lawyers, and I learned that it was a profession he shared—another piece of the puzzle that I meticulously filed away. He was shocked to find that my grandfather had been honored by the NAACP for his civil rights work in Kansas. Still anonymous, he wrote this message to a researcher who was looking into the ways Westboro used Twitter:

> I became aware of WBC via Anonymous. I immediately sent MPR a nasty tweet. She responded in a charming way. I was charmed. I wiki'd WBC which led me to wiki Fred Phelps. I learned that he, like me, was a lawyer. I learned that he was a civil rights pioneer in Kansas, which was contrary to what I expected. I studied more. During that study, WBC won a Supreme Court decision I didn't realize was pending. Whether you love them or hate them or think they're good or evil, you can't deny that it's a fascinating, complex American story. If MPR hadn't sent a witty, charming response to a nasty tweet from me, I wouldn't know the first thing about WBC, and I wouldn't have written this to you. That's the power of Twitter. That's influence. That's the power of an @.

Witty, he said. *Charming.* I found myself blushing at his compliments, but failed to recognize the deeper import of what he was saying. It was only much later that I noticed the pattern, that the dynamic he described had played itself out repeatedly during my time on Twitter—among many others, it happened with a friendly college student in Canada, a sassy start-up employee in Chicago, a hilarious Australian guy who tweeted political jokes, even an American soldier to whom I had sent a care package in Afghanistan. At the time I had been vaguely aware of the changes that communication on Twitter was working in me, but it was only in hindsight that its effects became clear. The 140-character limit caused me to drastically cut back on my use of insults, which Westboro members made a habit of stringing together in long, alliterative lists: "bombastic, blowhard, bigmouth, bimbo, bastard." Not only was there no space for insults in tweets, there was also an almost immediate feedback loop: unlike with email, I could watch a Twitter conversation derail in real time whenever I included personally disparaging language. The exchange would swiftly devolve from a theological debate to a playground quarrel. It became clear to me that causing offense with needless ad hominem attacks did nothing to communicate our core message, and I learned to avoid it. Hostile tweeters became almost like a game to me, and I delighted in learning to use humor, pop culture, and self-deprecation to diffuse and disarm antagonism. To change the nature of the conversation and convey our message in a way that outsiders could better hear it. The tongue might be a fire, I was learning, but it didn't always *have* to be.

"So, when do you drink the Kool-aid?" one guy tweeted at me.

"More of a Sunkist lemonade drinker, myself. =)" I told him.

By long forbearing is a prince persuaded, and a soft tongue breaketh the bone.

Somewhere along the line, my anonymous lawyer bragged about his Words With Friends prowess, and I impulsively responded with my username in a hashtag. Two days later, he started a match with me, and the game began in earnest.

———

I was about six when I first thought seriously about marriage. Gramps had spoken from the pulpit one Sunday morning about the foundation for proper marriage: serving the Lord together. Marrying an unbeliever was verboten, and for us, that meant only other Westboro members were permissible partners. Since the church was composed almost entirely of my immediate and extended family, it occurred to my child mind that if I were ever to marry, it would have to be someone from outside, someone who hadn't grown up in this peculiar faith of ours. I'd been seeing outsiders on the picket line for about a year by then— angry, screeching, violent, wearers of neon muscle shirts and fanny packs—and I was afraid.

"What if I get married to someone who *acts* like a good person, but then it turns out they're bad? Gramps says you can't get divorced. What will happen to me, Mama?" I was clutching her hand as we walked down our street after school one sunny afternoon, my little tum churning with dread at the thought of being hoodwinked by one of Satan's boys. I'd only just conjured this scenario, but my thoughts were already tumbling all over themselves, my tendency toward melodrama completely unhelpful. Instead of seeming like some far-off possibility, the danger felt real, immediate, pulsing from heart to limbs and back again.

"The Lord will keep you, little Meg." My mama's voice was gentle, reassuring. "He knows the hearts of all men. If you're supposed to have a husband, the Lord knows how to make sure he's a good one. He won't let us be tricked." Her quiet certainty was calming. *She's right,* I thought. *The Lord will take care of us. We have to trust Him.* They were the words I always heard the adults repeating.

My tiny death grip on her palm must have given away how truly scared I was, because she shook her head, laughing indulgently, and went on: "And anyway, you won't have to think about that for a long, long time."

———

I can't remember exactly when or how I learned what sex was, but I was still six when I discovered that it was how babies were made. My mom was pregnant with her seventh child, my baby sister Grace, and I gasped vociferously, with stark realization and something akin to horror. "So you *have* had sex with Dad!" I accused her. *"Seven times!"* I knew sex to be acceptable within the context of marriage, but only just; the practice was still highly questionable and suspect to my mind, and I couldn't understand why anyone would risk it—especially my smart and pious parents.

I soon learned that sex wasn't the only thing that could get you into trouble, though. "Lust," too, was dangerous and forbidden. My mom explained it carefully to my siblings and me sitting around the living room during one of our daily Bible readings. "Lust is a strong desire for something you're not entitled to. You cannot be said to 'lust' after your spouse, for instance, because that's something you *are* entitled to. The word doesn't apply!" I vaguely understood that the context here was boys and girls, but my mind went straight to my little sister's Barbies. Bekah refused to let me play with them, but I'd always dreamed of combining our dolls into one giant collection, which I would then apportion between us as I deemed appropriate (the naked ones with the ratty hair and missing limbs would be hers, obviously). I *strongly desired* to take control of her toys; was this lust? I wasn't positive, but Mom had already moved on, so it didn't seem like the perfect time to ask.

"Then when lust hath conceived, it bringeth forth sin: and sin, when it is finished, bringeth forth death." She was quoting James 1:15. "You need to understand this, children. Lust is the *beginning* of every sin, and death and Hell are the *end* of every sin. Every evil thing arises from lust. We have to be vigilant about it. Don't think that you're special or strong, that you can just go down a lustful path in your mind and not have it affect your actions and behavior. This is a truism: *Then when lust hath conceived, it bringeth forth sin: and sin, when it is finished, bringeth forth death.* Make no mistake: lust *will* bring sin, and sin *will* bring death. You have to cut it off, and not let it take root in your heart."

She paired this verse with another, and they will be forever linked in my mind: *Can a man take fire in his bosom, and his clothes not be burned?* It's one of the Proverbs, captivating in its simplicity. The imagery clearly hearkens back to Hell again, where most of our conversations eventually led.

The discussion continued one day when my mother came to my kindergarten class to have lunch with me. On our way to the cafeteria, she spotted my first-grade cousin walking down the far end of the nearly empty hallway. Mom suddenly seemed disturbed and disgusted. "The way she walks is so inappropriate!"

"What do you mean, Mama?"

"She swishes her butt when she walks. Do you see that? She does it on purpose. No one walks like that."

I watched my cousin as she disappeared into the lunchroom, try-ing to see what my mother saw. As far as I could tell it was the way she'd always walked, and I said so, confused.

"No. She walks like that to get attention from boys."

Ah, it dawned on me.

Lust.

Suddenly very aware of my gait, I began to walk stiffly, keeping my little hips as still as I could make them. I asked my mom if I did that sort of thing when I walked, too. She shook her head. "No. I'll have to talk to her mom about it. I'm worried about that girl."

———

As my childhood years passed, and then my teenage ones, ever more praise was heaped on virgin marriages, and ever more vilification on any relationship outside of that. There was no such thing as "dating" in this context. God hated fornication, and having dinner alone with an unrelated member of the opposite sex would inexorably lead to fornication—or at the very least, it had *the appearance of evil*, which we were strictly instructed to avoid. Even if a couple was engaged, there would be no kissing, and certainly no time to themselves, until after the vows. If they didn't have a chaperone at all times, there was *the ap-pearance of evil*: the presumption would be that the betrothed had been in flagrante, their undefiled status would be called into question, and the church would have to suss out exactly what had happened during the time in question.

And although marriages weren't terribly frequent at Westboro, it seemed like there was never any shortage of such matters for the church to suss out. Before I was born and as I was growing up, several women in the church had relationships and children outside of mar-riage. These affairs were calamitous and fearsome to behold, their dev-astating consequences seared into my young psyche like a white-hot brand. I listened to the hushed conversations of the adults one evening, learning they centered around an aunt of mine who'd been wonderful and close with me since I was a babe; she'd take my siblings and me on drives to the park, recounting stories that sounded fascinating even though they were several levels above anything we could really grasp while our ages numbered in the single digits. I didn't understand all that had gone on with her, but words like "shameful," "deliberate," "willful," ". . . with *him?*" and "I can't think of anything worse" were thrown around, and I knew they meant sex.

For if we sin wilfully after that we have received the knowledge of the truth, there remaineth no more sacrifice for sins, But a certain fearful looking for of judgment and fiery indignation, which shall devour the adversaries. The ominous warning, terror, and despair of this passage were all over my aunt's face when it came time for the church to sit in judgment of her for the intolerable sin and havoc she'd wrought among the congregation. We filed into the church sanctuary and took our places in our usual pews, the atmosphere filled with a dreadful heaviness. For what seemed an excruciatingly long period, the adults soberly and dispassionately discussed the fate of this woman, whether she should be stripped of church membership in order to keep the church pure and to drive out the evil inside her. *Concerning him that hath so done this deed . . . deliver such an one unto Satan for the destruction of the flesh, that the spirit may be saved in the day of the Lord Jesus.* To be excluded from the church was a terrifying proposition, the worst fate imaginable for a member of Westboro—a sure sign that you weren't one of God's elect but a reprobate destined for Hell. If an excluded person found a way to convince the church that he'd truly repented, he could be granted membership again, but there were no guarantees. As it became clear that the church was leaning toward excluding her from membership—unless and until she found a way to sufficiently demonstrate her repentance to them—anguished sobs racked her, contorting her face with shame and desperation as she begged for mercy and forgiveness. Her young son, also, not yet a teenager, pleaded through tears that they not do this terrible thing to his mother. But the church body, undeterred by their supplications, voted her out with no further discussion.

In the wake of this trauma, the behavior of my cousin became petrifying to me. Jael, my dear friend the butt-swishing first-grader, grew into a coquettish middle-schooler, and the shenanigans that resulted were cause for great concern. *Abstain from fleshly lusts, which war against the soul.* She seemed to be constantly in trouble because of boys she was "messing around with." In our lingo, this could mean just about anything from simple flirting to sex. I always figured it couldn't have been more than a kiss in Jael's case, though that was still a sin egregious and inexcusable, a flagrant display of lust and *the appearance of evil*. We saw these "innocent" flirtations as the beginnings of real danger that would end with the shame of being an unwed mother and the desolation of being voted out of the church. When Jael got detention for a silly incident that involved hurling a spit wad at a boy, we were all deeply worried for her soul. Her classmates from the church—my older brother and a few other cousins—were charged with keeping an eye on her at school and reporting any suspicious behavior.

The following year, I joined the middle school crowd and that responsibility fell to me, as well. A few weeks before I was set to start at my new school, I walked across our backyard and into the church. My siblings and I would take turns having sleepovers there with Gran and Gramps, often several times a week during the summer months. Gramps's room was the master bedroom upstairs, but Gran usually slept in a recliner in the downstairs room with the fireplace. We would always join Gran and watch marathons of *I Love Lucy*, *Bewitched*, or, if we were unlucky, *Bonanza*. On this night, Gran and I stayed up late watching *Lucy*, and when the time came, she turned off the TV, I flipped off the light, and we each settled under our covers. To lie in the dark and talk with Gran—wise and soft-spoken, keeper of stories and resolver of spats—was a privilege. That night it was a quiet, considered admonition she had for me. "You're such a good girl, Meg," she half whispered across the room. "You're a good friend. You're such a blessing to your parents. You help your mom so much." She was silent for a moment. "Please promise me you won't ever change. A lot of people, when they get to be your age, start to change. They start getting into a lot of trouble." I thought of Jael and felt myself beginning to panic. She was warning me, I realized, because I was on the cusp of dangerous territory. I felt the force and weight of her charge, assuring her over and over again that I would not change. That I would not be a burden to my parents. That I would watch out for myself and my loved ones. That I would be good.

Despite my fears, I settled into the rhythms of sixth grade without so very much trouble. Middle school made me feel official and grown up, but the very best part was getting to spend time with my older cousins. I cherished our newfound closeness, and so was completely thrown when, months into the school year, a mutual friend accidentally made reference to "Jael's boyfriend" in my presence. How could I have missed this? The girl immediately tried to backtrack—it was widely known among our classmates that the Phelpses weren't allowed to date—but it was too late. I was sick with worry and fear, but also pleased to have discovered valuable information that could help save my cousin from the clutches of this vicious sin. I colluded with other church members to surreptitiously question classmates about the dalliance, and then reported back to my mother that afternoon after school.

I don't recall the consequences of this incident except as they related to me. There was joy at being the object of my mother's pride; instead of following my cousin's bad example or trying to hide her wrongdoing, I'd been responsible and cautious and was looking out for the soul of my friend. There was hope against hope that sweet Jael would be saved from her concupiscence. And there was determination to never allow myself to be in her position, to never repeat the mistakes of the dearly beloved women in our family. I never felt superior to them, no—on the contrary, the moral missteps of such strong, godly women made me fear all the more for the safety of my own soul. I was female, and therefore easily deceived, and I prayed that God would deliver me from such sinful thoughts and desires. My mom, my aunts, and my Gran warned me in mostly vague terms about the sensual sins that had befallen the most devout of women. And as with Gran, I heard such expectation and hope in their voices as they spoke to me: that I wouldn't fall to the obstacles that had caused so many before me to stumble; that the standard was higher for me and my generation. With the Lord's help, I would make absolutely certain that my own thoughts and behavior were above reproach.

———

As it turned out, I didn't have much to worry about. From middle school through college, there was really no one in the church whom I could conceivably marry—it was still almost entirely my relatives—so I didn't entertain any serious thoughts of relationships. I had hormones as a teenager, of course, and a couple of boys at school caught my eye—

but in addition to being terrified of lust and of falling out of favor with God, I was a realist. We protested every single day in our hometown and across the country, and our church was universally hated for it. I understood that the likelihood of any of my classmates being interested in me was essentially nil—especially after we started protesting outside our high school during lunch period—and I also knew that the odds of any of them joining the church were even lower. I knew a hopeless situation when I saw one. I also knew that I was far too young to be thinking about boys anyway, so the whole idea was mostly off my radar.

I got older. A crew from the BBC came to Topeka to film their documentary about Westboro in 2006, the year I turned twenty. Louis Theroux, the wily but affable presenter, spent a great deal of time talking to me and the other young adult women in my family. He and the rest of the crew seemed fascinated by the fact that our church was populated almost entirely by the children and grandchildren of the only pastor it had ever had—an especially salient consideration given the dearth of potential spouses for us, the grandchildren. We would likely never marry or have children of our own, which Louis saw as a huge problem for us, both personally and as a church. To him, the desire for companionship was in the essential nature of humanity, and without it we young, vivacious women would grow to be bitter spinsters, old and alone. He pointed out that our doctrines and strict policy of marriage only to church members were against our interests as a church body, too; they effectively cut off new blood that the church would need to grow. We would all eventually die off without it, and then Westboro would be no more.

We dismissed Louis's arguments as utter poppycock. First of all, we told him, only the basest of humanity is ruled by carnal lust. There is no true member of God's church who is so lascivious as to *need* marriage, and certainly not one who would be willing to defy God and marry an unbeliever. *Be ye not unequally yoked together with unbelievers: for what fellowship hath righteousness with unrighteousness? and what communion hath light with darkness? or what part hath he that believeth with an infidel? Wherefore come out from among them, and be ye separate, saith the Lord, and touch not the unclean thing.* The Apostle Paul's second letter to the Corinthians is infinitely clear: no matter the circumstances, a

desire to marry outside the church is dispositive evidence of one's lack
of salvation.

Second, we argued that God is entirely sovereign and controls the
minds of all humankind. Of course, He'd chosen to harden the hearts
of the vast majority of them—that's why our church was so small—
but with God, all things are possible. If He so chose, he could easily
bring any or all of us a husband or wife. They would become believers and join the church, and then they would be suitable spouses for a
servant of the Lord.

Finally and most important, we were living in the last of the Last
Days, and Jesus would soon return through the clouds and save His
people and dismantle the foundations of the earth. Who cares about
marriage when the world will *imminently* be destroyed by God?

But when Louis approached Jael with questions of marriage and
the future, she didn't respond with a Bible verse—just a gentle laugh
at his ignorance and a rhetorical question or two of her own: "Are you
kidding? Who is gonna marry us?!"

After so many years, Jael had become a realist, too.

———

At twenty-four, I had a major stumble. It was a short-lived infatuation
with a young, foreign salesman who approached my seventeen-year-old
sister, Grace, and me while we were walking through the mall (in a
hurry, as always, because we couldn't be out by ourselves for too long).
He convinced us to let him do a demonstration on Grace's hair of the
curling iron he was selling, and we phoned home to get permission.
The only reason we could even hope for a green light was that the
salesman was Israeli. At that time, our church was exploring the book
of Revelation, and many church members believed that we would be
the instruments used by God to save 144,000 Jews. The whole doctrine was incredibly strange to me—it certainly wasn't theology that
I'd grown up with—but I wanted to understand it. I'd also never met
an Israeli Jew, and he seemed different from the American Jews I'd
met at pickets (which may have had something to do with the fact that
I wasn't holding a GOD HATES JEWS sign and singing an anti-Semitic
parody of "Hatikvah," but I digress). My mom was curious, too; it
seemed like both of us were thinking something along the lines of

"Maybe we'll meet a saved Jew right here in Topeka!" So Grace and I got the go-ahead. Mom even told me to invite him and his colleague, also Israeli, to church on Sunday.

We sat there talking for about an hour while he worked through my sister's impossibly long locks—a woman's uncut hair being a sign of her obedience and subjection to God and to her father or husband. Looking back, there isn't anything about this guy that I can point to as having been especially appealing. I could tell that he was interested in me, but more to the point, there was a slim chance that he could be saved—a hope I hadn't dared to have for any guy outside the church in all my years. More than anything, the feeling I had sitting in that chair was simple *possibility*, and it was electrifying—like nothing I'd ever felt before.

The Israelis couldn't make it to church two days later because of work, but they did come to Sunday dinner at my house. When they walked in with homemade falafel, the sweet, spicy scent of barbecue already permeated the kitchen. After dinner, we sat around the living room all evening—the salesmen and my parents and siblings—talking about God and Judaism and Israel and the Bible. Hebrew was their first language, which made Google Translate a necessity and deep discussion well-nigh impossible. Neither side walked away convinced by the other's beliefs, but it was a noteworthy conversation—less because of its substance and more because of its tone. It was contemplative rather than contentious, which wasn't generally the norm when it came to Westboro members and theological debates.

A few weeks later, I was out for a solo bike ride around the campus of my alma mater, when suddenly the Israeli pulled up next to me in an old car and said I should come see him. I told him I couldn't, but he pointed toward a nearby apartment building and said I'd only be there for just a minute. The tiny spark of excitement that shot through me was more than dwarfed by an overwhelming sense of foreboding and dread; I felt physically ill. I pedaled on for a moment, then turned around and headed toward his building. I tried to maintain some sense of propriety by resolving that I wouldn't go *into* his apartment. This was already *the appearance of evil*, but I felt that going inside would be unforgivable, my chastity essentially assumed to be forfeit.

It was early evening, but the sun was still hot, the extreme humidity of our Kansas summer still stifling. I found him sitting in the shade of the apartment building when I pulled into the parking lot. It was late July by then, and I was halfway through a fourteen-mile ride; beads of sweat were forming and falling all over my skin, deeply tanned that far into the season. I got off my bike and sat down on the curb next to him. We talked for a minute. I showed him photos of the results of my own amateur attempts with the curling iron. He laughed and then stood up and said we should go inside where it was cool. I demurred, my heart pounding steadily in my ears. It felt like the world was moving in slow motion.

Just then, the other salesman darted outside and teasingly grabbed my little black backpack, absconding with it back into the apartment. It was a flirtatious move, but I protested angrily—my phone and wallet were in there, and I couldn't leave without it. I followed them into the apartment, the corrosive acid in my stomach seeming to multiply with each step until I thought I would vomit. The blast of air conditioning that hit me when I walked in was welcome, immediately bringing goose bumps to my skin, but it was almost completely dark inside. The lights were off and the curtains drawn, so it took my eyes a minute to adjust from the brightness outside. His roommate had thrown my bag into his bedroom, so I followed him there. He sat on the bed. I pleaded with him to just give me the bag, but he insisted I sit down next to him, facing him. I sat. He said sweet things I wanted to believe—that I was beautiful, that he cared about me—and then tried to kiss me. I evaded awkwardly, tucking into myself and bringing my arms up as if to protect my face.

No. I could not cross this line.

He tried again, and again I evaded. I stood up. He gave me my bag. I let him hug me. We walked outside. He hugged me again. And then I was off.

I biked straight home feeling sick and shaky and tortured with guilt. I cried as I rode, overcome with shame and panic that God would curse me for what I'd done. I had let my whole family down. My parents. The church. Myself. I was no longer unsullied. It wasn't just my actions that were so exceedingly sinful; it was the indefensible thoughts that had led me to them. *But I say unto you, That whosoever looketh on a woman to lust after her hath committed adultery with her already in his heart.* According to Jesus, the fact that I'd had those feelings in the first place made me guilty of adultery.

I felt broken, but I tried to clean myself up as best I could, to pretend like nothing had happened. When he emailed a few days later—"You don't understand how I think about you all day long."— I couldn't stand it anymore. I showed the message to my mom and begged for help and forgiveness. She was understanding and kind, but I thought I saw doubt in her eyes when I explained that I'd only hugged him twice, that I hadn't done anything else (why would I feel so guilty and afraid if that was all we'd done?), and that pained me all the more. She sat down beside me and read me a passage from the book of Isaiah: *Neither let the eunuch say, Behold, I am a dry tree. For thus saith the LORD unto the eunuchs that keep my sabbaths, and choose the things that please me, and take hold of my covenant; Even unto them will I give in mine house and within my walls a place and a name better than of sons and of daughters: I will give them an everlasting name, that shall not be cut off.* My mama wasn't excusing my behavior, but she was trying to tell me that she understood, trying to help me find comfort in the very likely scenario that I would be a "eunuch" for the rest of my life, trying to help me see that having a place in the house of God—His church—was better than having a husband or sons or daughters. She was preparing me to accept that this was a sacrifice I might be required to make for the kingdom of God's sake, as several of my aunts had been called to do. I squeezed her hand and cried quietly, something I found myself doing each time I encountered that verse thereafter, without ever quite knowing why—just a nebulous, fleeting sense of loss that I neglected to pursue.

It was even worse when my oldest brother, Sam, called to talk to me. He's seven years older than me, and I'd always admired and looked up to him as a near-perfect example of a true servant of God. He kindly chided me, and told me that I couldn't pursue this. That by wanting something that God hadn't given me, I was murmuring against Him. That the people in the Bible who'd murmured against God had been destroyed. That I needed to get back to single-hearted fidelity to God and put away this sin. Whether or not I ever got married was God's decision alone, Sam reminded me. If He chose not to give me a husband, then I should be thankful, because then it would be my happy lot to serve Him without being encumbered by *the cares of this life*. He reminded me of the Apostle's words: *The unmarried woman careth for the things of the Lord, that she may be holy both in body and in spirit: but she that is married careth for the things of the world, how she may please her husband.* We don't get to be mad at God for not giving us what we want, Sam said. How dare we? God is Perfect, Sovereign, and Just—and we are His to do with as He pleases.

Of course it was true, all of it. I knew all the words by heart. Sam was right, and I was so grateful to my big brother for bringing them to my remembrance, for helping guide me back to sanity and away from sin.

We got past it. I didn't bike by myself anymore. Of my own accord, I installed a tracking app on my phone so that I could show my mom where I'd gone if I ever had to leave the house unaccompanied. I wanted to be on *the strait and narrow path* Jesus spoke of, the one to salvation and eternal life. I wanted to prove—to myself and to my family—that I wasn't going to continue down a path that would lead me to Hell and destruction. I would pray, and the Lord would help me. I would be vigilant. I would stay close to home. I would avoid going anywhere alone. I would keep my distance from anyone who could trip me up.

I would be safe.

———

My phone vibrated briefly and played the already-familiar trill of the Words With Friends tone. I glanced at the screen and read the notification, though I knew what it said:

"Your move!"

It's vaguely suggestive, which I noted and then pretended I hadn't—as I had every day for the past week we'd been playing. It happened the same way each day: there was no play during the daylight hours, and then at some point in the evening, he'd make a move in the game and we'd start to chat. He'd question me about theology, ask me to explain more about the pickets and verses I'd posted on Twitter that day, and make vague references to his life as a "country lawyer." I'd answer his questions, describe Westboro's history and doctrines, and tell him about walking out of the Kansas City premiere of Kevin Smith's film *Red State*. (Smith had taken to Twitter to invite me to review the Westboro-inspired film onstage after the showing, and my parents had agreed to allow it. But when we caught sight of two former church members—including my brother Josh, whom I hadn't seen in seven years—my mom sensed a setup and the whole group of us bailed.) We made our moves so quickly that we'd get through an entire game each night, and then begin again with a new game the next evening.

In all our conversations, I was careful to maintain propriety; I still knew absolutely nothing for certain about this man—including whether he even *was* a man. I was hyper-aware that he could be a journalist or otherwise trying to entrap me, to trick me into revealing some titillating piece of information about "The Most Hated Family in America." I wasn't terribly worried about this possibility, though; I wrote everything with the assumption that it could be published in a newspaper—exactly as I would respond on Twitter, but without the 140-character limit. "If you ever have a question about whether it's appropriate to say something," my mother always said, "just add the word *judge* to the end of it—as if you were addressing a judge in the middle of a courtroom." I took my mom's advice to heart, but I was still amazed at how quickly I had fallen into this pattern with my anonymous friend—and in complete denial about how much I was coming to crave my interactions with him.

There was also something illusory about talking with a person who was faceless and (presumably) far away. Before Twitter, friendship with outsiders had always been easy to avoid; I'd chat with classmates during school, but since there was no interaction outside of that, the relationships always fizzled. All I'd ever had to do was keep a little distance from them, and outsiders would always be at arm's length, never close enough to hurt me. And when physical separation failed, like at the salesman's apartment that summer day, I was still mostly protected; as a child, I had donned guilt, shame, and fear—of God, of Hell, of the church—and I wore them like an impenetrable cloak that could never be shed.

But this was not like that. It felt different. Is it even real when half of the conversation comes from a person completely shrouded in shadow? Is it real when the words themselves and all evidence of their existence disappear forever after just a few hours? Lying prone on my bed in my pajamas, perched on my elbows with phone in hand, it was easy to believe that it was not—that the vast distance between us made me safe.

Distance, as I would come to learn, is a relative concept in matters of the heart.

—

"You're too much."

It became a frequent refrain of his, and one that I adored (vastly superior to the other expression he was so fond of: "You're okay."). After playing and chatting for a few weeks, I understood this saying to mean that my attention to detail and ridiculous enthusiasm at the most insignificant of occurrences were a joy to him—or, as he'd put it himself a few times, "I love the way your mind works." This was a shock, and touched me in ways I could not have anticipated. I'd been getting in trouble all my life for talking too much and too fast, rambling on and on about subjects and ideas that almost no one else cared about—but this anonymous stranger wanted to hear them. Which is how I ended up telling him silly stories like:

"This morning I was trying to think of an economic principle to describe a situation. I learned it in Microecon, but couldn't remember the name of the principle. Eventually, I did. I just got to my bed and found an exam from Microecon. The one with the answer I was looking for (principle of diminishing marginal utility). Haven't seen this in 5 years, and have no idea how it got here. No one even knew I was looking for the answer. Weird stuff!"

As much as I enjoyed sharing my stories with him, I wanted to hear *his* stories, too—but it seemed hopeless. I was already consumed with curiosity, and his refusals to open up just made me all the more determined. Since he always balked when *I* asked questions—especially ones that might reveal more of his identity—I stopped asking (or at least reduced my questions by half; I was truly desperate, though I couldn't allow myself to admit it). It was clear that my fear that he was an insidious deceiver had a twin: *his* fear that our friendship—the deepest friendship I'd ever had outside of Westboro—would reflect poorly on him if it became known in his small community. I realized

I just had to be patient and not too probing, to let him share *what* he wanted *when* he wanted.

"Do you play an instrument?" I asked him one day.

"No, but I have DirecTV."

I found him ridiculously clever.

As the weeks and then months passed, my patience paid off. In addition to the information I'd already gleaned, I discovered that he was from a very small town (though not in Nebraska, I was relieved to learn; I still harbored many hard feelings for the state after police officers in Bellevue arrested my mother for lawfully protesting). I knew he was somewhat older than my twenty-five years—early thirties, I guessed. His family had always had a farm, but his parents were professionals: a social worker and a nursing professor. His only sibling, a brother, lived in Chicago with his wife and three children. His family was of Norwegian descent, and he was very tall, with blond hair and blue eyes. I even got part of his name: his initials, C.G. His fear of being connected to WBC made even more sense when I discovered that he was an elected official. I didn't like his reticence, but I could see where he was coming from.

Most of our discussions revolved around Westboro and theology, which he wasn't terribly familiar with. I tried to educate him, but no matter how tenaciously I defended our positions, he just couldn't get past some of them—especially the funeral protests. "But what about the family?" he would press me. My answer to this question sounded more and more hollow as time went by, but I refused to admit how uneasy—almost guilty—this line of questioning was making me feel. I argued the position I'd believed since I was a kid: that the definition of love was "truth," and that any expression of truth was, by definition, loving. Truth was love regardless of context, target, or tone—even when it involved holding a sign that read THANK GOD FOR DEAD SOLDIERS on the sidewalk near a military funeral, while singing praises to the homemade bombs that killed them. C.G. strongly disagreed, and it became a point of contention that came up more often than the rest of his objections. When I wanted to talk about commandments and truth, C.G. was focused on humility, gentleness, compassion. To him, our message and methods clearly lacked these qualities—no matter how truthful we believed our words to be.

I've commented on the signs/picketing several times. You've never given quarter to any real discussion. (They're biblically supported, etc.) I've said and continue to believe that it's just BS designed to gather attention. I understand that you need attention to deliver your message; however, I've never encountered a family as intelligent or creative as yours.

You are carrying those signs because of circumstances 20 years ago in a city park and subsequent momentum.

You can do better.

I had been raised to view life as a battle between good and evil, and I knew that every person fit into one of those two categories. "There is *only* Jacob or Esau! Elect or reprobate!" as my mother would say. C.G. didn't see it that way. He suggested a third group: people who were decent, but not religious. Why would God condemn people who had lived decently in the world? In truth, C.G. seemed to find shades of nuance and complexity in *every* situation—even when it meant reversing himself on opinions he'd previously expressed in strong terms. I found this tendency perplexing at first—as if I could never know for sure what he was *really* thinking—but I soon came to admire this quality, too. He was always reevaluating, never so committed to a position that he couldn't assimilate new evidence.

As I came to appreciate him more and more, it became distressing to hear of his distress. When Amy Winehouse passed away that summer, my family celebrated: she was a whore and a drug addict, and her death was God's punishment. But like so many others who filled my Twitter feed, C.G. lamented her early demise—a tragic loss of life and the beauty that her immense talent had brought into the world. How very *young* twenty-seven was. When a far-right terrorist murdered seventy-seven in a car bombing of Oslo and subsequent attack on a youth summer camp, church members rejoiced again. "My entire Facebook wall is shattered Norwegian innocence," C.G. told me. He simply could not imagine telling the parents of murdered children to PRAY FOR MORE DEAD KIDS. I insisted to C.G. that God was good and that all His judgments were righteous. I quoted verses wherein God laughs at the calamity of unbelievers because they rejected Him. *Because I have called, and ye refused; I have stretched out my hand, and no man regarded; I also will laugh at your calamity; I will mock when your fear cometh.* But watching my family track the rising body count with glee, I felt mournful.

The truth was that I had started to feel sad in response to tragedies even when C.G. wasn't there to prompt me. On Twitter, I came across a photo-essay about a famine in Somalia, bursting into tears at the sight of the first image: a tiny emaciated child. My mother heard and immediately walked over to my desk, asking what was wrong. I pointed to the photo on my screen and shook my head. "Would you send me that link, hon?" she said eagerly, "I'm going to write a GodSmack about it!" The disparity between my response and my mother's gave me pause, but she didn't seem to notice. She was already caught up in composing a celebratory blog post. In the past, this discrepancy would have made me wonder what was wrong with me, but now I thought of the prophet Elisha, weeping at his prophecy of the destruction of Israel. As I watched my mother's fingers fly over the keys, a small part of me began to wonder if there was something wrong with Westboro.

I couldn't acknowledge any of this to C.G., of course, or even to myself. Instead I quoted Bible verses and insisted that he needed to stop substituting his judgments for God's.

When our discussions became thorny like this, as they inevitably did, he directed us back to music, books, movies. He introduced me to David Foster Wallace and Norwegian cookies, writer and comedian Jake Fogelnest, and the music of John Roderick, Blind Pilot, the Avett Brothers, and Foster the People. They became special to me for the simple fact that they'd come from him, but I also discovered that I really enjoyed them, too. I didn't want to forget anything he told me, so I started recording everything in a Field Notes Brand notebook— the notebook itself being another item he'd introduced me to. He was a hipster through and through—I'd never known one before—and I quickly came to love all things I-heard-about-this-cool-new-group-months-ago. I was saturated in his digital presence, even though we were worlds apart.

Throughout it all, we approached each other with the deliberate caution one might employ in the presence of a dangerous, frightened animal; a single false step could be one's undoing, or it might send the beast hightailing it into obscurity, never to exploit another Triple Word

Score again. This sense that so much was at stake with each word was unwavering, almost palpable, and the thrill of it was combustible. There was no thought of speaking openly or directly about any feelings we might be developing, because to do so would be to acknowledge that this was about more than just God, and that would mean the end of it. And yet the subtext was always there, simmering just beneath conscious thought; I saw it, and I refused to see it, limerence disguised by equivocation and the purposefully easy cadence of our conversations. It was in the words we chose to deploy on the game board ("UNREQUITED"). It was in the songs and lyrics we shared (*I've put no one else above us / We'll still be best friends when all turns to dust*). It was in the way we mocked each other with doting nicknames masquerading as insults ("circus monkey," "old man"). It was in the literary quotes we presented without comment or preamble ("I am also inclined to overuse the word 'old,' which actually has less to do with age, as it seems to me, than it does with familiarity. It sets a thing apart as something regarded with a modest, habitual affection. Sometimes it suggests haplessness or vulnerability. I say 'old Boughton,' I say 'this shabby old town,' and I mean that they are very near my heart"). We were offering the words of writers and journalists, musicians and comedians, in order to convey what fear and decorum prevented us from saying ourselves.

I never allowed myself to imagine it, but it would be foolish to deny the secret hope that I came to harbor: that he could be mine someday. That he would eventually rip off the mask and appear at church one Sunday morning. That was the only way it could happen, of course; he'd have to join Westboro. I knew this was the only way, and I did what I could—keeping my words as disciplined and proper as I could make them—to sway him in that direction. In the subtlest of ways, I was trying to convince him of the rightness of our doctrines, the necessity of the protests, and the magnificence of life at the church. I never directly encouraged him to come to Topeka. Westboro had always frowned on attempting conversions; we didn't want to guilt or cajole people into joining our ranks, because we believed conversion was God's job alone. Still, I insinuated that it was the right move— and because he was responding with curiosity instead of condemnation, I continued to hope. I told several church members about him, even, as honestly as I could bring myself to be. I didn't tell them he was the most captivating person I'd ever known. I didn't tell them I loved my conversations with him more than just about any other part of my day. I didn't tell them what he had promised me when I worried aloud that he would one day decide I was evil and stop talking to me ("I never will unless you want me to"). Since I was hiding the depth of my infatuation even from myself, it wasn't so very difficult to hide it from the rest of my family, too.

The latent dream of my waking hours became impossible to ignore one night in late September. Seven months of these conversations had left me impossibly intrigued and altogether obsessed, and as I slept, I dreamed. In the dream, I'm standing on the driveway outside my house one summer Saturday; the grass is a vibrant green, the neighborhood alive with activity, and the noonday sun is beating down unmercifully—just like I like it. A black car with darkly tinted windows pulls up beside me, and a tall, blond man opens the door and steps out of the backseat on the driver's side. I can't see his face and we've never met, but I know his name: Chad Garrett. Suddenly I'm on the other side of the block, on the front lawn of the church itself. There are church members all around working on maintenance—mowing the lawns and cleaning the inside of the building and playing with the kids out back—but I'm looking for him. He comes around the corner looking for me, too, and we're alone for a moment. He walks over and embraces me, his hands tangling in my curls as he holds me against him. I'm keenly aware that we're on the church's security cameras, and I know I'll be in trouble when everyone finds out, but I can't bring myself to stop. I want this so badly. I've waited so long for him. It is undeniable.

When I awoke, I was shaking. I could still feel his hands in my hair. It was September 30, and I spent the day fighting back tears, my stomach constantly on the verge of spilling its contents, though it was empty. When he started a game that night, I told him I couldn't talk to him anymore, or ever again. That I was deleting Words With Friends. We went back and forth about the whys and the wherefores for a little while, but I knew I was right. It had become undeniable.

This could not be. It would destroy me, body and soul, just like God had promised.

Then when lust hath conceived, it bringeth forth sin: and sin, when it is finished, bringeth forth death. Can a man take fire in his bosom, and his clothes not be burned?

I'd already let this ungodly affection for an unbeliever take root in my heart. If I didn't rip it out with both hands, I would fall away and lose everything—my family, my friends, my whole life in this world—and in the world to come I'd be tormented in Hell for all of eternity, where the worm that consumes your flesh never dies and the fire is never quenched.

I didn't imagine it was possible for this to be any more gut-wrenching than it already was, but I was swiftly corrected when the messages kept coming:

You know I love you. You know I do. It's not just the idea of you. I know you.

You also know I'm not coming to Topeka.

My heart hit the floor with a sickening thud. It was what I'd uncon-sciously ached to hear for so many long months, followed by what I'd feared was true all along. I thought bitterly of Jack Boughton, a character from *Gilead*, the first book he'd ever recommended to me: "I think hope is the worst thing in the world. I really do. It makes a fool of you while it lasts. And then, when it's gone, it's like there's nothing left of you at all."

I hated myself.

Just before I deleted the app, he said, "South Dakota."

It took me less than two minutes to find his name. On a list of South Dakota State's Attorneys, there it was: "Chad Fjelland, Clark County." C.G.'s username included that foreign letter combination—"F/j"—and I was sure this had to be him. I looked him up on Google and found a photo: there he is, sitting in an office at a big wooden desk with papers strewn about, law books filling the shelves against the far wall. He's wearing a white button-up shirt, his tie thrown casually over his shoulder. I stared for a minute, feeling so strange to finally have a face.

I had to cut him out of my life forever, but first I had to know more. I wanted to know if he'd been honest. Online research had al-ways been a strength of mine, so I spent a few minutes using my talents to uncover as much about him as I could, to see if he'd told me the truth. My mind swept through seven months of talk and came to rest on three data points that could possibly be confirmed independently: the size of the community he lived in and two deaths that had occurred there.

First, I looked up the funeral home's website and searched through the obituaries. It only took a moment to find what I was looking for, and my heart swelled a little.

He'd told me the truth.

"Clark, SD" was my next search term. Population: 1,139.

Truth.

I felt frantic, pathetic, and out of control. I was entering true stalker territory, but I couldn't stop; I paid $6.95 for a public records search.

POSSIBLE ALIASES: Chad G Fjelland.

"C. G." Truth.

AGE: 39.

Older than I'd believed—fourteen years my senior—but he'd never told me otherwise. Truth.

MARRIAGE INDEX: No Records Found.

The most important part. Truth.

There was a list of addresses and phone numbers, but they meant nothing to me. I sat in the empty office staring at my computer screen for a long time. In the span of twenty minutes I'd gone from total ignorance to stalker-level scrutiny, and I finally had answers. I had a name and a face, proof that I'd been conversing with a real man who really existed in the real world. His name was Chad, even, just as I'd dreamed.

And now he was gone forever.

I crawled into bed and cried until I slept.

———

I tried to undo it all the next night, to take back my insistence that we never speak again.

No, he said, we couldn't talk anymore. It had all become too much.

I agreed. What else could I do?

I didn't tell him I'd hunted him down and discovered his identity, but I did tell him I'd dreamed the name "Chad Garrett." I didn't know whether the middle name was correct, because the records search had only said "G." Within half an hour, he'd sent me an email: a list confirming all the personal data I'd found the day before and more. The only thing that didn't match was his age.

"Age 38."

I shrugged it off. The public records search must've been based on the year, and his birthday just hadn't come yet this year. Our age difference was unexpected, but by then, I just couldn't bring myself to care.

And anyway, my eyes kept returning to the first line of the email: "Chad Garrett Fjelland."

Chad Garrett. Chad Garrett. Could it possibly be that my dream had been right? It felt like a sign from God. It gave me hope that maybe the rest of my dream would come true someday, too.

He said, "Believing in your heart that you'll always be anonymous, and then to give that up . . . I think that maybe that's really the only way that a human being can share their heart. I never planned on surrendering that anonymity. You have what's left of mine. Just never hurt me."

It was late. He made the last play of the game and won.

Ever the tease, he said, "Finishing second in a two-person word game only hurts when you're better at making words. Here's three: goodbye, dear Megan."

Ever the know-it-all, I corrected his grammar: "Here *are* three."

"You passed the test," he said. "Unchanged from the day I 'met' you. Unchanged."

For the second night in a row, I cried myself to sleep.

———

Months went by. I was depressed and missed him terribly for a while. I came to hate the Internet, because I couldn't ever get away from him.

He'd deleted his Twitter account—my Gatsby was gone for good—but there was a new one whose tweets and favorites I checked obsessively for months after we stopped talking. And then there was his Spotify account. His Instagram. His Facebook, though he didn't friend me. But even apart from the Internet, he seemed always near at hand. His hipster music began to play on mainstream radio stations, eventually becoming fodder for Westboro parodies. My brothers had taken a liking to his little Field Notes notebooks, too, and I loved and hated the sight of them strewn about the house. *Pathetic.*

Eventually I lost hope. Life went back to normal, but it was grayer than before. I'd finally seen what I was missing, and my world felt impoverished without it. Without him.

It got easier with time, but I woke up one morning the following June feeling altogether desolate. A dream again, though I couldn't remember it. The house was silent so early in the morning—most of its eleven inhabitants were still asleep—and I traipsed down the stairs to find my mama sitting in our office in her pajamas, her face lit up by her computer monitor. She looked over at me with a wide smile that morphed into maternal concern when she saw that I'd been crying. She rose immediately and hurried over to put her arms around me, rubbing circles on my back. "What is it, sweet doll?" she asked softly. I couldn't talk through the tears, and she just held me tight for a long moment. Finally I managed to choke out between sobs, "I just feel so alone sometimes. I didn't know it was possible to be around so many people and feel so alone."

She squeezed me and didn't let go. She understood. "Oh, love bug." She was so gentle. *"The arm of the Lord is not shortened.* He will comfort you. He does comfort you. I love you. We have a wonderful life."

She was right. She had always been right. Outsiders had scoffed at the long years of my mother's anti-lust entreaties, the hysterical ravings of a Puritanical sex-obsessed hypocrite: "Really?" they'd ask, "God is going to send you to Hell for going on a date? What exactly is the harm?" But they knew better. The truth was memorialized everywhere from Leo Tolstoy's *Anna Karenina* to Leonard Cohen's "Hallelujah," King David's gaze lingering on Bathsheba as she bathed on the roof, *Her beauty and the moonlight overthrew you.* Chance encounters igniting obsessions that shatter into heartache. The most pitiful part was that mine hadn't even needed a face or a body to root its hemlock inside me. He was just words on a screen, and more than half a year had passed since I'd said goodbye to him. *Can a man take fire in his bosom and his clothes not be burned?*

I squeezed my mother and buried my face in her shoulder.

6. The Appearance of Evil

Right around the time the world began to unravel, my mother was recovering from surgery. She was supine in the king-sized bed she shared with my father, one set of pillows stacked beneath her knees and another propping her torso up against the tall, chestnut-colored headboard. My father was always on the lookout for ways to make her life easier, and he'd found her a small bed-desk from which she was now working. Aside from the whirring of her laptop, a companionable silence filled the room. I sat in the chair at her bedside with my feet tucked under me, writing a letter to my sister.

Dear Grace Eliza, Sister-mine, Trouble-maker, Friend—

Photography is where you shine, but you also have a way with words that's truly your own. I think this [Field Notes Book] is perfect for you, and I hope you'll write down the story of the little orphan girl who wanted to be a pirate (changed my life!) and Adventures of Mini Megan and other important things that strike your keen eye. I'm so thankful to walk this path with you, dear heart. So. Very. Thankful.

With all my love to my baby sister (and favorite shopping partner ☺), I am

Yours always,
Megan Marie

I was newly smitten with my anonymous friend, and he had just turned me on to these pocket-sized Field Notes Brand notebooks. The one in my hand was a special edition allowing for custom headlines, and to its blank cover I had delicately applied dry transfer decals to give it the title THUG LIFE in the chic Futura typeface beloved by hipsters everywhere. All for the irony, of course. My eighteen-year-old sister was no more a thug than I was a hipster, but it was fun to knowingly pretend, mocking both ourselves and the identities we took on. In spite of our skinny jeans and liberal deployment of gangsta rap lyrics in daily conversation, we had the self-awareness to know that we could never convincingly pull off these characters—"The Notorious M.E.G."—all of which were especially ridiculous and giggle-inducing given that we were members of a despised religious group, both of us still living at home and required to obtain our mother's permission to leave the house even for short periods. The juxtaposition was the joke. "The world is doomed, but check out these shutter shades and old-timey newsie outfits!"

I looked up from the notebook as my mother set aside her computer, her eyelids turned down at the corners. Exhausted. Uncomfortable. Impatient. We were in the throes of the travel and media frenzy following the Supreme Court arguments, and this compulsory downtime was getting to her. The surgery had aimed for pain relief in her lower back, and as she curled her body away from me in preparation for a brief afternoon nap, I eased myself into the space beside her and pressed my thumbs firmly into the flesh on either side of her spine. Ours was a physically expressive family, my parents and the sisters in particular: Bekah, Grace, and I. Massage had long been a casual, regular occurrence in our home—so common, in fact, that I'd developed a Pavlovian response to my sister's approach: goose bumps would appear all over my skin even before Bekah had begun to smooth away the tension she found in my neck and shoulders. She and I often spent evening Bible studies standing over our parents as they read aloud, working through the knots that had collected in their muscles as they spent long hours sitting at a desk, or laboring in our overflowing vegetable garden, or picketing on a breezy day with two signs in each hand ("the Butterfly"), or—in our father's case—commuting 140 miles round-trip each day for his job in Kansas City.

"Thank you, sweet doll," my mother mumbled into the pillow. My hands began the familiar trek around each shoulder blade in turn, along the spine, across the span of her low back, and then reversed direction upward, returning to the pliable skin of her neck. The pressure I applied was alternating at regular intervals, muscle memory taking over, and I continued until her breaths came slow and steady. A few minutes longer to ensure she wouldn't rouse, and then I slowly, deliberately disentangled myself.

———

My mother's troubles began with an email. My parents tried to keep it under wraps at first, and they managed to shield my siblings for a short time, but I was twenty-five. For years I had spent most hours of most days directly in my mother's orbit. Though I didn't know its cause, her distress was apparent to me. She and my father were spending an inordinate amount of time in heated conversation that became hushed on my approach.

After a day or two of gentle pressing on my part, my parents finally allowed me to see the message—just once, and only on my father's iPhone for a few short moments. He hovered, antsy, so I read in haste before he could take it back. It was a disciplinary email from my eldest brother, Sam—just thirty-two at the time—and Steve, a former documentary filmmaker who'd converted and joined Westboro a decade earlier. My stomach turned as I read the accusations, which primarily surrounded the harsh, unmerciful way she could treat others in the church. I knew as well as anyone that my mother could be too zealous in correcting other church members. I'd frequently found myself on the wrong end of her sharp tongue, and I'd had a front-row seat as most of the others had, as well. Still, no one could deny that her vehemence was borne of a desire to do right by the Lord and by us, and that—as Margie had rightly noted in her message to me the year before—my mother's hard edges had been softening for some time now. She had a remarkable tenderness that had been an example for me all my life, the very embodiment of *God loveth a cheerful giver*. She sacrificed for our loved ones tirelessly, the result of an uncanny ability to discern our needs and an unparalleled determination to fill them, no matter what it cost her.

I felt strongly that the case against my mother was overstated, and I was upset that these two men had chosen to stir things up while she was still recovering from surgery. It was a cowardly assault at a time when she was most vulnerable. My father seemed to agree. I could see that he and my mother were gearing up for a fight, preparing her rebuttal—which was also disheartening. I didn't want my parents to *completely* discount what this email was saying, because there was some truth to the criticism. I wanted my mother to hear the legitimate critique at the heart of this email, but in overplaying their hand, Sam and Steve had offered distraction that allowed for easy dismissal. Was someone finally going to address this issue that had been a grief of mind to so many of us at various points, only to blow it with narrow-minded and overblown contentions?

It took time for me to recognize this disciplinary message for what it was: the cynical use of a genuine problem—my mother's abrasiveness—to upend the existing structure of the church. From the moment he'd joined Westboro, it had been apparent to me that Steve wanted to take over. He'd stated his desire for leadership plainly, but was thwarted by the biblical requirements of a church leader—that he could not be *a novice, lest being lifted up with pride he fall into the condemnation of the devil.* I'd viewed this naked ambition as an awkward fact of church life. Now that he was *not a novice*, however, he appeared to be shifting focus to the other obstacle to his rise to power: the longstanding influence of my mother. For Steve, it seemed to me, her sidelining was a stepping stone.

I'll never know exactly what occurred in the conversations that followed this email, because a fundamental transformation took hold of the church almost instantly. Throughout my life, constant, unguarded communication had been all but an object of worship at Westboro. Dozens of emails and text messages flowed through the church's distribution lists each day, covering everything from media and lawsuits, to childcare and lawn maintenance. Members saw one another at protests, hymn-singing gatherings, the family law office, and in our common backyard. We ate dinner together, read the Bible together, exercised together. We congregated frequently for "work crews," where teams of us would put up drywall, paint fences, make signs, mow lawns, and have "cleaning parties" at construction sites to build additions onto members' houses. At 6 A.M. on snowy winter mornings, roving bands of young men and women would wander the neighborhood with our shovels to clear sidewalks and driveways so the mothers wouldn't have to work so hard to get their children to school on time. And throughout it all, we spoke openly of our struggles and triumphs, the state of our souls, the focus of our recent Bible studies and how these ancient lessons applied to current events and our own lives. "Communication is the key!" wasn't just an incidental part of our culture—it was how a group of eighty people managed to maintain such remarkable unity in executing both the endless logistics of communal living and an astonishingly effective worldwide preaching campaign. *Then they that feared the Lord spake often one to another: and the Lord hearkened, and heard it, and a book of remembrance was written before him for them that feared the Lord, and that thought upon his name.*

This email marked the end of an era, though I couldn't know it at the time. Since I wasn't privy to the discussions about my mother's behavior, all I could do was watch with trepidation as events unfolded in front of me. First there were the apology emails from my parents to the church: "Beloved of God—I have offended people over the years with a hard, undisciplined tongue. It is so very wrong and shameful. Please accept my apology and please forgive me. Self-justification is an amazing thing. Please pray for me that the Lord would take away the blinders and heal me of this most important of all illnesses. I love you. I'm so very sorry for the offense I have caused." Then there was the response from an aunt: "We will do better to help you both because we love you dearly." And then came the punishments.

My mother would no longer arrange the pickets in Topeka. She would not prepare the monthly events calendar. She would not orchestrate our cross-country protests. She would not coordinate childcare or media schedules. For the foreseeable future, my mother would not be allowed to give interviews at all. My father tried to defend her against the onslaught, to push back against the extreme penalties, but this only resulted in threats of further punishment: if my parents failed to submit to the judgment of the church, anyone over eighteen who was living in their home would move out and live with other church members. My parents would be shamed and ostracized by their own children.

That final threat was reported to me via a phone call from an aunt who spoke in a reassuring voice. I stood in the dark in the office I shared with my mother, staring out the window into the spring afternoon as my aunt explained that my parents were "in a very bad way." That I shouldn't worry, because the church was not going to let anything bad happen to my siblings and me. As if our parents were a threat to us. I was stunned listening to the sudden shift in how the elders spoke, their tender and heartfelt praise for my parents' boundless dedication and sacrifice abruptly decaying into a noxious contempt. The rot had set in almost overnight. I'd kept quiet for days as I tried to understand what was happening, but when my aunt explained that they'd threatened my parents with removing us from our home, my response was visceral. I felt my lip curl as I nearly erupted in a menacing "Just you fucking *try.*" The thought shocked me into keeping my silence—had I ever in my life felt such a thing against the Lord's church?—and a moment later my aunt ended the call.

———

We may have reached the age of majority, but I couldn't bring myself to employ the term "adult" in reference to myself or any of the siblings now staring at me expectantly. I'd called them together as soon as they arrived home, two brothers and two sisters, all between the ages of eighteen and twenty-four: Bekah, Isaiah, Zach, and Grace. We stood in the back living room, and I closed the door so as not to alert our four youngest brothers, who were doing homework and playing video games in the next rooms. I looked around before opening our meeting: Isaiah and Zach wore stoic expressions, Bekah's brow was deeply furrowed, and Grace—the only one already aware of our purpose here—was unsuccessfully attempting to mask her outrage. I tried to be neutral, but I couldn't keep the edge out of my voice as I recounted the day's events.

During the discussions among the elders, it had apparently occurred to someone that my siblings and I might have an opinion about being forced out of our parents' house. The home we had shared every day of each of our lives. I'd received a follow-up call asking that I speak with my siblings so that we could come to a decision—which was yet another bizarre development. Children were never asked to make independent decisions. As baptized members of the church, the five of us had a duty to shun those who *walk among you disorderly*. The question for us seemed to be: Did the Phelps-Roper children feel we could live with our quarrelsome parents and still serve the Lord as we ought?

I posed the question to my siblings, concluding with a firm "I see no reason to do this, and I have absolutely no interest in leaving."

"Me, neither," Grace piped up. Isaiah and Zach agreed.

Jaw set and brow still furrowed, Bekah looked perturbed but nodded slowly. The pressure to punish our parents was evident, and we all felt it. I was proud of my siblings for resisting.

"Okay," I said. "I'll let them know."

Grace trailed me out the door and up the back steps to my bedroom. My parents had renovated it for my birthday several years before, replacing the carpet with a serene shade of lilac that complemented the beige drapes. I loved this space. At the southwest corner of the second floor, it was far from the common areas where my family spent most of our time, a calm among the chaos. I'd lie in bed on warm nights with both windows thrown open to the epic storms of my Kansas summers. Just before a downpour the air would be suffocating, so heavy I could hardly breathe . . . and then the sky would open and the lightning would flash and the peals of thunder that had spooked me awake as a kid would lull me to sleep.

"What the fuck is going on?"

The "f" word was not really an acceptable use of language in our house, but Grace dearly loved it anyway. It was a pantomime of mischief and defiance; the accompanying wink was always implied. Not today, though. My sister sat down on the bed next to me and held out her hand for my phone. I gave it over, and she began squirreling through my emails and text messages to question me about what she found there. Grace was curious and engaged, and since I was so heavily involved in the central work our mother had always done, there was always more detail about church activities in my messages than there was in hers. She'd been reviewing my phone regularly for a couple of years now, ever since we'd become close—but this would be the last time I gave her free rein. I had grown possessive of my communication with C.G., and though I cherished having no barriers between my sister and me, I did not want to share him. This should have been a neon warning sign to me, but the roiling turmoil in the

church was a distraction from my growing feelings for him and en-
abled my denial.

Grace and I were in a state of disbelief at what was happening to
our parents, convinced that it was undeserved and unduly harsh—but
there was something else, too. It picked at me the longer we spoke, my
apprehension mounting until I finally identified its source:

"Wait a second. Who exactly is *making* these decisions about Mom
and Dad?"

My grandfather had long preached that Westboro was the quintessen-
tial New Testament church: "local, visible, autonomous, self-governing,
exercising discipline over her members." The verses addressing church
decision-making were myriad, and they made it clear that consensus
was required. When church matters came up—especially disciplinary
matters—active participation was the duty of every member. Everyone
had to vote. Everyone had to agree. Without exception. If even a single
member disagreed, no action would be taken. This had been the standard all my life. *Fulfil ye my joy, that ye be likeminded, having the same love,
being of one accord, of one mind.*

The need for church unity was one of our animating principles,
the reason we were in constant communion and communication with
one another. It's why we often answered questions from journalists and
passersby using the same words in the same order with the same tone.
To some, this phenomenon was evidence of indoctrination and coer-
cion, but I never saw it that way. We were *of one mind* as the Lord required us to be, and these verses showed that each of us had a voice
that was integral to the church's success.

So why were the meetings about my parents taking place behind
closed doors?

Grace shook her head, looking as disconcerted as I felt.

———

In spite of our refusal to leave our home, the threat had its desired
effect on our mom and dad: the willingness to distance my siblings
and me from our parents sent a clear signal that their exclusion from
the church was an imminent possibility. Faced with the apparent fact
that the congregation was in full agreement as to the enormity of my
parents' sin and the righteousness of their punishment, my mother and

father could reach only one conclusion: that God had blinded and deluded them as to their grievous faults. That their judgment was impaired, their thoughts fatally compromised, and that the only way forward was to trust and submit to the collective wisdom of the church without question. My parents seemed lost and dejected that night when they pitifully thanked my siblings and me for choosing not to leave them. My heart ached for them. They seemed broken—and that was exactly the point. The fight had gone out of them.

Inexplicably, it had not gone out of me.

On an evening walk with my sister-in-law Jennifer, I raged. Working myself into a frenzy, I argued that *no part* of this process was being done in a Scriptural fashion. Jen kept saying, "You need to talk to the elders."

"I have! I've talked with Margie and Lizz and—"

"*No,*" she insisted, "the *elders.*"

I paused, confused. Jen held forth for a few minutes, and it soon became clear that she was not referring to "the elders" as the term had always been used at Westboro: an informal descriptor of all of the older people in the church, men and women of wisdom and experience. Instead she was referring to "the elders" as if they were the holders of a formal position in the church. *What . . . ?* I thought, surprised and shocked into silence yet again.

At the next break in Jen's diatribe on submission, I asked, "And who are the elders?"

Fred Jr. Jon. Tim. Charles. Ben. Sam. Steve.

"Your dad is, too," Jen said, "but he needs to get his house in order."

All of the older, married men.

I felt sure that my father could not have been involved in this decision, but I was aghast at the rest of them—both the ones who had orchestrated it and those who had acquiesced. It occurred to me that over the course of just a few days, these men had managed to overturn the democratic system, gleaned from Scripture, that had ruled Westboro all my life. Only then did I understand that *this* had been the ultimate purpose of that email. No doubt they believed they were assuming their rightful place at the head of the church, and Sam and Steve must have seen that my mother had been the only member of the church with enough influence to take a stand against such a hostile takeover, so there were no two ways about it: if these men were going

to supplant the church's long-standing decision-making practices, she
had to be neutered.

The new hierarchy they had instituted made it instantly apparent
where the rest of us now stood.

They hadn't even bothered to let us know.

———

My mother had always laughed at the remarkable resemblance between her sense of humor and Grace's. Whereas Bekah and I tended
to view life through rose-colored lenses, wanting our stories tied up
with big red bows and happily-ever-afters, the thought patterns shared
by Grace and our mother were often morbid, endlessly playful, and
frequently resulted in a group of siblings laughing ourselves to tears.
Grace was forever plotting, her mind spinning tales for us at every moment. One day I returned to my desk and found money she owed me
for a pair of jeans she'd bought on my credit card. Attached was a note,
typical of her mischievous machinations, written as if to a loan shark
with a plea not to "hurt my family."

Sisterhood had not always been so agreeable to me. I could never
identify precisely when it happened, but somewhere along the line, my
eight younger siblings had—mercifully—ceased devoting their every
waking hour to fighting and fits. I had always felt protective of these
adorable nuisances, but now they had grown into clever and creative
human beings whose minds I'd want to know even in the absence of
our genetic connection. I'd spent my early years seizing upon every
opportunity to spend time away from them, desperate to be free of
responsibility for them and to be a Big Kid. Now we sought each other
out whenever we had free time. We'd walk to the bakery for cake pops
and frosting shots while Noah pontificated on *Captain Underpants* and
The Hunger Games. We made time for family movie night most week-
ends, parsing scenes from films like *Inception* and *Never Let Me Go* for
weeks afterward. On more than one occasion, I reached my arms out
to my sides to stretch only to have Luke mistake it as an invitation
for a hug. The nine of us were easily a self-sufficient picketing team,
a formidable crew of laborers, people who could work together mostly
drama-free to get things done, with good-natured teasing and banter
all along the way.

Sunday afternoons would see us hiking together with our parents along the trails by the Kansas Governor's Mansion, chatting and laughing and tripping over each other in the waning sun, throwing ourselves onto the train tracks and feigning looks of abject terror for an impromptu photo shoot. Our parents would hold hands, contentedly watching over the whole brood of us and laughing at our shenanigans. The lessons that brought us to this place hadn't come easily, but they were among my most treasured. Being part of a family this size—especially with our imaginative and ever-attentive parents at the helm—had helped to teach us humility and patience. We had each come into the world with a strong personality and an outsize sense of justice, but as we grew, we learned to pick our battles, not to throw down at the slightest provocation. We learned to yield to each other. *But the wisdom that is from above is first pure, then peaceable, gentle, and easy to be intreated, full of mercy and good fruits, without partiality, and without hypocrisy.*

In the months that followed the installation of the self-appointed elders, I dedicated myself to employing these lessons in the face of escalating confusion and frustration. The elders issued new edicts on an ad hoc basis, and always via direct, in-person communication; gone were the days of church-wide emails and meetings where important matters were hashed out for all members to hear and weigh in on. Instead, members would learn of decisions from an assigned elder: one's husband, if married, or father, if not. For the few members who had neither husband nor father as a church elder, an elder was appointed to disseminate information to them. Questions and concerns, once freely discussed with all other church members, were now confined to our assigned elder or parents only. My brother Sam had been my friend and counselor for many years, but when I asked him about a new decision in the early stages of this process, he shut me down: "You need to talk to Dad about that. He's the one you should be addressing such things with." Joy, contentedness, submission—these were the only acceptable communications among the church body as a whole.

Not even *Gramps* was an appropriate audience for questions or doubts, as he was kept only minimally aware of all the maneuverings of the elders and the day-to-day happenings of the church. This had already been a trend for some time. My grandfather was getting older,

and my family had taken an example from the book of Exodus, when
Jethro, the father-in-law of Moses, saw that the job of leading the Israelites had become too much for Moses to do alone. *Thou wilt surely wear
away, both thou, and this people that is with thee: for this thing is too heavy
for thee; thou art not able to perform it thyself alone.* Jethro proposed that a
system of lesser judges be instituted beneath Moses, *and it shall be, that
every great matter they shall bring unto thee, but every small matter they shall
judge: so shall it be easier for thyself, and they shall bear the burden with thee.*
The new elders seemed to see themselves in this manner, relieving my
grandfather of the burden of leading the church. To go over their heads
and seek aid or comfort or understanding from our pastor directly—to
call the elders' judgment into question in any way—was not allowed.
Even as the cruelty toward my mother continued and increased for
months on end, and even though she and Gramps were close, she dared
not be open with him about what was happening to her. If she had, her
exclusion from the church would have been all but certain.

I struggled to conform to our new paradigm, and I struggled to
understand and articulate why I was struggling. Theoretically, it was
possible to implement a change like this in a biblical way. There were
plenty of verses in the New Testament about elders, and I realized
for the first time that at least some of them were referring to a specific office in the church—not just to "older people." *And when they
had ordained them elders in every church, they commended them to the Lord.
Let the elders that rule well be counted worthy of double honour.* But unlike
in that passage, *we* hadn't ordained these elders; they had ordained
themselves—a fact that would have been easier to accept if I hadn't felt
conflicted about nearly every decision they issued.

One of the first came just before the Royal Wedding, the marriage of Prince William to Kate Middleton. Per our usual practice,
the church issued a news release and announced on Twitter that we
would protest the affair: "Wedding vows mean nothing to these royal
mutts!" We had no intention of actually traveling to London—not
least because the United Kingdom had banned church members from
entering the country—but even the announcement of a protest was
enough to generate significant media coverage. We were engaging in
what we called "virtual picketing": protesting a faraway event in a local space, and reaching the target audience by publishing photos and

messages on the Internet and through the media. There was nothing inherently dishonest about this tactic—injustice in one city often inspires public demonstrations in others—except, of course, that our intent was to deceive.

We had employed this strategy before, choosing words that were technically true, but designed to leave an impression that was not: that we were actually present outside the event. I'd thought this was funny when I was younger, viewing it as a prank or a trick, rather than a lie. The behavior seemed questionable to me now, but all doubt left my mind as soon as I saw my cousin Jael abandoning the "technically true" for outright lies: she was posting tweets about being on a plane to London. My heart sank when I received a group text from Steve instructing everyone with a Twitter profile to republish a post from an account he had just created: @UGNewsWire. The account purported to be an "Int'l News Service," complete with a fake logo to make it appear as if it were a legitimate media outlet. Its posts read:

WBC members (of 'God Hates Fags' infamy) picket outside Westminster Abbey day before #RoyalWedding

Westboro Baptist protesters outside Westminster Abbey - singing songs & chanting 'God Hates the UK'

The infamous Westboro Baptist Church is on the ground in the UK - protesting the Royal Wedding:

Each of the posts included an image of Westminster Abbey that had been digitally altered to include picketers with signs. I saw that Steve had sent them to the BBC, the Associated Press, *USA Today*, and other news organizations.

I was mortified. These lies were idiotic, not only violating the Scriptures but offering the hordes of people who hated us a legitimate reason to impugn the integrity of the church. It undermined our claim to being messengers of God, and it was the picture of a verse my mother quoted often: *Give none occasion to the adversary to speak reproachfully.* I had several thousand followers on Twitter, and though I angered them on a regular basis, I had a growing sense of community with the people

I encountered there. I felt like I owed them the truth, and I didn't want to be attacked for being dishonest. And on top of everything else, I didn't want them to think I was the type of person who would tell ridiculous lies for the sake of publicity.

In a pique, Grace found me at my desk not long after Steve's message came through: "Did you see Steve's text?!"

"Yeah," I sighed. "Yikes." Grace and I talked it through and were in agreement that the whole situation was petty, wrong, and embarrassing. We also knew that we would hear from Steve if we didn't retweet him, and that we couldn't decline his order without support from our parents. If we refused to obey—even in the matter of a simple retweet—there would be trouble. I briefly considered pretending to have missed Steve's message, but that *also* would've been a lie, and it wouldn't have worked, anyway: I had at least a few thousand more Twitter followers than all other church members, and he would certainly check my account to see if I'd done his bidding.

As if on cue, a follow-up text from Steve popped up on my screen.

I went in search of my mother and asked if we had to follow Steve's instruction, explaining the objection that Grace and I shared. This was just a week after my mother had sent her apology email to the church, and though she agreed with us, she had no standing to question or correct another church member on any matter—especially an elder—no matter how egregious. She contacted my father at work, and returned later to report that we just needed to do what Steve had directed.

I picked up my phone and tapped the "retweet" button feeling utterly disgusted with Steve, with myself, and with the state of the church. What was the *matter* with these elders? Our integrity, our fidelity to the Scriptures—these were our foundation and our only defense against the accusations that the world was forever hurling in our direction. Our signs were plastered with the wrath of God, but here we were, hypocritically ignoring one of the clearest declarations of God's hatred in the Scriptures:

> *These six things doth the Lord hate: yea, seven are an abomination*
> *unto him: A proud look, a lying tongue, and hands that shed innocent*
> *blood, An heart that deviseth wicked imaginations, feet that be swift*

*in running to mischief, A false witness that speaketh lies, and he that
soweth discord among brethren.*

Not just one but two of these seven abominations addressed lying.
A lying tongue. A false witness that speaketh lies.

Just as I'd known they would, Twitter users quickly discovered
the truth and began to call us out for the lies and manipulated photos.
They quoted Bible verses to me, the same ones I had quoted to my
mother. Ashamed and angry, I repeated the party line about "virtual
picketing" and Steve's ridiculous claim that the fake picket was never
meant to be taken literally—that the photos were so poorly Photo-
shopped that no one could possibly have been taken in by them—but
this, too, was demonstrably false. When someone on Twitter pointed
out to @UGNewsWire that Westboro members were banned from
the U.K., Steve had tweeted back, "it was reported that the ban was
lifted, but authorities can't confirm." *Of course he meant to deceive people,* I
thought, *he just did a shitty job.*

Lying on my bed that night, Grace wasn't spinning her absurd
tales, and I wasn't twisting her hair into French braids the way I'd done
since she was a little girl. It felt foolish to be worked up over something
as small as a retweet. Was our father right when he accused us of carping and self-righteousness? He had reminded us that we knew these
people in the church, that they were kind and thoughtful and trying to
do right by the Lord. They were working hard to preach to this Godforsaken world, and the two of us were sitting on the sidelines looking
down our noses and sniping at them. What was our problem?

Grace and I stared at the ceiling for a time, talking quietly until
we came to the answer:

For the first time, we had been told to do something unscriptural
by someone in a position of authority.

For the first time, we had no way to make our objections heard by
the church.

And as always, we had no choice but to submit.

———

By July, three months after the initial disciplinary email, visible signs of
the elders' influence were multiplying. A new, stricter modesty standard

for women and girls had come first, implemented within days of the elder takeover. Before that, the general rule had been to cover the "4 B's"—"breasts, back, butt, and belly," my mother recited—but its enforcement had never been draconian. Now, showing any hint of skin in these areas—as, when reaching into the truck bed to grab a picket sign, a girl's shirt rose and briefly exposed an inch of her stomach—was cause for censure. Legs, too, had become a problem. My parents sent my sisters and me to the mall in search of longer shorts, and we found several pairs that reached below mid-thigh. Our father approved, but he had been given to understand that his judgment was suspect. The process became even more demeaning when he sent me down to model the new shorts for my eldest brother. I was twenty-five. Sam was thirty-two. He did not approve. Modesty required high-necked blouses, dresses or pants that covered our legs down to our knees, and covered feet—no sandals—during the Sunday church service.

My mother's disappearance from the media was another outward indication of the shift. She had represented the church in newspapers and radio interviews the world over on an almost-daily basis, but now Steve had taken charge. I was humiliated on her behalf as I watched her awkwardly turn away from a swarm of media that had surrounded us at a protest in Ohio. They were clamoring for interviews, baffled and trying to understand our message—but preaching the Gospel was clearly less important to the elders than bringing my mother to heel. Because she had been stripped of most of her other church-related duties, as well, the Phelps-Roper home grew eerily quiet as the constant flow of reporters, cousins, and other church members ebbed to a trickle.

As sudden and jarring as these changes were, there is an image that stands out in my memory as most clearly signaling the distress of this transition period: a close-up of my littlest sister's fingers. Grace and I paid close attention to the elders' decisions, and the more we saw, the more troubled we became. I was practiced at justifying Westboro's doctrines, but the cracks forming in our fortress of logic and Scripture were becoming ever more difficult to ignore. Why would we be punished for unintentionally flashing an inch of skin on our back or belly, while our brothers were permitted to swim shirtless, with all of theirs on full display? Why were girls in other Westboro families subject to more lenient rules of modesty? How could the standards of God differ from house to house? *Let us walk by the same rule, let us mind the same thing.* Sam dismissed our objections, seeming to believe that they originated from a desire to dress like sluts. Grace and I knew better. That the problem went far deeper: hypocrisy, and the dawning realization that the rules we had been taught—the divine rules of a sovereign God—were being systematically replaced by the caprices of fallible men. Church members had always denied that we were "interpreting" the Bible, insisting that we were only reading and obeying what was *plainly* written in the Scriptures. But once I was excluded from the discussions, it soon became obvious that interpretation was inescapable—that it was happening daily, hourly, and always in ways that protected and expanded the authority of these eight elders.

Holding signs together at the pickets, sitting at our desks at home, lying side by side on my bed, Grace and I floundered, trying to make sense of it all and coming up empty. And all the while, she picked. The bits of skin around her fingernails were tiny at first, but she picked at them for weeks, tearing them off again and again until all of her fingers were scabbed and bleeding. "How did it go today?" Grace would ask in resignation when she returned home from school. I'd describe watching our mother stare unmoving at her ringing cell phone again, and then she'd answer it quietly, disappearing to the far corners of our empty house to have another conversation with my dad. Always more trouble, though she was trying to keep it from me. I'd tiptoe after her to eavesdrop on her side of the conversation—a habit I'd picked up from Sam growing up—to learn the source of the conflict. My mother was defensive, disbelieving the complaints my father was receiving: an aunt who disapproved of my mother's tone, another vaguely unsatisfied that her mannerisms demonstrated sufficient repentance. It was as if they were actively looking for reasons to be offended. Despair was creeping toward the deepest parts of me, but I fought to keep it at bay and to comfort my sister. As I relayed the day's events to Grace, she would pick. *Pick. Pick.* My reassurances about the necessity of submission—our own and our mother's—began to sound hollow even to my own ears, and I could never say enough without resorting to lies. Instead, I bought her a box of hot-pink Hello Kitty Band-Aids and covered the tips of all ten of her mangled fingers.

"The Megan Solution," she called it. A tendency I'd developed without realizing it.

Cover it up, and it will go away.

———

As it turned out, 2011 was conducive to cover-ups.

June marked the beginning of the most ambitious construction project we had ever undertaken: an enormous house for my aunt and uncle and their seven children, to be built on a concrete foundation directly across the street from my front door. The entire frame of the house would go up in the first eleven days—"Push Week"—which were full of scorching sun and ninety-degree temperatures that had us all baking. Sweat and sunscreen soaked through our clothes, but the work site was alive with the high-pitched buzzing of table saws and the insistent instruction to "Measure twice, cut once!" from the men who'd taken vacation days from work to lead the project. By the time we installed the roof trusses, we were sunburned down to the last minion and an accident with a framing nailer had sent a cousin to the emergency room—but the frame was up. Push Week was a success.

Amazingly, there were several unfamiliar faces around the construction site, too. In an unprecedented turn of events, new members were joining the church at an astonishing rate. Ten years had passed since Steve and his family had joined Westboro—the only outsiders who had come to stay in the quarter-century I'd been alive—but in the span of just a few months, a flood of new people arrived. A twenty-something man from the U.K. Another from a suburb of Chicago. A young woman my age, along with her three children. And an older couple from rural Kansas who had divorced before joining Westboro. It was the second marriage for both husband and wife, and—as our sign paraphrased Jesus—DIVORCE + REMARRIAGE = ADULTERY. *Whosoever putteth away his wife, and marrieth another, committeth adultery: and whosoever marrieth her that is put away from her husband committeth adultery.* It seemed impossible that anyone would make such a sacrifice—a happy marriage that had given them two sweet young boys—in order to join our church. After a lifetime of hostile rejection of our beliefs, we took this sudden profusion of converts as a clear sign that the Lord was with us, and that the end of all things was at hand. *The fruit of the righteous is a tree of life; and he that winneth souls is wise.*

My work for the church also expanded during this period. Most of my mother's tasks had been reassigned to other church members, and several of them had fallen to me. In addition to coordinating the creation and publication of our news releases, I was now the keeper of Westboro's picket schedules, both local and national. If I had questions, I was to report to my father or Steve, rather than to my mother—still sitting at her desk five feet from mine. It was a relief to have a degree of freedom from her intense overmanagement, but I could never feel good about it. I had been taught all my days to honor and obey my mother. I felt a growing sense of disgust at her shaming, and I wanted desperately not to contribute to it. Whenever I made or received a call about church matters that my mother had once overseen, I walked out of our office in haste. I would not cause her more pain with pointed reminders of the position she had lost.

Meanwhile, the unusual success I was finding on Twitter and in the media had caught the attention of the *Kansas City Star.* They sent a reporter to Topeka, and I spent many hours during that spring, summer, and fall giving interviews for a profile. The reporter shadowed me at work and at protests, and came to hear a sermon one Sunday. He even attended one of our summer birthday parties, watching me play volleyball and sit poolside with my cousins and nieces, happily fielding requests to tame their long hair with French braids. His questions were typical and without end, and I reflexively responded in the same way to the same pressure I had always felt when representing the church: to present a strong, united front. To show no weakness. To never admit—even to myself—that the church could be wrong. "There's something wonderfully liberating in the notion that you're one hundred percent right," my grandfather often noted with calm and confidence. It was another conundrum—"mindfucks," as Grace began to call them—that I wouldn't see until much later: That we could experience such a deep sense of personal shame and humility, saying with the Apostle Paul that we were *the chiefest of sinners,* while simultaneously declaring that God had given us the *most* righteousness and insisting that the world obey our understanding.

Our position was inherently arrogant and full of hubris, but we *felt* humble.

Between my conversations with the reporter, with all of the new Westboro converts, with outsiders on Twitter, and with C.G. on the back side of the Words With Friends game board, my growing doubts were crowded out by eternal justification. My attempts to convince them of our piety served to focus my attention on the aspects of the church that made life there so large and extraordinary. The camaraderie. The sense of family and belonging. The wonderful and smart and kind and generous and supportive church members. And the incredible feeling of being in a large group of people functioning almost seamlessly, as one, doing meaningful work as the earthly representatives of the Creator of all mankind. We weren't just holding signs on street corners. We were preaching the standards of God, "maintaining and defending pure Gospel truth," as Gramps always said from the pulpit. *The Wars of the Lord.*

"I'm here because I want to be here," I told the *Star* reporter. "Because I believe these things. Because I love these words."

My regular conversations with C.G. had ended two months earlier, but he sent me a message the day that the profile was published.

"She has no real friends," the article read. "Few acquaintances. The majority of her outside interactions comes with the people—journalists, mostly—who stop by to profile the family."

With characteristic brevity, C.G.'s response was a link to a video clip on YouTube. The farewell scene of *Dances with Wolves*. Sitting horseback atop a snowy cliff is a Native American called Wind In His Hair. He had initially been hostile to the man leaving the tribe via a trail far below the cliff—a white soldier who became known as Dances With Wolves—but now yells out to him in the Lakota language: "Dances With Wolves! I am Wind In His Hair. Do you see that I am your friend? Can you see that you will always be my friend?" Shouting it from the mountaintop, as it were.

My heart soared, and it made me ashamed. I stifled the feeling as soon as I could, steeling myself with the words that concluded the profile:

"I'm all in."

—

In C.G.'s absence, I threw myself back into the work of the church and found an even greater sense of my place within the body. By visceral instinct more than conscious deliberation, I understood that no force silences doubt as effectively as zeal—a passionate clinging to familiar and reliable truths that quiets dissonance and snuffs out uncertainty in an avalanche of action. I was eager to be useful to fellow church members in every way that I could, and my obedience was rewarded with a deluge of tenderness from my loved ones. My twenty-sixth birthday arrived in January with a "text bomb"—the coordinated arrival of dozens of messages from church members, all popping up on my screen at once. My mother had implemented the practice for Westboro birthdays a few years earlier, but the outpouring of love was overwhelming this time.

The message from my dear friend and cousin Jael began: "Dear MegHeart, I have never known a better friend than you."

From my beloved Gran: "Dear little Meg, you have always been a sweet, precious child; & for many years, a faithful & loving servant to our Lord! Gramps & I love you very much! Happy Birthday! You are GREATLY blessed!" She was eighty-six, but had learned to use emojis on her iPhone, her message sprinkled with happy faces and flowers and musical notes.

My mother wrote the story of my life in a series of tweets, which I copied into a Field Notes, fixing her typos as I always did:

> Twenty-six years ago, God loaned us a baby girl. She's comforted us always. We had great hopes for her and called upon the Lord for wisdom to teach her.
>
> Her dad and I had only ONE hope for her: That she would have a tender heart from God, toward Him and His word, and that she would serve His people!
>
> God moved us to sanctify her in her comings and goings, and to teach her line upon line and precept upon precept all of His counsel and ways.
>
> Our little @MeganPhelps has evidence of grace from God and loving kindness, showing a work of God upon her heart, causing obedience to God.

One more tweet on the early days of @MeganPhelps on her God-appointed path: The HUGE happy personality is still with us!

And Grace:

26 years ago, @MeganPhelps was born. I am above all blessed to have her as my sister, friend, counselor, teacher, +, +, +.
    Boaz said to Ruth, ". . . for all the city of my people doth know that thou art a virtuous woman . . ." The same can be said of @MeganPhelps.

Accompanying Grace's tweet was a birthday gift on the same theme: a painting based on an album cover I loved, from a band called "Sons of an Illustrious Father." Grace had replaced the name of the band with a new one: "Daughters of a Virtuous Mother," in the radiant colors of sunset. It was beautiful, but I sensed in this gift a small act of defiance, too: unqualified praise of our mother, who was still an object of scrutiny and judgment by church members. Though I felt confident in condemning the whole world, the pronouncements of the church were sacrosanct and I had always been terrified of contradicting them in any way. *For rebellion is as the sin of witchcraft, and stubbornness is as iniquity and idolatry.* But in that moment, my sister's subversion lit me from within. She was defending our mother.
    And she was not afraid.

———

As the months ticked by, my vague hope that life would eventually return to some sense of normalcy began to dissolve. The shaming of my mother continued into the spring and summer of 2012, more than a year after it had begun. The church was caught in another incident of lies and Photoshop, and it became an international news story that we had pretended to protest Whitney Houston's funeral. After this fiasco, and at the risk of getting ourselves into more trouble with our father, Grace and I were finally able to convince him to represent our concern to the rest of the elders. They agreed to end the public lies and manipulated photos, but only because they were deadlocked about the issue: four of them were against it, but four had no qualms. I was relieved that they had decided against continuing the practice, but I simply could not fathom that *half* of the elders saw nothing wrong with it.

Somehow, the situation deteriorated further still. A cousin of mine, then a woman in her early thirties, admitted to committing fornication and other sins, and she was ostracized and isolated by the church for months. The elders deemed her unrepentant. Just before the church-wide meeting that was to be her final warning from the congregation, I spoke with my brother Sam. I explained to him that I hadn't been allowed to speak with our cousin for nearly half a year, and that I had no way of knowing the state of her heart and mind. She and I were both members of the church, and didn't I have a duty to *love one another with a pure heart fervently*? But on the elders' command, I hadn't even spoken to her. I told Sam that I needed to actually interact with her to know how she was.

"You mean, 'trust, but verify'?" Sam scoffed. He shook his head dismissively. "Nah." He made it clear that I just had to take the elders' word for it and accept their judgment that she was unrepentant. This was the clearest repudiation yet of the unanimity called for in Scripture. I was stunned.

We walked across the backyard in the cool air of late April—almost a year exactly after that email to my parents—and joined the meeting in the church sanctuary. My cousin pleaded sorrow and repentance for her misdeeds, and I heard true shame and sincerity in her voice. The elders were unmoved. The meeting quickly became a campaign to exclude her that very night, in spite of the fact that three church members spoke up in her defense. I was grateful when one elder voiced the same objection that I had: that my cousin had not been given the biblically required third and final warning from the church body—her last opportunity to demonstrate repentance.

All of her defenders were overruled.

"You need to be instructed in this matter," one of my uncles said with stomach-turning condescension.

After thirty-odd years at Westboro, my cousin was kicked out of the church, her home, her family, and her life—all in violation of the very Scriptures we claimed to champion.

My sisters' responses to these events reflected the internal struggle I was experiencing. For many years, my perspective had been
much aligned with Bekah's. We both felt a deep sense of inferiority
when it came to matters of Scripture, and we were willing to yield
to the judgment of older church members—even in cases where we
at first felt discomfort or disagreement. The church had taught us to
distrust our own judgment from the time we were children, and we
had taken the verses to heart. *The heart is deceitful above all things, and
desperately wicked: who can know it?* When I spoke with Bekah about
the doubts I was having, she responded in the same way that I always
had: to see herself as insufficiently spiritual to question the wisdom
of the elders. "We must be missing something," she would say. "The
elders must know something we don't." She trusted them, but little
by little, my trust was eroding and withering. I wanted to believe
Bekah, but for the first time in my life, I couldn't shut off the questions running through my mind. I couldn't identify the source of my
new willingness to challenge the church, but I wanted it to go away.
I wanted the simplicity of my old position—"trust and obey"—but
it was proving elusive no matter how many times Bekah inspired me
to reach for it.

Grace was another matter entirely. She had always had a unique
role in the Phelps-Roper family, and I'd watched her grow into it with
joy. As the seventh child of eleven, Grace tended to have fewer of the
more mundane household responsibilities, because those generally
fell to the older ones of us. Instead she had more free time and fun
projects: arranging creative portrait sessions for other families in the
church, painting street addresses onto the curb outside each Westboro
home, and entertaining our little brothers. She was full of mischief and
dubbed the "Pied Piper" by our mother, because the four youngest boys
would follow her anywhere—including into the girls' bathroom on one
memorable occasion. Whereas Bekah and I were regarded as submis-
sive and obedient, Grace's free spirit and apparent lack of discipline
earned her a reputation in the church as willful and coddled. It was
a branding I considered undeserved: though it appeared that Grace's
daily tasks were more distraction than discipline, she was doing all
that our parents required of her.

I felt motherly toward all my youngest siblings, each of whom I had read to and sung to and rocked to sleep when they were small, but Grace would always be special to me. She was the youngest of us three sisters in a family full of boys, and her name suited her well: she was graceful both in features and manner. My sister's beauty and charm could be almost unnerving at times, though we never spoke of such things in our home. Any discussion of beauty was limited to an oft-quoted admonition about its emptiness. *Favour is deceitful, and beauty is vain: but a woman that feareth the Lord, she shall be praised.*

It was hard for me to hear the way our aunts and uncles impugned Grace's obedience, and I became her champion of sorts, subtly pushing back against their disparaging words. I wouldn't realize until much later that the protectiveness I felt for Grace wasn't just because she *was* following the rules. It was because she was managing to do so without losing herself. I adored Grace's creativity and free spirit and the dreams she would so casually mention—of traveling to Paris or Rome to see the sculptures she was studying in art history, or off to Russia, home of Pushkin and Tolstoy. I loved her dreams even though I knew them to be impossible. We could never leave the United States and the broad protection of the First Amendment, and the church's ban on international travel was just one of the innumerable limitations on our lives that I had long ago assimilated. But because "Grace flies under the radar," as my parents often noted, she was somewhat insulated from our mother's watchful gaze and need for submission. She hadn't yet been broken. She'd made it to age nineteen with her will intact, and she was the only person with whom I could speak openly about my concerns— the only one willing to express disagreement with the elders' positions without including the standard caveat: "The elders know better. We must be missing something."

Neither of us was prepared when Grace became their next target.

———

"Megan!"

Grace urgently called me to her room early one morning in late May, and I found her on her bed looking panic-stricken and ready to vomit. She was hysterical, telling me she had just received a call from the wife of one of the new Westboro converts. Justin and Lindsey [names changed] were about my age. We saw their conversion as a testimony to the power and sovereignty of God: He had turned their hearts to His truth.

The couple and their baby boy had rented a house from my parents located just a few doors down from ours, and Bekah, Grace, and I visited often. We liked them immediately and were in awe of their lives and talents. In contrast to the lives we had led at the church— structured, protected, controlled—theirs had been full of exotic places and experiences. Their transition in forsaking that worldly life to stand with us on the picket line was mind-blowing to my sisters and me, and we wanted to understand their conversion in every minute detail. In Lindsey we recognized the same creative energy that animated Grace, and the two bonded over their mutual love of style and art. Lindsey's repertoire of skills was broader than my sister's, and they made plans for Grace to take lessons from her—drawing, painting, sewing. We would have dinner together, watch movies at their house, and stand together on the picket line in Topeka, Grace and I quizzing them end-lessly about their life before Westboro.

The alacrity with which we took to this new family was remark-able, but not unusual. I wasn't aware of the pattern at the time, but Grace and I often bonded with outsiders in this way. We harbored a deep curiosity about the world outside, and we indulged it as much as the constraints of our lives would allow. She and I would sit on the floor of my room or hers and read books and stories aloud to each other for hours, not just the Bible but everything from *Anna Karenina* to the fairy tales of Hans Christian Andersen. When it was Grace's turn to read, I'd pull my hands through her long, dark waves to detangle and braid them, or massage her scalp in slow, methodical motions, or paint her nails in one of the colors approved by our father—light pink, nude, or clear—while we contemplated the curious lives and ideas of these characters. Whenever journalists and filmmakers came around for interviews, Grace and I would ask almost as many questions about their lives as they asked about ours, and we grew attached if they spent more than a few hours with us. On the day that Louis Theroux and the BBC crew departed after three weeks of filming, we exchanged gifts— including baby clothes and blankets for the sound engineer, soon to be a father—and then I retreated into my house to cry in my bedroom. The four of them had been so kind to us. I believed their choices would lead them to Hell, but I cared about them. I didn't want to say good-bye forever, and it frightened me that I regarded them with such affection. *Love not the world, neither the things that are in the world. If any man love the world, the love of the Father is not in him.*

But now with Justin and Lindsey, we didn't have to say goodbye. They had had as many fascinating experiences as the journalists we encountered, but here there were no limits or constraints. We didn't have to keep them at arm's length, because we were *allowed* to cultivate friendship with them. They were part of our community. They were safe.

All of that ended on the morning of the phone call. Lindsey had discovered that Grace and Justin had been texting extensively and was convinced that my little sister had designs on her husband. The two had class together at the university and had grown closer over the course of the semester, conversing often about everything and nothing. I'd had no idea how frequently they'd been texting, but when I listened to Grace describe the messages, I instantly thought of C.G.: The discussions never touched on "inappropriate" topics, but the closeness itself felt improper to me. The fear on my sister's face twisted my insides, especially since I knew what was coming. I wanted to defend Grace to our parents and to the elders—"She didn't know what she was doing!"—but an angry call from a jealous wife was a scandal that couldn't be smoothed over by a plea of ignorance, no matter how genuine. It wouldn't matter to the elders that Grace had seen no distinction between a friendship with an unrelated man and a friendship with one of our cousins. Why would she? We had been told all our lives that church members *were* our family, and that's how we had always seen them—related or not. *For whosoever shall do the will of my Father which is in heaven, the same is my brother, and sister, and mother.* The same verse that justified cutting our brother Josh out of our family was the one that instructed us to bring these strangers into it. And more, the fact that Justin was married gave Grace an even greater sense of safety in their closeness. It was unthinkable that anything improper could happen with him, *because he was married.* The line was so bright and crossing it was so far outside the realm of possibility that she simply didn't believe it could be improper.

Punishment was swift. Grace was forbidden from having any

contact at all with either Justin or Lindsey, not even to apologize. Instead of chasing after children as she did every summer, Grace would be required to take a temp job at the Kansas Department of Revenue, sitting at a desk doing data entry work for eight hours each day. My siblings and I would no longer be permitted to spend time with Justin and Lindsey, but instead would avoid them—except that we could say hello if we happened to pass them at church on Sundays. Because Lindsey had not asked to be baptized since she'd arrived six months earlier, the elders decided that it was time to isolate her from the rest of the church. She was a negative influence. "What makes her any different than the rest of these heathen, except that she's related to a member of the church? That doesn't confer any special benefits to her."

New restrictions kept coming, growing increasingly draconian all the time. Sam and Steve had never approved of Grace's freewheeling spirit, and they encouraged my father to rein her in. It seemed to anger both men that Grace had opinions and that she was willing to ignore their advice—even when the smallest issues were implicated. Two years earlier, Grace and I had decided to switch to Apple computers. Steve advised against it, and I yielded to his recommendation immediately and without complaint. Grace, on the other hand, thanked him for his input and explained that she would be getting a Mac. Steve pestered my parents for weeks afterward, strenuously arguing that his reasons for remaining with the status quo were worth following. It had seemed embarrassing at the time, because it was clear to me that Steve only cared about the issue because he wanted to be obeyed. My mother eventually came up with an excuse for why it *had* to be a Mac ("It will help Isaiah learn another operating system for his job!"), and though I didn't care about the computer either way, I was glad that my parents had pushed back against Steve's bullying.

But my father couldn't really do that anymore. His judgment had been so severely called into question by the church that he had seemed unwilling to trust himself—or my mother—ever since. Instead he listened and followed the recommendations of his fellow elders, even when they were contrary to his instincts. Most of these new rules had no specific foundation in Scripture—just a reference to a broad passage calling believers to *abstain from all appearance of evil*. When Sam and Steve learned that Grace was using her required twenty-minute work break to explore the area around her downtown office building, they prompted my father to forbid it. He did. *The appearance of evil.* She began spending those breaks sitting on the couch in the twelfth-floor bathroom. When Grace asked to take our brothers to a park to climb trees, our father forbade that, too—not just on that day, but ever. That Grace would request such a silly thing was taken as evidence that her heart wasn't in the right place. *The appearance of evil.* When our father instructed Grace to choose a degree other than art, Sam and Steve advised him that he hadn't gone far enough—that her options should be limited to the study of nursing or computers only. The fact that both of those studies were anathema to my sister was almost the point. In the words and actions of these men I could not help but see that, above all else, their desire was to break her spirit. Any comfort she found in her old ways—exploring and adventuring, even within the extreme confines of our sheltered lives—had to be taken from her. It was as if that phone call from Lindsey had given them an excuse to impose upon Grace every unreasonable limit they could dream up in order to quench her spirit. It was as if they were saying, "You see what happens when you let a young woman have her way?"

Still, I understood that Grace wasn't perfect, and that my father was trying to help her to grow—to learn to discipline herself and her mind, and to see that necessary courses of action aren't always fun or enjoyable. Sometimes, you just had to do what you were told. Bekah and I had learned these lessons when we were young, and our lives had become much more pleasant as a result. In learning to conquer our wayward emotions, we had found peace, and I tried to encourage Grace to seek it, as well. As much as I disagreed with so many of the elders' decisions, I still believed that submitting to God meant submitting to church leaders, and I sent her quotes about the importance of training our hearts and minds to yield to them. Just by virtue of their authority over us, I fell back into the position that they were right, that our doubts were wrong, and that any disagreements we had were the rebellious impulses of disobedient children. How dare we think that we knew better than the leaders God had set over us? I wanted to yield, and I chided myself for any thought that contradicted the church.

"I just don't *understand* this, Mom!" She and I were in the kitchen getting things ready for dinner. A month had passed since Lindsey's call
to my sister, and Grace and I hadn't exchanged a word with her since.
I had asked repeatedly for permission to apologize, to explain that our
sudden disappearance hadn't been a choice to punish Lindsey for the
understandable outrage she'd unleashed on my sister, but because the
elders had decided it was best. With increasing anger at my persistence, my father refused. Echoing the other elders, he insisted that
Lindsey deserved neither explanation nor apology: she was no concern
of ours except inasmuch as she had an interest in the Bible and our
doctrines. "We've put Lindsey in an impossible situation!" I told my
mother. "We've almost completely cut off her interactions with church
members because she isn't baptized—but we've also told Justin that
if he's *ruling well his own house*, he'll be keeping Lindsey from having
relationships with friends or family *outside* the church, too! She's just
supposed to stay at home all the time and only have her husband and
toddler around? Steve would *never* have accepted that kind of treatment if we'd done it to *his* wife when he first came here!"

My mother was quiet. I could feel myself spinning out of control, despair and bile rising in my chest, but I couldn't stop myself
from continuing. "*What are we doing?* There is *nothing* Scriptural about
what's going on here! The elders act as if their judgment is infallible
and they refuse to listen to anyone else—even when they're *directly*
violating the commandments! All the verses about being of one mind
mean nothing to them! The women are angry and spiteful and *always*
finding reasons to be offended!" I was crying now, filled with a desperation so choking I could hardly breathe. I quoted the verses I knew
my mother already knew. She'd turned to them often over the past
year, trying to maintain hope that her situation would improve. My
heart twisted into a knot of despair knowing that the past year had
been so much worse for her. I was only a witness to the cruel treatment of the elders and other members. She was their primary target.
By this shall all men know that ye are my disciples, if ye have love one to
another. In lowliness of mind let each esteem other better than themselves. Put
on therefore, as the elect of God, holy and beloved, bowels of mercies, kindness,
humbleness of mind, meekness, longsuffering; Forbearing one another, and for-
giving one another.

Mercy. Humility. Meekness. Compassion. Where were they among this church body?

Almost as soon as the thought formed in my mind, another took its place:

I sounded like C.G.

———

The Fourth of July arrived. We'd stopped celebrating American Independence after the September 11 attacks—dispositive evidence that our nation was fully and finally doomed—but we still got the day off from work. Grace and I had volunteered to spend some of ours painting the basement walls in the home of our friend Jayme, a new church member, so we changed into old clothes after the noontime pickets. We headed out into the afternoon heat, across the street, down the path of stone steps that led through the shade of my aunt's front yard and then my brother's, and into the dark house that sat three doors west of ours. The basement's dim lighting felt especially depressing after the blinding sun outside. We lined the floor by the walls with garbage bags, and I poured white paint into an empty cottage cheese carton that Grace held out to me. Neither of us spoke. I connected a portable speaker to my phone—the new album by Blind Pilot, another of C.G.'s recommendations—and pressed play.

Grace had misjudged again, and she'd received an ultimatum from the elders: one more wrong move and she would be excluded from the church. This time, my sister's crime had been failing to turn Justin in for reaching out to her. He'd used Twitter to send her a private message asking how to fix the situation his family was in. Justin and Lindsey seemed baffled by and resentful of the isolation that the church had imposed upon them—an obvious and entirely reasonable response, as I'd argued to my mother just days before. Instead of reporting Justin's message to the elders, Grace had sent a brief response explaining that she couldn't talk to them, and to please just talk with our parents. He'd followed up with an email, and Grace had called him to repeat the same message: Talk to my parents.

After a couple of guilt-filled days, she'd turned herself in.

The elders considered Grace's actions depraved enough to warrant abridging the biblically mandated disciplinary process, jumping directly to the final step before exclusion. And just as with our cousin, they'd made the decision without even meeting with the rest of the church. I knew that Grace should have reported Justin without hesitation, the way the rest of us had learned to do—*for they watch for your soul*—but in answering her mistake with more clear violations of Scripture, the elders continued to abuse the authority of their office. I had no idea if anyone else felt the same, because addressing grievances with other members—instead of one's elder—was not permitted.

I stared intently at the basement wall as I moved the brush over the deep purple stripes we were meant to cover. I watched the bristles leave their trails of white, but no matter how thickly I coated the brush or how many times I went over it—again and again and again—the darkness was still visible underneath. My mind spun through its familiar circuits, the same objections and doubts that had been brewing for over a year, grasping for something that would return order to the chaos. The futility of it all had been a heaviness in my mind for months, but it had taken on a physical dimension now, and it was suffocating—the dank chill of the basement and the shadows cast in the dim light and the impossible melancholy of the notes seeping out of the stereo. The weight of my arm and of the paintbrush seemed to grow with each stroke until I could hardly bring myself to lift them. An insurmountable burden.

I had never seen a member of my immediate family subjected to church discipline before, but it wasn't special family ties that made the situation untenable. It was the fact that for the first time in my life, the accused were people I lived with and knew most intimately. I had direct, firsthand knowledge of their daily lives and habits, and I knew that the judgments leveled by the elders were wrong. They were wrong about my mother. They were wrong about my sister. And I strongly suspected they'd been wrong about my cousin, too. I could not acquiesce to their conclusions the way I'd done with so many others before. I could no longer blindly trust the judgment of these men.

My arm continued to drag the paintbrush up and down, but my pulse and thoughts were racing. *By this shall all men know that ye are my disciples, if ye have love one to another.* I couldn't believe how our love within the church had been warped beyond recognition by the elders' unscriptural will to punish. By their implacable demands for unquestioning obedience. By their pernicious need for superiority and control. They had developed a toxic sense of certainty in their own righteousness, seizing for themselves the role of the ultimate arbiter of divine truth—and they now seemed willing to lay waste to anyone who disagreed with them. It was a heinous arrogance and sinfulness that could not be denied.

And in a moment of horrifying clarity, I finally saw what had eluded me for so long:

We had *all* been behaving in the exact same way toward outsiders.

It was as if we were finally doing to ourselves what we had been doing to others—*for over twenty years*.

My eyes widened and my face flushed hot, overtaken by panic and shame and regret and humiliation in the split second it took my mind to find a way to make sense of the chaos that the church had become:

What if we're wrong? What if this isn't The Place led by God Himself? What if we're just people?

And I felt sure that it was all true.

I crossed a chasm in that split second, pursuing a thought my mind had never truly imagined and now could never take back. With stark clarity I understood that whether the church was wrong or right, I was a monster. If we were wrong, then I had spent every day of my life industriously sowing doom, discord, and rage to so many—not at the behest of God, but of my grandfather. I had wasted my life only to fill others' with pain and misery. And if the church was right? Then asking those questions and even *beginning* to consider their implications was an unforgivable betrayal of everyone I had ever loved and the ideals I'd dedicated my life to defending. In my mind, I was a betrayer already. I thought of my mother, and the guilt was crippling. I didn't deserve to be part of this body of believers. The Lord was done with me—an Esau, after all. Already condemned. Overwhelmed by a sudden pressing need to leave *that instant*, every part of my body hummed with a single vicious accusation: *You don't belong.*

My eyes squeezed shut, my whole face twisting instantly into desperate sobs that I tried to suffocate by cutting off the air to my lungs. In the span of a few seconds, my world had disintegrated, slipping through my fingers like so much sand. I turned to put the paintbrush down and go home to pack—there was nothing beyond packing—but

I stopped short at the sight of my sister. Her back was to me as she worked the paint, shoulders hunched and limbs moving as if through quicksand—a visible reminder that she had been trudging through the same quagmire of depression, confusion, and despair that I had.

How could I leave without explaining to her?

How could I ever explain this to her?

Still sobbing, I turned back to the wall, and dipped my brush in the paint again. I was dizzy. Needed to calm down. Needed to think this through. My mind reached for solid ground, a way to explain to myself and my sister why I was suddenly doubting the church itself— the only truth we'd ever known. What did I know for sure?

The lying and Photoshopping were clearly wrong. *Lying lips are abomination to the Lord: but they that deal truly are his delight.*

The prolonged isolation and lack of grace toward perceived offenders were clearly wrong. *Brethren, if a man be overtaken in a fault, ye which are spiritual, restore such an one in the spirit of meekness.* Justin. Lindsey. Grace. My mother. My cousin. These situations were egregious, ongoing, and the list kept growing.

The endless proliferation of extra-biblical rules. *Ye shall not add unto the word which I command you, neither shall ye diminish ought from it.*

The exclusion of most church members from the decision-making process, and the inability to speak freely with non-elders. *Now I beseech you, brethren, by the name of our Lord Jesus Christ, that ye all speak the same thing, and that there be no divisions among you; but that ye be perfectly joined together in the same mind and in the same judgment.*

My heart hammered, full of terror at the seditious thoughts taking hold in my mind—would God snuff me out this very moment?—but I was growing bolder. I fought to stop myself from reverting to the mindset that had kept me from these questions all my life: certainty that the church was The Truth, and that I was a child, and that for me to challenge or contradict their established wisdom was nothing more than a tantrum.

I had to keep going.

I thought again of the arguments C.G. had made about our lack of compassion, gentleness, humility. How had I so easily dismissed him? How could I have missed what had been staring me in the face for over a year?

And most important: If the church was wrong about all those things, *what else were we wrong about?*

The question felt like an iron key sliding into the lock of a long-sealed door. I could almost hear it swinging open on hinges groaning with age, unleashing a surge of memories buried inside—as if they had been deliberately locked away so as to cause no disturbance. They flashed through my mind one after another:

- A pointed Twitter exchange with a Jewish blogger called David Abitbol: I was defending Westboro's call for the government to designate homosexuality a capital crime, in accordance with Levitical law—DEATH PENALTY FOR FAGS. David was an Orthodox Jew, and surprised me by quoting Jesus: *He that is without sin among you, let him first cast a stone at her.* I had seen this as a general call to humility, and I couldn't believe I had never connected that Jesus was specifically arguing against the death penalty. I was mortified. When I approached my mother, she doubled down. She repeated verses that seemed to support our position, but never answered what Jesus had said. Her stridency took me aback, and I walked away shaken. It was the first time I was consciously aware of inconsistency in our doctrine, but I was certain this sign was unscriptural. I had quietly stopped holding it—and put an end to my arguments with David—but this was a relatively small point of theology. I had set it aside, immediately and instinctively suppressing the memory.
- A conversation with my mother during a walk to an evening picket: Why did we have a sign declaring FAGS CAN'T REPENT? Couldn't God give repentance to anyone He chose? Isn't it misleading and dishonest to say otherwise? Again, she seemed not to hear me, repeating the verses we used to justify the sign, but not addressing the contradictory verses I had quoted. And again, I'd been afraid to pursue the objection—who did I think I was?—but I had stopped holding this sign, too.
- A Bible reading with my grandfather one summer afternoon: Gramps was making lunch in the church kitchen,

and I'd walked in with some papers my mom had sent me across the block to deliver. "What's that Matthew 5 say about divorce, love bug?" he asked me, pointing to the collection of super-large-print Bibles and concordances always stacked on the counter. I'd plucked one up and sat down and started to read to him, eventually coming to a perplexing phrase: *pray for them which despitefully use you.* We had been earnestly praying for the destruction of our enemies for years by then—but if that was right for us to do, what did *this* verse mean? My grandfather paused: "Well . . . it doesn't say to pray for their *good.*" In the context of Jesus's command to *love your enemies*, this argument made no sense. When I asked my father about it that evening and told him what Gramps had said, my father skeptically confirmed what I'd known was true: "That's clearly not what that means. It *does* mean to pray for their good." I was relieved to hear my father say so—but now that I'd resolved the immediate controversy in my thoughts, the contradiction flitted out of my mind like a butterfly, never to return again. *Why had I never pursued it?*

And with that, the most powerful partition in my mind—the one that had kept me from seeing the most grievous contradiction of all—dissolved.

We had been claiming to *love thy neighbor* all my life. We claimed we were the *only* ones who *truly* cared about anyone else. "We're the only ones that love these fags!" Gramps would say in his Mississippi drawl.

But at the same time, we had been wholly dedicated to antagonizing the world. We mocked and delighted in their suffering. We demanded they repent, and then asked God to preserve them in their sin. We prayed for Him to destroy them.

Two diametrically opposed positions, held strongly and sincerely by the same mind at the same time—just never in the same moment.

A deceived heart hath turned him aside, that he cannot deliver his soul, nor say, Is there not a lie in my right hand?

I felt deranged.

I numbly moved the brush up and down the wall, hot tears still sliding down my cheeks. My mind was finally settling on its inevitable conclusion: There was something terribly wrong at Westboro. God was not in this place. We were not special. Not hand-selected by the Lord to do His divine work. We were a deluded people.

As my thoughts slowed, I came back to the present, the melody of a new song drifting into my awareness. It was gentle and somber and yearning, and it sounded like I would never be happy again.

Will I break and will I bow / if I cannot let it go?

At these lyrics, I began to sob in silence again. I glanced back to see if my sister had noticed, but she was still blissfully unaware of my state. Of the fact that we were living a delusion. Even knowing how difficult things had become at Westboro, how could I drag her with me into this waking nightmare?

"When will these things change?" Grace had asked me after the ultimatum. When would the grip of the elders slacken, their control over our every movement? When could she say a simple "Hello" to Justin without the suspicion and wrath of the church falling on her? When would our mother be treated with the compassion any church member deserved?

I'd told her what I always had: that the Lord was with us. That everything would doubtless improve. I composed long messages to encourage her to take heart and continue in Westboro's way:

You must look on the great blessings you have been given, my sister. You must rejoice in those gifts and not continue to sorrow. You seemed to heartily agree with that recent line from Gramps' sermon: "I think unthankfulness may be the most disgusting sin of all." We don't want to anger the Lord with unthankfulness—for gifts and for deliverance and for all we have.

Remember what the Lord said to Joshua. Israel had trespassed against God and He cursed them in battle and Joshua mourned and prayed to God. "And the Lord said unto Joshua, Get thee up: wherefore liest thou thus upon thy face?" Instead of mourning, we have to get after what the Lord has given us to do. "Be not weary in well doing," dear girl, and "cast not away your confidence, which hath great recompense of reward."

In due season we will reap, if we faint not.

But the hope that inspired me to write those messages was now gone. We couldn't fix the problems in the church, because we no longer had a voice. When we objected, we weren't viewed as church members with legitimate concerns. Instead, we were disobedient children. I thought about the future, and there was nothing left.

If I could've known then we were dying to get gone . . .
I can't believe we get just one.

What if we *did* only have one life, and not eternity? How could we spend ours hurting people, picking fights with the entire world—not at the will of a Sovereign God, but for nothing?

How could I *not* talk to Grace?

I didn't know what we would do with our lives instead, but I thought of my sister's impossible dreams of exploring the world . . . and I suddenly realized that *maybe the elders had been right about her.* Maybe Grace didn't belong here, either. Maybe she had *already* come to the same conclusion I just had, but was afraid to leave on her own. Maybe *she* was afraid to tell *me*, because I had been such a zealous defender of the church for so long. If so, her fear was not unfounded. Our mother had taught us the same verses:

If thy brother, or thy son, or thy daughter, or the wife of thy bosom, or thy friend, which is as thine own soul, entice thee secretly, saying, Let us go and serve other gods . . . Thou shalt not consent unto him, nor hearken unto him; neither shall thine eye pity him, neither shalt thou conceal him: But thou shalt surely kill him; thine hand shall be first upon him to put him to death.

Our church wouldn't be executing anyone, but the standard was clear: if your closest friend or family member came to you suggesting defiance of Westboro's God, that person deserved to die—and *you* were responsible for turning them in. *Neither shalt thou conceal him.*

But Grace hadn't turned Justin in. Maybe she wouldn't turn me in. I needed to think before I spoke to Grace. Where would we go?

I forced myself to stop crying and let the logistical part of my brain kick in.

I immediately dismissed the idea of going to any ex-member of Westboro for help. We kept close tabs on the few who ever spoke up publicly about their time in the church, and it was clear that those people were awful. So many lies.

I thought a moment, and then went to pick up my phone. I switched the ringer to silent so that the telltale trill wouldn't sound over the speaker as I re-installed Words With Friends.

———

Grace came home on her lunch break the following day, and as had become our habit, I followed her up the stairs, down the hall, and around to my room in the corner of the house. We hadn't been eating much, and the heaviness of our silence had become habitual, too—particularly since the ultimatum. My sister had never been anywhere without permission, never been given any freedom or independence of any kind, and now she was on the cusp of being thrust into the world on her own at nineteen, with almost no practical life skills—for texting.

We sat side by side on the edge of my bed, staring at the wall in silence for a minute, and then I started to cry. I laid my head in her lap and sobbed for a few moments. She cradled my head and slowly dragged her fingers across my scalp, trying to comfort me.

"Grace . . ."

I tried to compose myself, but the longer I waited, the harder I wept. How was I even going to say this?

". . . what if we weren't here?"

I couldn't bring myself to say *What if we left?* aloud. I couldn't bring myself to make it real.

Her hand paused for a beat and then slowly continued its path through my curls.

"What do you mean?" she asked quietly.

What did I mean? My body was racked with sobs, and I tried to control them long enough to get the words out.

"What if we were somewhere else?" Slowly, slowly.

I don't remember any words after that. Only an eruption of despair. I tried to explain what had happened the day before in the basement, my terrifying realizations about the church, but what came out was almost entirely incoherent. I couldn't settle on any one idea long enough to articulate it, because I was overcome by a hysteria the likes of which I had never known. That familiar fear always just beneath the surface—the little voice accusing that in spite of everything, I really *was* a reprobate—had amplified a thousandfold. I knew logically that I couldn't escape the wrath of an omnipresent God, but the sense of His imminent judgment had kindled a fire in me, a desperate urgency to *get out*. I wanted to jump out of my skin. There was no way to consider the magnitude of the devastation that I would soon be forever cut off from everyone I had ever loved: my faculties simply shut down before I could even approach that reality. I was betraying my beloved *mother*—treated unconscionably by the church body and then abandoned by her own daughter. How could I leave her? *Monstrous.*

And all the while, Grace held my head in her lap, running her nails through my hair, periodically asking questions in a low, cautious voice. Distrustful. Why now? What has changed? Where would we go?

I had no other ideas, so I mentioned C.G. Maybe he would help us.

I didn't tell Grace that I'd spoken with him already, partly because both she and he were behaving as though they were afraid of me. As if they didn't know me. Their reactions were crushing, because they confirmed what I already believed: that outside of Westboro, I was nothing. Within the church, I was a cherished daughter—I wielded no power, but my skills were many and useful and valued. I was dependable, and trustworthy, and called upon frequently. I had built my life and identity around the church, and I was well-beloved. Who was I on the outside? I was the perpetrator of untold amounts of harm in the world. I was a lover of tragedy, cruelly attacking the grieving at their most vulnerable. I was a willing participant in the most aggressive anti-gay picketing campaign the country had ever seen. What reason did anyone have to give me a second chance?

Grace and C.G. had seen some of the very best parts of me. If even they thought me unhinged, there was no hope for me on the outside.

No one would ever understand.

All was lost.

7. Ye Shall Be Judged

It wasn't just in my mind. Grace was avoiding me.

Or at least, she was avoiding being alone with me. She *was* afraid. Each time it seemed we would have a chance to speak in private, she made other plans—heading off to read to our little brothers after Bible study in the evenings, or spending her lunch break in the kitchen instead of coming up to my bedroom. If I was going to the evening pickets, she would find a reason to stay home. If I was stuck working in the office, she'd grab a sign bag and volunteer to take the boys. I was in a constant state of attempting to mask my frantic anguish—so many people around, always; surely they could see the sedition in my thoughts?—and the panic was exacerbated by the knowledge that Grace could turn me in at any time. Only when we were together did I have any sense of relief that she wasn't reporting me at that very moment.

Why hadn't I left immediately?

It was C.G. who'd told me to slow down. When I re-installed Words With Friends and broached the subject of leaving the church, he warned me that this was not a decision I could make in an instant. If my existential crisis was just the result of a few squabbles with the new church leadership—if I still believed most of what I had been preaching for decades—then I would not find the world a hospitable place. Knowing how dedicated I'd been, he said I should think it through. That I needed to be certain. I saw the wisdom in

C.G.'s advice and would wait to make my decision until I knew for sure.

Still, there were a few things I *was* certain about, even in those earliest days:

I would not be attending any more funeral protests.

When my family prostrated ourselves after evening Bible readings, my prayers would no longer include curses for our enemies.

I would not be talking to the media, if I could possibly avoid it— there were too many land mines now, and if a reporter stumbled upon one, I knew I wouldn't be able to hide my misgivings.

And I would not hold any signs that I didn't believe, or preach anything that I didn't think was true.

The perpetual motion of the church never ceased, and outwardly I was still completely enmeshed in the flurry of activities that kept Westboro constantly in the news—but inwardly, my doubts were multiplying. For the first time in my life, I was allowing myself to ponder ideas that I had always instinctively shoved into the darkest corners of my mind. I felt like I was losing my grip on reality, my thoughts boomeranging back and forth between two extremes: (1) that Westboro was fundamentally right and that my mind was rebelling against God at Satan's direction, and (2) that the truths we held to be self-evident were entirely questionable, odious, and destructive—both for us and for the people we'd been accosting on the streets for more than two decades. I became consumed with questions, assaulted by every passing doubt I'd ever had. It had only been a few days since I'd been painting with Grace in that basement, but troublesome memories now seemed to appear in every quiet moment. I couldn't escape them.

Sitting at my grandfather's computer in the church library—typing Bible verses for one of his sermons—I flashed back to a drive to school one afternoon when I was in college. It was one of the first warm days that spring, and the windows were down, breeze ruffling my hair as I mulled over a point of doctrine. I was taking a logic course that semester, and as I pondered the argument, I became vaguely unnerved. We believed all outsiders hated us. If they said they hated us, we believed them. If they said they loved us, we believed they were either lying or delusional, and nothing could persuade us otherwise. I began to see that for many of our beliefs, there was absolutely no evidence that could be introduced to us that would cause us to change our minds. *Unfalsifiable.* My brows stitched together as I stepped out of the car— and then I had grabbed my bag, never to return to the question again.

Folding laundry with my four youngest brothers outside the up- stairs laundry room, I was abruptly transported back to my pew one Sunday morning a few years earlier. My grandfather was preaching about Hell again, expounding eloquently on what it entailed. *The same shall drink of the wine of the wrath of God . . . and he shall be tormented with fire and brimstone in the presence of the holy angels, and in the presence of the Lamb: And the smoke of their torment ascendeth up for ever and ever: and they have no rest day nor night.* In Hell, my grandfather explained, the damned would each in turn be put on trial: every wrong thought and word and deed that they had ever committed would be adjudicated in exhaustive detail. And the adjudicators? The people in Heaven. Each one of the Saints of God would have a caseload, as it were, person- ally condemning the reprobates to an eternity of agony and rejoicing at their endless suffering. It was a very real and present fear that my grandfather elicited with his detailed descriptions of torment—but the idea had been abstract to me until that moment. As I listened to my grandfather's words, it suddenly occurred to me to consider Heaven and Hell in practical terms: *I* would be condemning people to torture? And I would be happy about it? I couldn't even watch a torture scene in a film without jumping out of my seat, overcome with outrage, dis- gust, and revulsion that anyone could be capable of visiting such horror on a living, breathing human being. I didn't think I could condemn people to torture, and sitting in my pew that day, I'd wondered if there was something wrong with me. *No,* the thought resounded now. I picked up a stack of bath towels and handed them to my brother. *If Hell is real, then God is evil.* Terrified, I mentally backtracked. *Maybe.*

Walking with Grace and our nieces to the park that weekend, my thoughts veered to a letter to the editor published by the local news- paper when I was sixteen. It bore my signature, but my aunt Margie had written it. Though I had agreed with every word, there was one part that rang strongly discordant in my mind: "I've watched care- fully and listened to my grandfather and those who oppose him. My grandfather's Bible-preaching is more agreeable to my heart." We *never* appealed to our own thoughts or feelings as reliable evidence of truth, and we routinely disparaged others for doing so. The Bible was true because it was true, regardless of how I—or anyone else—felt about it or any of its teachings. This had been a theme of my life, oft-repeated by my mother: *The heart is deceitful above all things, and desperately wicked: who can know it?* There was always urgent warning in my mother's voice when she quoted this passage: we could not trust our hearts. Our feelings would lead us astray. Why had Margie written that sentence? I'd been almost physically repulsed by it, and watching my nieces bound across the field as we arrived at the park, I was finally able to pinpoint why: my sixteen-year-old self had started to recognize the contradiction. We used our hearts to authenticate the moral truth of the Bible—the same Bible that told us our hearts were deceitful. I shook my head as I realized that all we *had* was our hearts. In writing that sentence, Margie had unwittingly betrayed that at bottom—resting beneath all the chapters and verses that we'd spent years quoting and memorizing—the foundation of it all was a belief that our hearts had led us true when they told us the Bible was the answer.

Our unreliable, desperately wicked, deceitful hearts.

——

The few weeks following that Fourth of July were the longest I'd ever lived. Whenever Grace couldn't avoid being alone with me, our conversations followed a predictable pattern. I would attempt to dissect the problems at Westboro, and she would nod in agreement at my analysis—but then she would insist on addressing the consequences that I could not bear to consider. Our family. How worthless our lives would be without them. The pathetic emptiness of a life without this divine purpose. And eternity in Hell. These were unfathomably horrifying, but I could not let go of the failures of Scripture and logic that I now saw so clearly in the church. How could we go on living like this?

But how could we live outside of this?

Whether we stayed or left, our prospects were bleak.

There was no containing the despair and devastation that seized my body each time I imagined leaving, so Grace and I resolved not to think about it unless we had the space to mourn without an audience. She was still avoidant and seemed afraid of me, but we both knew that public displays of unhappiness would raise suspicion in a

hurry—accusations of discontentment and murmuring against God—
and there was still so much to think through. When Grace and I were
apart, we discussed our doubts by text messages that we deleted shortly
after sending. We agreed that I would keep screenshots of the conversations so that we could examine them later, but that I would transfer
them to a hidden folder on my computer in case my parents came to
examine my phone. I had never been subjected to such scrutiny, but
others had—and if the request was made, it couldn't be denied without major trouble. I hated the deception, but I knew that regardless of
what we decided, we needed to be as sure about it as we could be.

For his part, C.G. was full of gentle, sometimes pointed questions.
He was trying to discern what was happening in my mind, and since
my thoughts were swinging back and forth like a pendulum, I was
grateful for his calming influence. Explaining myself helped me to focus. It gave me something to hold on to.

> **C.G.:** What do you believe?
> **MEGAN:** I can't call my whole life a waste. I've learned so very
> much. And I never would have met you if I weren't me. I really
> believed those things, and there really is a lot of good in it—
> about caring and looking out for people. These are good
> people. I wonder if I'll be able to stand without their support.
>
> I've thought before, "Who cares?" re: whether some-
> one is gay. It was a knee-jerk response, and I'd put the ki-
> bosh on it. I'm not sure what all I believe. I'm working on it.
> **C.G.:** This doesn't seem real. You must understand that.
> **MEGAN:** Which part? I know, though.
> **C.G.:** All of it. I'm watching True Blood right now, and, as you
> know, "God Hates Fangs." That's you. That's crazy.
>
> I know you from YouTube and your voice there is dif-
> ferent from the one I hear when I read your words. It's all
> crazy. You aren't real to people. You're an idea.
>
> And what about Bekah? She just stays there and lives
> happily ever after?

Lying in the dark late at night, tucked away with phone in hand, I
pondered C.G.'s questions and tried to make sense of them. I thought

about Bekah. I had always seen myself as much more like her than like Grace—far more willing to yield than to challenge—and I wondered again how I had become so unruly. The elders weren't the first major transition in the church, nor were my mother and sister the first close loved ones targeted for church discipline. In the past, no matter how much I initially doubted a position taken by the church, their justifications always made sense eventually. Could I even recall the last time Bekah and I were completely in sync in this shared tendency? Certainly before Twitter, I knew.

> **MEGAN:** Bekah is just like I was not so very long ago. It will be horrible, and she will take it so hard, and she will blame herself. She is so tender-hearted. I love her so.
>
> **C.G.:** Why can't you get her out, too?

I clicked my screen off and squeezed my eyes shut, willing myself not to cry. Exhausted of tears. My bedroom suddenly felt stifling, and I opened the window in search of a breeze. How to explain to him? I lay back down and stared at the ceiling, now bathed in the orange light of the streetlamp outside.

> **MEGAN:** She wouldn't come. She just wouldn't. As ardently as I fought you, she would fight any notion that this isn't the way. She would be scared of me and for me and would enlist the aid of the whole church to recover me (before I left, I mean). She is exactly where I was—but she is less confident in herself and therefore even more willing to distrust her own thoughts and judgments. I wish she would leave—and maybe she will one day. But I don't think it will be soon.
>
> Life is short. And getting shorter all the time.
>
> **C.G.:** Then show empathy for people rather than mocking them.
>
> This isn't my place. At least not tonight. Good night, sweet, confused girl.
>
> **MEGAN:** I'd be offended, except I know: you only know I want to leave, but not all the reasons. One reason: it does

not make me happy to see people killed or starving or maimed. I don't want to mock them; I want to help them.

It is your place. You're a friend. Sleep well.

———

Between Grace, C.G., and the news, I was presented with fresh opportunities to stew in my confusion and despair daily. Grace was stewing, too, sending me text messages fretting about Hell as she sat at her desk doing data entry work downtown. As I struggled to answer my sister's pressing questions about our eternal fate, my thoughts returned to Margie's letter to the editor—that contradiction of relying on our hearts when our hearts were evil. It had not occurred to me to see that paradox to its logical conclusion, but now a new question dawned on me:

What if the Bible *wasn't* the literal and infallible word of God?

At home in my bedroom, I froze. This was the sine qua non of our belief system, the foundational truth of the life I had led since I was capable of conscious thought. I was surprised at how noiselessly it shattered.

Not a single breath passed before my mind pulled forth a Bible story that had rankled me since the first time my mother read it to my siblings and me when I was a little girl.

In the book of Judges, the final three chapters tell the tale of a Levite and his concubine. We are not told their names—only that she *played the whore against him*, and retreated to her father's house in the city of Bethlehem. There she remained for four months, until her husband went after her, *to speak friendly unto her*, and to bring her home again. By the repeated entreaties of his father-in-law, the man was convinced to stay and eat and make merry for several days. The fifth day arrived, and as they prepared to leave that afternoon, the woman's father pressed him again: *Behold, now the day draweth toward evening, I pray you tarry all night.* But the man would not. He and his concubine and his servant departed, though it was too late in the day to make it home by nightfall.

That evening, rather than spend the night in a city of strangers, the Levite decided their group would press on to the city of Gibeah, of the tribe of Benjamin. They arrived just after sunset. When an old man saw them preparing to sleep in a street of the city, he drew near.

"Let all thy wants lie upon me; only lodge not in the street," he warned them. The old man brought them into his house to care for them and their animals.

As they were *making their hearts merry*, the men of the city surrounded the house, beating at the door and calling out to the old man: they wanted to rape the Levite. *"Bring forth the man that came into thine house, that we may know him."*

The old man begged them not to do such a thing: *"Behold, here is my daughter a maiden, and his concubine; them will I bring out now, and humble ye them, and do what seemeth good unto you: but unto this man do not so vile a thing."*

But the men of Gibeah wouldn't listen to the old man. The Levite took matters into his own hands, delivering his concubine to the men beating at the door.

And they knew her, and abused her all the night until the morning: and when the day began to spring, they let her go.

As the day dawned, the woman collapsed outside the door of the old man's house. Her husband arose and opened the door to leave, only to find her there. Her hands were on the threshold.

And he said unto her, Up, and let us be going.

But none answered.

The Levite picked up the body of his concubine, carried her back home, and hacked her into twelve pieces. He sent one to each of the twelve tribes of Israel. *Consider of it, take advice, and speak your minds.* The tribes gathered and sent messengers to Benjamin: turn over those men of Gibeah so that we can put them to death.

The children of Benjamin refused, and civil war ensued—the eleven tribes against the one. Benjamin dominated the first two skirmishes, annihilating forty thousand men. The Israelites wept and fasted and made offerings to God. Should they go to battle a third time? *And the Lord said, Go up; for to morrow I will deliver them into thine hand.*

The next day, the children of Israel killed twenty-five thousand men of Benjamin, and their animals, and their women, and set their cities on fire. Six hundred men fled into the wilderness, and they were all that remained of the tribe of Benjamin.

Having prevailed, the Israelites faced a new problem. They could not allow an entire tribe to perish, but there were no women left to re-populate Benjamin: all their women had been killed, and all the men of Israel had sworn an oath to God not to marry their daughters to the sons of Benjamin. *Cursed be he that giveth a wife to Benjamin.* Instead they found one city in Israel that had sent no men to battle—and thus, had made no oath. Twelve thousand valiant men were dispatched to the city to kill every man, woman, and child, except the young women. They found four hundred young virgins in the city, brought them to the camp, and gave them as wives to the surviving men of Benjamin.

Still, two hundred men remained without wives.

Therefore they commanded the children of Benjamin, saying, Go and lie in wait in the vineyards; And see, and behold, if the daughters of Shiloh come out to dance in dances, then come ye out of the vineyards, and catch you every man his wife.

And thus they did.

This story flashed through my mind in a moment, and I thought—like exhaling a breath I'd been holding my whole life—*That is bullshit.* It wasn't that I didn't believe it. It was that every part of the story disgusted me, from God all the way down. I had forever repressed the outrage and disgust I felt at reading it, and though questioning the Bible like this shook me to my core, I also felt a glimmer of re-lief. Of liberation. I didn't have to believe that this story was anything but awful—and not just the senseless carnage that left tens of thou-sands dead. Every woman in this story had been treated unconsciona-bly: Men snatching unsuspecting women to force them into marriage. Other women given as gifts, having just witnessed all of their loved ones slain and their city destroyed. The old man offering his virgin daughter, and the woman sacrificed by her husband to a feral mob, raped to death. The husband then—finding her fallen *with her hands on the threshold of the door*—responding with *"Up, and let us be going."* I'd wanted to punch him or vomit every time I'd read the words. Others might place the blame upon the men in the story, but as a predestinar-ian, I was most repulsed by the God who had instigated and orches-trated the whole thing.

Disgusting.

What if the God presented in this story—in this Bible—was not the real God?

I sat down on my bed, reeling. How could I suggest this possibility to Grace? If it frightened *me* so, there was no question it would scare her, too—especially coming from me. She might wonder whether I was being influenced by Satan. It would sound like every argument we'd spent our lives learning to dismiss out of hand. People who discounted the Bible were angry, just trying to evade the truth of the Scriptures because they were convicted by them. Of all the questions and doubts I raised, doubting the Bible itself would surely be the most preposterous to my sister.

GRACE: Eternity scares me.

MEGAN: Me, too, sometimes. I think there must be God because of existence ("science" doesn't have answers about Creation). Then I think, what if the God of the Bible isn't the God of creation? We don't believe that the Koran has the truth about God. Is it just because we were told forever that this is How Things Are?

It's comforting to think we have all the answers.

Does it really make you happy when you hear about people dying or starving or being maimed? Do you really want to ask God to hurt people?

I ask myself these questions. I think the answer is no.

When I'm not scared of the answer, I know the answer is no.

GRACE: What does that last text mean?

MEGAN: It means: I know that saying that (that it doesn't make me happy when people die) is against what this church believes. To go against that scares me (sometimes, but not always anymore). But I know it's the truth to say that it doesn't make me happy.

GRACE: I just don't know anything.

But what if we are wrong and we go to hell?

MEGAN: Why do we think it's real? It's starting to seem made up to scare people into doing what they say.

GRACE: But what if?

MEGAN: Then it would be horrible.

If someone told us we had to obey Artemis or we'd be

tormented by Hades when we die, we'd laugh at them. I think we worry now because we've believed it was real forever.

I didn't want to tell her these things, but getting these ideas out of my head—giving them form—was the only thing keeping me sane.

Grace refused to let me off the hook: How would we know any God besides the one of the Bible? If "decency" is the standard, how could we say what violates it if there are no Scriptures? Is homosexuality wrong? And adultery? And abortion? Without the Bible, how do we know when we make mistakes? What made you change on July 4? All these questions you ask me, wondering how we know the God of the Bible is the right one—did they come from C.G.?

I had never felt so ignorant, but I was glad she was forcing me to think on these questions. I answered, trying to deduce principles of morality as best I could. I knew that Grace was suspicious of C.G., that she hadn't approved of the closeness she'd sensed between us the year before—but when she asked about him, I told her the truth: that he'd never said anything of the kind. That he'd been shocked when I messaged him that day. That it was reason that brought me here.

My sister was unconvinced.

Meanwhile, C.G. had questions of his own. Two weeks had passed since I first spoke to him of leaving, and on the news that day, a tragedy: twelve people had been murdered—a shooting at a movie theater in Aurora, Colorado. One of the victims had been an active Twitter user named Jessica Redfield. The words of her friends and colleagues were circulating on the platform, and like so many others, I found her profile and read. It shook me to see the words of a woman who had been alive not twenty-four hours before, to know that she had no idea what was about to befall her. Even more chilling was the fact that just the month before, she had escaped another shooting at a mall in Toronto: she'd gotten a strange feeling and walked out just seconds before someone opened fire in the food court. My heart ached for her and her family.

MEGAN: I just starred a tweet about @JessicaRedfield. Had you seen that? Look at her timeline. She had no warning. Scary and sad.

C.G.: I heard about her. I will.

I still don't know if I know you. 30 days ago, you'd have been saying "God sent the shooter" today. Today: I just sense that you have empathy and that's it.

Which?

MEGAN: The latter. I just feel disconnected from all that. It was kind of happening a little at a time (e.g., on issues like tragedies; I told you it didn't make me happy). As soon as I started to actually let myself second-guess it, it's just drifted so far away . . .

I don't know that I could get it back even if I really wanted to.

———

Grace and I had been close for years, but after those few weeks of avoidance, this period brought us physically closer than ever before. When we weren't arm in arm, we walked close enough to stumble over each other's feet. At pickets, we stood inches apart, holding two signs each in the outside hand—as if they were a buffer to keep anyone from penetrating the protective cocoon we were building around ourselves. She had slept in my bed on occasion, but now it was almost every night. Always trying to discern which way was up. I even took to carrying her on my back, like I'd done when we were kids. It was comforting to think that among all the casualties we were about to sustain, at least we would get to keep each other.

Neither our closeness, our sadness, nor our joy was acceptable to the elders. My father got wind that Grace had sat in my lap at our hymn-singing one evening, and instructed us not to do it again. He did the same when he found out she was sleeping in my bed. When an uncle of ours caught us jumping on the trampoline one evening at dusk—a momentary release of pent-up anguish, frustration, confusion, and fear—he stared us down as he made his way from the church to his home across the yard. Grace was "in trouble." Everything she did was suspect—and the fact that I was comforting rather than ostracizing her made me suspect, too.

As much as I tried not to imagine the actual act of leaving, Grace seemed determined to make me face what it would mean. She would text me from work, detailing all that we would lose if we walked away from the church. What comfort would there be in a world without the prospect of eternal bliss alongside our loved ones? How could we depend on mere humans for anything? And in the event that we some-how managed to withstand the storms of life—death, illness, injury—and make it to old age, how meaningless would our lives have been? If we missed all those years watching our little brothers grow up and our parents' hair turn gray, what would we have to look forward to at the end of our lives? "I weep," she wrote.

Running errands for my mother, I pulled my car into the nearest parking lot and wept, too.

—

We decided to stay.

Ultimately, Grace and I could entertain the possibility of leaving for only a few weeks before it became too much. We were each inhabit-ing two minds: the one that was trying to make things work within Westboro's framework, and the one that was preparing for the worst. It made me question my sanity, unsure of every thought that crossed my mind. *A double minded man is unstable in all his ways.* Grace pointed out that although leaving was unthinkable, despair awaited us no matter which option we chose. "How can we be happy?" she asked me.

> MEGAN: For now, we can try to avoid situations where those problems come up. Keep a low profile. Stay close to home. That kind of thing. And for the future . . . we don't know for sure what's going to happen. I have a feeling it's going to get worse re: Steve, et al, but maybe it won't. We could deal with that when we come to it. We can also do what you said—organize our rooms/things. Save money. Make and keep memories. All those things are good no matter if we left or stayed. We're just going to keep trying.
>
> GRACE: Thank you.
>
> MEGAN: I love you, G. I'm sorry I put this burden on you.
>
> GRACE: I love you, double. No apology necessary.
>
> MEGAN: Had you thought about it at all—even as a vague, remote possibility—before we talked in my room that day?

GRACE: Not really. Maybe because I thought if I ever did, I'd be alone.

MEGAN: Me, too.

"If we go, we'll go together."

If something happens with me and they make me go, I would understand if you wanted to stay.

GRACE: Quidem. Together.

This was the plan we came up with: Stay. Attempt to convince the rest of the church to hear our objections. Pray for the best.

And only if our best efforts failed would we again consider leaving.

I also had to stop pursuing my questions about the Bible and where it stood on the spectrum of truth. Permanently dethroning the Scriptures I had so revered was inconceivable. They contained too much good to come down definitively against them, and Hell was a looming possibility that felt far too real. *Know thou the God of thy father, and serve him with a perfect heart and with a willing mind: for the Lord searcheth all hearts, and understandeth all the imaginations of the thoughts: if thou seek him, he will be found of thee; but if thou forsake him, he will cast thee off for ever.*

Not long after we made our decision, C.G. disappeared without warning. I hadn't told him we were planning to stay, and he gave no explanation for his sudden withdrawal. He simply stopped answering my messages. My sister did not delight to see my despair compounded, but I knew she was glad it was over. She wanted me to be committed to our life at Westboro, and she perceived that I would be distracted so long as I had even a shadow of hope about C.G. Grace's intuition was correct, but the ache in my chest was as deep as it had been when he and I had said goodbye the year before—and that told me all I needed to know. In spite of my hurt and anger at his sudden dismissal, I understood that the end result for me—that I would be forced to come to grips with the church and my beliefs without outside influence— was the best possible outcome. My decision had to be untainted. If we did eventually leave, it could only be because it was the right choice to make—because the church had replaced the Scriptures with the word of these fallible men—and not because I wanted something to which I wasn't entitled. *But every man is tempted, when he is drawn away of his own lust, and enticed. Do not err, my beloved brethren.*

And—I thought bitterly—whatever else C.G. intended, he was teaching me a valuable lesson: on the outside, Grace and I could count on no one but ourselves.

———

Having established our intention to stay, Grace and I found ourselves right back where we began: in an intolerable situation that had to be confronted. But how? We decided to start slowly at first. Rather, we decided that *I* would start slowly. My sister was still the subject of ongoing church discipline, and like our mother, had no space at all to object. No matter how legitimate the complaint, she would be seen as recalcitrant and almost certainly excluded from the church without delay. I had only marginally more leeway, and I was well on my way to losing even that. Grace and I had refrained from using Twitter almost entirely since July 4, though she had a good excuse: as part of her punishment, the elders had forbidden her from doing so. But given my generally prolific use of the platform, my sudden lack of Twitter activity—combined with an inability to hide my heavy heart—had almost immediately become cause for worry. I began to receive concerned text messages, phone calls, and visits from other church members, with Steve at the head of the pack.

He called me up one day in late July. I was out at the noontime pickets with two of my cousins when my phone rang—and though I wanted badly to decline the call, I picked up. Delaying the discussion would only make things worse. I could never stay still when stressed, so as soon as I answered, "Hello, Steve?," I began dragging myself up and down the sidewalk in the heavy humidity, pacing in front of a church we'd protested every single day since I was about six. Steve said I seemed down. *No shit*, I thought, but held my tongue. He said he was worried because I didn't seem as unguarded as I'd always been. I didn't attempt to deny it, but I focused on the safer sources of my despondency: the difficulty of watching my mother go through this long period of transition and general fatigue from all the work on my plate.

"You didn't mention Grace," Steve said flatly.

Suspicious.

I mumbled for a moment, unsure of how to proceed except to say that I was weary and wary, and then he jumped in again.

"It's not a *doctrinal* thing, is it?" He was incredulous at the thought, but before he could make me answer, he launched into a diatribe about the importance of regularly engaging other members of the church. I wanted to shoot back that he and the other elders had made that impossible. That they had created such a sense of fear within the body that there was no way to speak openly about any objection to their actions. An Orwellian level of control over our every word, our every movement.

But I kept quiet. When he finished, I thanked him kindly, hung up the phone, and made a decision. I had already suspected that doctrinal errors would be the most difficult to change, because they were seen as coming directly from the Word of God: "Death Penalty for Fags," "Fags Can't Repent," "Pray for More Dead Soldiers," "Pray for More Dead Kids." What if I focused instead on the application of doctrine? Not theology. Not major foundational principles or anything that required extensive exegesis. Just kindness within the church—the lack of which seemed to me the clearest and the simplest example that Westboro had veered far off track. This was the place to start.

Grace and I also decided that our mother seemed the safest person to approach first. Although she, too, had been deprived of her voice in church matters, she was the one who had helped convince our father to hear us out about the Photoshopping incidents. I had to believe that she knew her treatment to be unscriptural, no matter how often the elders made her profess otherwise. I was cautious at first, asking more questions about the details of the incidents that continued to occur almost daily, just interminable pettiness. I knew she was trying to hide her sorrow from me and my siblings, but she was no more successful than I was—especially since I was paying closer attention than ever. What did my mother really think?

As the weeks passed, I expanded the scope of these discussions to include the treatment of Justin and Lindsey, as well. And then Grace. Even the cousin who had been voted out a few months earlier. I started with my mother, and then continued with my Gran, both of whom were sympathetic. Neither of them disagreed with my analysis and both understood my despair—but whereas Gran would shake her head and agree that things looked very bad indeed, my mom would mostly listen. The rest of the church—including her own husband—presented a united front as to my mother's grave sins. They made her believe that if she felt any offense or sense of unfairness with respect to their treatment of her, then it was completely a result of her pride, not because there was anything unjustified about their cruelty. They ascribed ill motives to many of her actions—even *positive* actions—and then they retaliated against her on that basis. And if my mother tried to dispute their analysis, there would be even more trouble. As I came to appreciate these dynamics, my outrage increased and I grew bolder. *They were making her believe that she was literally insane.* That is—as I would later learn—they were "gaslighting" her. I became the only person in her life willing to confirm, directly and unequivocally, that the accusations against her were unwarranted, off base, and often *utterly deranged.*

Although my mom avoided saying so directly, I eventually came to believe that she and I were on the same page about the unscriptural nature of so many of the actions and decisions implemented by the elders. We would talk, and then we would pray together that the Lord would fix everything. The only difference between us, I realized, was that she had no doubt that God was with Westboro. It never seemed to occur to my mother that all of this misconduct might be evidence that we were wrong—that there was something rotten at the core of our beliefs.

With my brother Sam, I presented my disputes as hypotheticals or general curiosities. I led with few specifics, lest he end the conversation and send me back to our dad—but he sensed there was more to my questions than I was letting on and pressed me to come out with it. Standing outside a Topeka church during our Sunday morning pickets, I nearly broke down in tears of desperate frustration as I spoke of the cousin who'd been kicked out. I made my case, citing verse after verse that showed how we had done her wrong. I tried and failed to be calm, and he erupted in response, justifying it all: the church had made a decision, and God was with us, and that was that. He was angry, but he also seemed genuinely perplexed that I had a problem with what had been done. I knew I was getting into dangerous territory and backed off again.

At first, I steered clear of mentioning anything to Bekah, because I was afraid of what she would do. With every good intention, she would surely have turned me over to the elders for what I now saw as "re-education," putting me solidly on their radar as a troublemaker. But if Grace and I decided to leave, I knew that I would then regret it forever if I didn't try to talk to Bekah about what was happening. Driving around Topeka with her, running errands after church, I poured my heart out. I was cautious at first, restrained, describing everything as clinically as possible, the whole litany of misconduct going all the way back to the Photoshopping—but the longer I spoke, the more desperate I became. As I parked the car in the Office Max parking lot, my words came faster and faster, rising to a fevered pitch until I was sobbing hysterically. She reached over to hug me as I finished my jeremiad. ". . . and I just don't have any hope that it'll ever be fixed!" She started crying then, too, and we stretched across the front seat in an awkward embrace. I knew I was scaring her, but I had to lay it all on the line. "I'm so sorry," I whispered.

"It's okay," she said, weeping. "It's okay if you break my heart." I had said all I could say. She walked into the store while I tried to compose myself, and on our drive back to the house, her focus was on encouraging me to speak to the elders. If I could just *tell* them these things, surely there would be a good answer. I told her I would keep trying, and she seemed relieved—not particularly worried about the troublesome case I had made against the elders themselves. So confident that all was well in the Lord's church. *Trust and obey* was second nature.

Finally, after several weeks, I went to my father. Again, I tried to be calm and reasonable. I limited myself to subtle questions and gentle pushback—possible only thanks to Herculean efforts to swallow the panic rising in my chest—but at every turn, I was shut down. As day after day, week after week passed with no improvement and no obvious way forward, I began to despair again.

———

As September rolled in, my mantra changed. Gone were the days of *Grace . . . I don't think I can do this forever.*

"Grace. I can't do this forever."

We sat together in Grace's bedroom, she at the foot of her bed and me on the floor staring up at her. This room still felt very much like a child's—white curtains with little blue stars printed all over them, her

walls and ceiling painted in bright, primary colors. It had been such a
happy time when we'd repainted it two years before. All of the siblings
had been obsessed with a bizarre YouTube cartoon called *Charlie the
Unicorn*, and in one corner of the room, I'd used a tiny brush to paint
cheery polka dots and quotes from the show: "It's a land of sweets,
and joy, and . . . joyness." It hit me again how very young she was. I
couldn't ask her to leave. I wouldn't pressure her.

But I also couldn't keep walking this fine line. How long would
I be able to avoid media and funeral pickets without detection? How
long until someone handed me a sign I believed unscriptural? How long
could I continue to choose my words ever so carefully—like some dishonest politician? I largely escaped explicit lies, but I grew ever more
uneasy as I faced the fact that I was deceiving everyone both within
the church and without. I might be limiting my own behavior, but
with my presence and assistance, I was endorsing the rest of Westboro's
behavior, too. The church had always been all or nothing—in or out—
and this was no-man's-land. I could not survive here.

Grace and I eventually decided that unless something major
changed, and soon, we would have to leave. We would begin to prepare in earnest, and in the meantime I would also take greater risks
in raising these objections with others. The closer we came to walking
out the door, the less I had to lose by sticking my neck out to petition
the others. And what if Grace somehow managed to get kicked out
before we could actually leave? We started a new game of Words With
Friends, and Grace changed her username so that it was unidentifiable.
No matter what happened, we could always communicate privately
there.

As soon as the decision was made, my first course of action became
immediately clear: apologize to Justin and Lindsey. Mindful that I was
now in the territory of direct rebellion against my father's instructions,
I drafted a text message to Justin explaining why we had suddenly
disappeared from his and Lindsey's life. Even as fearful as I was, I knew
that reaching out to our erstwhile friends was the right thing to do. I
should have done it months ago.

That I had to *rebel* in order to apologize struck me as hopelessly
corrupt.

I thought my heart would stop while waiting for Justin to respond.

Again, the prospect of imminent doom hung over my head—whether destruction from God or discovery by my family—and I tried to still my shaking hands as I unloaded the dishwasher. Perhaps Justin had learned his lesson last time, and was already turning me in. Perhaps the elders were launching an investigation this very second. My fear got the better of me, and I texted again to beg for a response—ironic, considering that I had left them hanging for over three months.

When Justin finally returned my text, it was everything I had been trying to tell my parents for months: That he and Lindsey had had no idea why they were being treated this way. That the last time he had tried to reconcile, it had gone horribly awry. That it had been painful to be left in the dark, "tossed off and forgotten," and that his wife was angry about the way the church had managed things. Justin was afraid of getting into trouble for this text exchange, too, and promised not to tell anyone but Lindsey.

At least we had that assurance.

But from what Justin said, Lindsey seemed done with the drama. She saw no hope for change. Justin told me that the elders had even forbidden sewing lessons with some of the younger girls that Lindsey had planned with their parents. She and Justin had planned a "double date" with another young couple, and that, too, had been disallowed. I was baffled. Having meals together was a regular part of our fellowship, and had been for as long as I had been alive. To my mind, it was now undeniable that the elders' decisions were primarily driven *not* by Scripture, but by a need to keep church members in our place. To make us understand that bending to their will was the only option. Nothing else mattered.

Justin and I tried to orchestrate the circumstances of a church-sanctioned apology from Grace to Lindsey: we would each separately and cautiously reach out to my parents. We were still trying to make it fit. Still hoping we could make it work.

But it wasn't to be. When I gently approached my father that evening, he blew up. He had heard enough from me about the issue. I retreated with the same feeling I'd gotten almost every time I'd challenged his decisions over the previous year: that hardliners like Steve and Sam were behind this new authoritarianism. When I disputed elder edicts, my father's choices were limited to either shutting me down

or resisting the militant faction among the elders—and we both knew
how the latter would go. He also just seemed convinced that their
collective wisdom *had* to be correct. After all, this was the Lord's
church.

And on top of everything else, he was surely as exhausted with the
whole mess as my mother, Grace, and I all were.

"Time to despair," I wrote to Justin that night. "There was a blowup
(no one knows about any of our discussions, though). Abort mission.
I'm so sorry, friend." Justin responded that he was at a loss. Miserable.
Hopeless. We'd reached the end of the line, but he thanked me for
even making the effort.

"Take care," he said.

I told Grace everything just before bed, breaking down when I got
to the part about our father. In our estimation, he was one of only two
or three elders who took to heart that verse about humility—*in lowliness of mind let each esteem other better than themselves*—and it contributed
to his unwillingness to challenge the others. "*They* should have been
learning *his* compassion!" I wept bitterly. Instead, they had insisted he
take on their severity.

I slumped onto the bed beside my sister and pressed my face into
a pillow. She reached over to stroke my back, and as we lay there in
silence for a moment, I realized it wasn't just the change in my father
that I was mourning. It was the final crumbling of an image I had held
so long in mind. Westboro Baptist Church. Special interest of the Almighty. Uniquely guided to eternal triumph by God Himself.

Sordid. Base. Banal.

Human.

———

Making the decision to leave gave me greater boldness in my futile attempts at reform, but it also introduced yet another impossible question:

When?

Neither Grace nor I had an answer—just a growing list of reasons that it couldn't be *now*. We couldn't leave before Mom's birthday,
surely. And what about our parents' anniversary? How cruel it would
be to ruin everything right at *this* moment. And then there were the
things we couldn't bear to leave without, all that we would forever lose

access to once we left. What about family recipes? And home movies? And old photos? We should wait just a little while longer . . .

There was no denying that this was partly a stalling tactic, based on a dwindling hope that drastic change would occur and save us from our plans.

At the first prospect of losing everyone back in July, Grace and I had become painfully aware that there was so much we didn't know about our parents' lives, and our grandmother's. What did we know about our Gran's life before Westboro? My sisters and I had begun interviewing her almost immediately after I spoke my treason to Grace. We'd file across the backyard in the evening, past the yellow slide and the pool filled with splashing cousins, and into the church. We'd find Gran upstairs in her bedroom next to the church library where Gramps held a Bible study at 7:30 each morning. At eighty-six, our grandmother was so quiet and gentle. Smaller than I'd ever seen her because of the deep curve in her spine. Stooped with age. She'd lie on her bed, and Grace would lie next to her, Bekah on the floor at the foot of the bed and me at its head. I'd switch on my iPhone's recorder, and we'd take turns asking questions, and I'd try not to choke at the thought of losing my Gran, at the tsunami of guilt washing over me for even thinking of betraying her.

I started recording everything. Hymn-singing practices. The sounds of our monthly birthday parties. Evening Bible study. My mother's stories about my siblings and me when we were young. A prayer she said for me. The din inside the van on picket trips. Bekah reading aloud. The repartee of my little brothers. Even if I somehow got them back later—even if they eventually left—all the years of their little-boy voices would be gone.

An endless stream of photos. A family kickball game. Mom and Luke getting ready to walk to school one morning. My parents holding hands as they walked through a department store. A family visit to our favorite art museum in Kansas City. Milkshake parties with Gran and Gramps. Walks to the park with my nieces and nephew. The front porch where Grace and I ate breakfast each morning. A trip out for snow cones with Luke.

In those months, every joyful experience became a torture that left Grace and me in tears and gasping for breath. We'd huddle together on my bed like that, trying to remember what it was like before all this. What it was like to be happy without the inescapable sense that we were watching the slow, excruciating deaths of everyone we loved. I began obsessively taking notes to chronicle every moment. I filled notebooks with descriptions of routine interactions, terrified of losing even a single one. As if clinging to these memories might alleviate the agony. As if recording it all could keep them from slipping from my grasp.

I made a list entitled "Funny/Nice Things Said During Hugs." Gran, on how she could always count on me to smell good. Gramps, on how my curls in his face made it difficult to breathe—how he was going to drown in them someday. Mom, on how she didn't mind being smothered by them. Dad, on how he loved it when I finished his sentences. "I love you, Mimi," he said. It was the name Luke had given me as a toddler, when he couldn't pronounce mine correctly. "We're very fortunate to have you as a daughter." I wrote it down before he could regret it. Before he could take it back. Before he could take down the photos of me that hung on the walls, before he could repurpose my bedroom, before he could spend the rest of his life erasing me from his memory as much as possible.

I started to clean out my room. I had never moved anywhere in my life, and I didn't know how anyone ever did it. It took weeks, because I pored over everything. Old photo albums. Shoeboxes full of birthday cards and thank you notes I'd been saving since elementary school. I scrutinized every page of the baby book my father had been maintaining for me since I was born. He added to it every year, and it was full to bursting by now, outgrowing the three-inch leather binder he'd bought to expand it. Our family grew larger each time I flipped to a new page, until I came to something I didn't recognize. A note my father had slipped in two months earlier, back in August.

Dear Miss Megan,
    Thank you for all the kind things you do for me. I love you dearly. I don't say either of those things enough. We are so fortunate. Your mother and I love you so much!
    Love, Dad

A little at a time, Grace and I began packing our things in boxes. My sister made labels that said things like "shoes" or "books." I numbered my boxes, meticulously cataloguing every single item that went into each one ("Shoes—Blue Wedge Heels from Jael's Wedding"). I tucked each piece of jewelry I owned into a tiny white envelope labeled with the date and occasion on which I'd received it. If I ever forgot any detail, there would be no one around to remind me. I copied sixty-three DVDs' worth of home movies, watching scene after scene play like a funeral reel.

And all the while I knew what would happen when we left. I knew the heartbreak they would feel, and the betrayal. I had felt it when Josh left eight years earlier—a devastating postmortem that went on for weeks after he left. We had racked our brains looking for every sign of his duplicity. And with each new instance we found, we had transformed our horror into outrage. All of us who remained were disgusted with his perfidy. How could he? What sort of monster could pretend to be one of us, knowing all the while that he was going to abandon us forever?

It did not occur to us to think of *his* devastation. We couldn't see his terror, or his despair, or his desperation. It was so much easier to rewrite history and cast him as a villain. To insist that he didn't care about us. That he was a selfish jerk who wanted only to pursue his own lusts. We could not imagine that this nineteen-year-old boy could have a legitimate reason to leave the only Church of the Lord Jesus Christ in the world today. We could not consider that there was anything truly wrong with us.

My parents, my brothers, my sister, my Gramps and my Gran— they would all look back just like I had. They would see me copying those home movies. Interviewing Gran. Cleaning out my bedroom. They would search through all the text messages and emails I had sent. They would remember my tears and my refusal to tweet, and they would wonder how I ever could have looked them in the eye. They wouldn't understand that I'd wanted to tell them everything. That I'd tried so hard to keep them. That I'd been begging for change.

That I'd wanted to stay.

———

November dawned, and Grace and I couldn't hold on anymore.

Steve had announced a new round of Sign Movies—short videos, each featuring a member of the church explaining one of Westboro's signs—and asked all members to choose which sign they wanted to address. Grace and I both signed up, but we knew we wouldn't go through with it. The videos would be filmed November 23 to 25, so we had until then.

Less than three weeks.

We didn't know it yet, but we wouldn't make it even that long.

At the end of September, as Grace and I were starting to plan our exit in earnest, it became clear to me that Justin and Lindsey wouldn't last at Westboro. Especially from the perspective of an outsider, their treatment must have seemed so bizarre and unjustified. Why would they tolerate it indefinitely? So I reached out to Justin, ever so cautiously, to see if they were going to leave, too.

They were.

We started talking. First Justin and I. Then Lindsey and I. But Lindsey still didn't want to talk to Grace. She was still suspicious. I told Lindsey that Grace had assured me there had never been anything more than friendship with Justin, and that I believed her. On the day that Grace finally spoke with Justin for the first time since May, I sent her a message:

MEGAN: Dear Gracie, Just in case I don't get back before you leave, a word of caution (as if you needed any more . . .): be careful with what you say to Justin. I know you're cautious and discreet, and I know you wouldn't deliberately do anything to hurt a friend. Just be careful not to put him in a position to be secretive or duplicitous to his wife; distrust—especially in that kind of relationship—is poison. No matter what, you're a likely temptation. Sweet, charming, beautiful, talented, funny, and more. All those things + closeness to Justin = easy for Lindsey to suspect something. Make your conduct above reproach, and (if she'll give you the opportunity again) be her friend. Make sure she knows she can trust you. You're a good person. And you want good for people, and you want to *be* good to people. It's hard for me to believe that there's a person in the world you couldn't win over.

>You probably didn't need all this—but sometimes you
>say obvious things to me, and it helps me be focused and
>think clearly. Love you, Sun.

Given that we still weren't allowed to speak, the four of us began
a disjointed discussion about our plans. Justin and Lindsey wanted to
move to North Carolina, and at first the dream was for the five of us
to buy a house together. I would get a job, and the other three adults
would go to school, and Grace and I would help take care of Justin and
Lindsey's sweet baby boy. If we were living with our good friends—
people who knew this life, who knew our family, who understood what
it meant to leave them—then maybe we wouldn't be so lonely. The
problem was that the more time passed, the more strained these relationships became. The four of us could hardly keep *ourselves* together
under the intense pressure, let alone be a support for the others.

Desperate for help dealing with the emotional fallout of our decision, Grace and I reached out to one of our old high school English
teachers. Whereas most of our teachers had preferred to ignore Westboro's existence while we were in school, Keith Newbery had been one
of the very few who hadn't been afraid of the subject. He was a bit of a
gentle giant—a former offensive lineman for Washburn's football team
when he was in college—and though he was less than a decade older
than me, I had a sense of him as an older, wiser, calming presence. In
school, he had never shared his beliefs or tried to shame us for ours;
he just asked thoughtful questions when related issues came up in our
homework or in the news. Twitter had opened an even closer line of
communication with Newbery, and we'd kept up with him there over
the previous year. He ran an account called @TchrQuotes ("Teacher
Quotes"), which he filled with sarcastic riffs on things his students
said. His posts were funny and inoffensive—"Nobody in this meeting
knows I have a McChicken in my pocket."—but whenever he tweeted
me in a friendly tone, he was vehemently attacked by Westboro's crit-
ics. That this cycle never dissuaded him from his kindness was part of
what made Grace and me believe that we could trust him.

Newbery was everything we could have hoped and more: a calm,
rational, dependable third party. Objective. Someone who knew us,
and our history, and our family, and who wanted to help us, whatever

we decided. We started moving boxes into his family's garage in late October, with the understanding that if Westboro changed, we would bring them all back. I could hardly think straight during that time, and I unleashed onto Newbery all of the thoughts and fears and sorrows and grief that I couldn't subject my sister to. He was a voice of compassion and reason when we needed it most—which was fortunate because confusion was mounting.

Justin explained that he and Lindsey were splitting up. The last several months had been too much pressure on their relationship. They were both planning to move to North Carolina, but now to different cities. Now what? I still wanted to help them, but getting into the middle of an increasingly messy situation seemed like a bad idea. I started to back off. Maybe we'd just have to go our own way after all.

But then Justin sent a message to Grace on her twentieth birthday: he wanted to be more than friends. I was aghast. He was a worldly twenty-eight-year-old, married, with a young son. She was naïve, much younger than her years, and was on the verge of losing everything, still living in an impossibly controlling home under even more scrutiny than usual. How could he possibly do this—especially *now*?

I thought of Lindsey. I had told her there was nothing between Justin and Grace. I could not imagine being in her place. She had come to Westboro looking for God, and she was leaving a year later with her world a shambles. I could not believe what had happened to her. I was ashamed of all of us.

Justin was not pleased to find out I was discouraging Grace. He insisted that he and Lindsey had been planning to split anyway, independent of Grace. He'd told me about their split weeks ago, remember? Why was I trying to control my sister the way our family controlled us? Hadn't I spent my whole life telling other people how to live? Who did I think I was?

It quickly became a moot point as everything unraveled at once. The relationship between Justin and Grace existed mostly by text, and lasted about two weeks before Grace ended it—but after it was over, Lindsey found out. The email came a few days later.

"Dear WBC . . ."

November 11, 2012. 3:55 P.M. Sunday.

I knew we had come to the end of the line as soon as I heard my father's voice. Stern. Gruff. Urgent.

He threw open the door to my bedroom, and my head snapped up. Grace and I were crying again, and she was scratching my head.

"You need to come talk." Eyes wide. He turned on his heel and headed down the hall. Grace and I looked at each other and tried to dry our faces.

We followed him to my parents' bedroom, where Mom was sitting in the new rocking chair. "It's okay, it's okay." Her words were quick and urgent, too.

We all sat down in their little sitting area, Grace and I on one side and our parents on the other. Dad started reading an email that Lindsey had sent him. About Grace and Justin. About our plans to leave. Things that were true mixed with things that were not. I was looking down, listening, shaking my head, knowing that we had to leave immediately.

I looked up, and my mother was holding her phone. A moment later, I heard the sound that an iPhone plays when you start recording a video.

"Please don't," I whispered.

She apologized. She'd meant to take a photo.

My father continued to read.

I understood why my mother had said, *It's okay, it's okay.*

Because there was hope for me.

I could have repented.

But there was no saving Grace. After this email, there was no possibility she wouldn't be voted out.

I looked at my sister and spoke in a low voice. "We need to go."

Our father hadn't heard. Our mother had.

I looked up.

I watched her mouth drop open in a look of shocked horror that will haunt me until I die.

I'd thought she might know. After all our talks, I'd thought she might see it coming.

She had not.

We filed back to our bedrooms to pack. We'd moved around twenty boxes out already, but there was so much more.

We tried to stay together. We knew people would come to try to talk us out of leaving. But we were sobbing, not thinking clearly, and Grace darted into her room next door.

Sam and Steve in the hall. Steve pushed the door open. I pushed it closed and kept packing. He pushed it open again, and wouldn't let me close it this time. They were yelling, saying that I knew better than this. My face was so contorted that I couldn't form sounds to make words. They left. Grace would tell me later that she'd asked our father to make them go. She'd heard them yelling in the hall. "She doesn't want to talk to them!" she told Dad.

My mom came in and asked that I go talk to Gramps. That didn't I owe him that? I'd known this was coming. Mom had made others on the cusp of leaving do it in the past. A last-ditch effort to convince them to stay. How could anyone look at our beloved Gran and Gramps and say they were leaving? I wanted to say no. I looked at her face. I couldn't.

I walked across the yard with her, not registering that this would be my last time. This path I'd traversed, often several times a day, since I was a child. Down the sidewalk, past the trampolines and the green cover over the pool, in the kitchen door, and up the stairs. My mother was telling me that I didn't have to follow Grace out the door.

We sat down with Gran and Gramps in his bedroom, the television blaring as always. He shut it off. Mom tried to explain. She thought this was because of Justin. She didn't understand that he was nothing. Absolutely nothing. That we would never give her up for a boy.

That we would never hurt her for a boy.

Gran, so quiet, disbelieving. "You don't want to leave us, do you?" I wept harder at her gentleness. I couldn't breathe. "You're not gonna do this . . . ?"

I hugged her as hard as I could. "I'm sorry, Granny!" I sobbed into her ear.

"Please," she whispered.

"Meg . . . ?" Mom said.

I had lived to support them. There was no worse anguish than causing them pain.

I will never know grief worse than seeing the pain I was causing. Hearing the hope in their words, and knowing that it was too late.

"We can't let you go, honey." Gran held me tight. "We'll be so sorry if you go." She paused. "Why?" Nonplussed.

I tried to explain. I had wanted to tell them openly for months. I had determined that if I couldn't make my objections while I stayed, then I would explain them in detail when I left. Maybe then they would listen. Maybe then they would understand.

But I couldn't say more than a few words at a time.

"She basically says that she feels hopeless," my mother said. "She has a litany of . . . She thinks that the . . . Well, I don't want to speak for her." Even now, after more than eighteen months of mistreatment, on the verge of losing two of her three daughters, her "right hand," she was too afraid of the elders even to relay *my* grievances about what they'd been up to.

"I've talked to Mom about this before . . ." I wept. I said a few words about the elders. About the way my mother had been treated, up until that very day.

"Well, this is not the way to treat your mom," Gramps said gently.

It was quiet for a moment. I couldn't speak.

He looked over at my mother. "Well. I thought we had a jewel this time, Shirl." How quickly his voice had turned. Cutting. Disgusted. "Looks like we got it all *wrong*."

Three elders walked in a moment later, including Sam and Steve.

I stood up. "I don't . . . I can't . . ." I was in no state to talk, and I would not be bullied. Not now. A conversation that was sure to go nowhere.

A singular urge to *run*. I turned—

"Megan!" My mom lowered her voice to an incredulous whisper, "Are you saying that your *pride* is more important than your *soul*?"

"No!" I whispered back. *Of course not.* I panicked. "I need to go—"

I ran out of the bedroom, down the stairs, out the kitchen door, and smashed into Jael on her way in. Jonah was right outside. It was so cold. I hugged him and told him I loved him so much, forever. That I was sorry. To please keep my phone number and to call me if he ever wanted to. He hugged me back, but he was only fifteen. He looked confused, unsure of what he was supposed to do.

I sprinted the rest of the way home, back up to my bedroom.

Margie appeared a few minutes later, crying as hard as I was.

"Please don't do this," she pleaded. "Please don't go. You've seen and said too much. You know this is right. Please don't go. I've never asked anyone not to go."

We held each other and wept.

"I'm sorry, Margie. I love you so much."

She let go after a long moment. She patted my back and walked away.

She walked away.

Jael came in a short while later, acting aloof and unmoved. She sat down on my bed, staring at her phone, typing away. She didn't look at me. She wanted to know why we were leaving. Her coldness in the face of my chaos was painful, but it made it a little easier to speak. I kept packing and answered as best I could through tears and grief. I spoke of the elders and their abuse of authority. I spoke of the mistreatment of church members. I spoke of doctrinal error, of unscriptural temperaments and picket signs. I told her I didn't think God was with Westboro anymore. She said little and stayed composed, but her voice broke when she thanked me for all the work I'd done on her wedding. How much time and energy I had spent to make it special.

"I only ever wanted to be good to you," I tried to say. I had to say it twice before she could understand.

"But friendship is a two-way street," she said, "and if I haven't been doing it on my side, I'm sorry." She was quiet for a long time, the only sound the *clack*ing of the hangers as I pulled shirts off them one by one. Bekah and I had shared a wardrobe for years—"the community closet"—and I had to decide what to take and what to leave.

"Have you been praying for the Lord to help you?" Jael asked.

I nodded. "And my mom and I would together."

My dad walked in to discuss my assertion that I didn't have a voice anymore. "Are *you* happy?" he asked Jael. She nodded. "Do you think you have a voice?"

"Through my husband," Jael said. Simpering.

"And is that acceptable or unacceptable to you?"

"That's the way it *should* be," Jael answered. "She has a voice through you. She *has* to submit to her father. That's her lot."

And that was how the elders had managed to pull this off, I thought. The conflation of parental and ecclesiastical authority was only possible in a church like ours, where nearly everyone was related. By rendering us "children" so long as we were unmarried, they thwarted all possible challenges to their control. There was no need to listen to what anyone else thought, because as our parents, they would *tell* us what to think. I shook my head involuntarily. My father had never been like this. I hated what this church had done to him. I hated what it had done to my mother. I hated what it was doing to our family, and to everyone we had taken aim at outside.

This place was toxic.

I ran downstairs to sort out my desk and found Bekah. She held out her arms and I fell into them, both of us openly weeping. She was getting ready to head out the door.

"I have to go drive with Jayme," she said, "and you gotta do what you're doing, so I guess we're parting ways."

"I love you so much, Bekah." Why didn't better words exist? *Your voice will follow me like a shadow for the rest of my days* and *I'll never be whole without you* and *The nights I dream of you will be my happiest.* I couldn't let her go.

"I don't know how you can say that and be doing this," she cried, "but Mom says you're always welcome back here."

"I tried to talk to you about all this . . ." I wept into her shoulder. Someone was playing a hymn on the piano.

"I hoped you just needed to get the right words from the right person," Bekah said.

We clung to each other until it didn't make sense, and then she tapped me three times—the way we always signaled the end of a massage—and she turned to go.

Noah texted me: "Pls turn around."

I looked up, and he stood there looking nervous. Afraid to speak to me.

I turned, and I saw Zach's computer from across the room. Noah often used it to play Minecraft, but now he'd set it up with a message for me. "MEGAN, LOOK" it read, with an arrow pointing to the second monitor. I moved closer. He had pulled up the *Kansas City Star* article from a year earlier. *I'm all in.* I wanted to tell him how often I had wished to go back to that place. How much I'd wanted to un-ask the questions, to un-see the contradictions. Instead, I hugged him. He was only thirteen. Maybe one day he would look back at this moment and understand. The way I had with Josh.

I texted him back. "I love you, my brother. Forever and ever. I'm so sorry."

One by one, I said goodbye to my siblings as I came upon them.

Three hours after my father walked into my bedroom, he was helping us load the minivan with our things. We'd have to come back the next day with a U-Haul. We couldn't stay in the house that night—our lifelong home was not *our* house anymore—so he would leave us at the motel next to our old middle school. He checked us in, helped us unload the minivan, hugged us, and left.

Room 108 was cold and sterile, entirely devoid of life, warmth, or happiness. It was everything I was afraid the world would be, and I couldn't bear to stay there, not then. I sent a message to Newbery asking if Grace and I could stay with his family that night, and then Grace and I sat on the bed, waiting.

A few minutes passed, and then my cousin Libby arrived with her husband. I hadn't spoken to her in the years since she'd left the church—she'd been cast as "Libidinous Libby" upon her exit, a selfish, self-important whore—but along with so many other of Westboro's judgments, I'd started to question their thoughts on her, too. I'd worked up the courage to reach out to her a few weeks earlier—a phone call to her office, because I was afraid she'd turn on me and publish my message if I emailed her. I'd told Libby that Grace and I were probably leaving, and she said, "I want you to come live with me," and we spoke like friends who hadn't just missed the last three and a half years of each other's lives.

In the howling, icy wind and the stark fluorescent light of the motel parking lot, the four of us loaded suitcases into the back of Libby's car. They'd take it all back to their home in Lawrence, thirty miles away. My sister and I would follow in the morning.

We hugged them goodbye, and they headed home with our things.

As Grace and I drove to Newbery's house in silence, I thought of a conversation I'd had with Bekah back in August. A letter had gone viral—a father disowning his son for coming out as gay—and she had called me into her office at the law firm.

"I can't believe it!" she'd exclaimed. "This guy actually says it right!" She started to read aloud, detailing the father's refusal to have any further communication with his son. Their happy times together were a thing of the past, and his son was no longer welcome in his home.

"If you choose not to attend my funeral," he wrote, "my friends and family will understand."

I'd felt my heart sink as Bekah read, but she was too excited to notice that I'd only managed a dull "Wow . . ." in response. I knew this letter was exactly the posture my family would take if we left. Grace and I had wept that night, realizing that it was gay people—I'd stopped using the "f" word by then—who would best understand what we were going through. The community we had antagonized more than any other. I hated that it had had to come to this for me to understand what the church had been doing to vulnerable people for so long.

For with what judgment ye judge, ye shall be judged: and with what measure ye mete, it shall be measured to you again.

I couldn't escape the sense of certainty pulsing through me as I pulled into Newbery's driveway.

No matter what I had intended, I deserved every bit of this.

Newbery opened the door. His two sons and his wife were already asleep. He led us down to their basement, a pile of linens in hand, and Grace and I each picked a couch and tucked ourselves in. This place was foreign, but unlike the motel, it was bright and cozy. And most important: we had friends here. I was ready to cry myself to sleep, assuming Newbery would leave us to our misery and head off to bed. Instead he sat down in a recliner and talked with us for a couple of hours. I hadn't known how badly I needed to talk to someone until he started asking his gentle, unassuming questions. How urgently I needed to mourn my family aloud, free of the need to stifle and camouflage every word.

Why had they made it so hard to tell the truth?

Just before 10 A.M. the following morning, I parked an enormous U-Haul at the end of our front sidewalk. Grace and I walked up to the front door like we had a thousand times before.

I rang the doorbell.

"Why did you ring the doorbell?!" Grace was incredulous.

"Because . . ." I had never thought to do otherwise. We were out-siders now. I had internalized my new status overnight.

My parents reinforced that status from the moment they opened the door. They stayed with us wherever we roamed in the house, appar-ently afraid to leave us alone. As if they couldn't trust us. It hurt my heart, but not like the jacket I found hanging on my bedroom door. Tucked into the hood was a sheet of paper torn from a notebook, with Bekah's handwriting: "This is yours, Meg." She had received the jacket as a gift from Jael several years earlier, but she'd shared it with me because she knew I loved it, too. We wore it so much that we'd put a hole in the left sleeve. The first moment I was alone, I slipped across the hall into Bekah's bedroom, pressed my forehead to the floor, and wept so hard no sound came out. At the thought of her lying in bed thinking about this the night before. At the thought that she wanted to give me this piece of her—of us—to take with me. At the fact that she couldn't say anything more than *This is yours, Meg* without running afoul of our family's expectations of her. I tore a page out of the same notebook, but my thoughts were a circle of *I love you I'm sorry I love you I'm sorry I love you I'm sorry*, and expressions of those thoughts were the only things to come out of my pencil.

Dearest sister-mine, Flor, Babi Lynne, Bobber Sue,
    I'm so sorry. I wish I could have been better. I love you more than words could ever say. I will love you and miss you forever, no matter what. I'm so sorry for everything, and for every offense I caused you. I'm so sorry. I love you.
    Swirl, MegHeart, Megabee, Megabus

I left the tears that fell on the page and on her desk. They would be dry by the time she saw my note, but I hoped she would feel them anyway, and that they would say more than my words.

As my parents, Grace, and I moved back and forth between the front door and the bedrooms, our timing became mismatched, and I found myself alone for another moment. I looked around, and then took off down the basement steps, rounded the corners, and ran into the darkened party room. Filled with a dozen long tables each encircled by chairs, this was a space we used to celebrate birthdays in the winter, and for meetings and Bible studies year-round. I flipped on the lights and pulled my phone from the back pocket of my jeans.

Photos of my grandparents and their children hung all along the room's two longest walls. I had wanted to take photos of them all before I left, but there hadn't been time. There was never enough time. I pressed record and made my way around the room as fast as I could, afraid I'd be caught and told to stop. Still filming, I switched off the lights and continued to move quickly, back through the laundry room with the drain that had terrified me as a kid, back through the rooms that Josh had lived in just before he left, back up the fourteen steps, and into the kitchen. Weeping now, I moved through the downstairs, carefully avoiding my parents and sister.

This could not be happening.

Making my way around the upstairs next, I stopped at the photos of an exuberant baby Gabe. They were taken before his headful of blond curls had come in, back when he was bald and so fat he had three chins. I wondered if we would ever be friends before he grew bald again. I choked on the thought.

I made it back to my room. Grace and our dad were outside loading a piece of furniture into the U-Haul. Hesitant, my mom pushed open the door to my rapidly emptying bedroom. I looked up and stopped moving. She stayed just inside the door. She looked like she wanted to come closer, but was afraid. Her tone was cautious.

"What will you do, Meg? You've loved these doctrines. You were a little girl, walking around the park—"

Her voice broke and her face twisted in despair. Gage Park. Our earliest pickets, back when I was five. She finished the sentence in tears.

"—and you were so happy."

She turned to go, and all I could do was weep. I had no idea what I was going to do. I just knew that I would never be free of the pain of causing her pain. Of all the dreadful things I had ever done or ever would do, nothing—nothing—would be worse than this.

The van was filled too quickly. We asked for our Bibles and headscarves and hymn books, and our father ran down to the church to get them. We met him and our mother outside by the garage. No hymn books, he said. Those belonged to the church. I thought of the blue hymnal that I'd written all over when Grace was born: "Megan Phelps-

Roper + Grace Phelps-Roper" with a heart drawn around them. If they didn't cover it up, it would be an object of scorn and pity for its new owner. *Those two foolish girls.*

It was time for final hugs. Dad first.

"Well, we're not gonna be doing this for a while." He didn't mean it unkindly.

And then Mom.

"Goodbye, doll."

I was shaking. I don't remember if I said anything. I just held them tight for as long as they let me.

Grace and I turned to cross the yard to the van.

"Girls?" Mom called out.

We turned.

"You can always come back."

Her hope broke me more than her tears.

8. Strangers and Pilgrims

We'd been on the road for a few hours by the time I realized I was white-knuckling the steering wheel. There weren't many cars at that early hour, but the image would have seemed comical to anyone passing me driving north on I-29. Leaning forward with my face hovering just behind the dash, whole body clenched, I looked like the stereotypical grandmother with poor vision trying to navigate during rush hour. Had my sister not been sleeping in the passenger seat, she surely would have made fun. I unclenched my fists and tried to relax in my seat—only to realize a few minutes later that in the absence of conscious effort, my body had resumed its original position. I gave up.

It was mid-December, and Grace and I were more than ready to get out of Kansas. Just over a month had passed since I'd last seen my parents, and confusion had reigned in the interim. After so many years of a life micromanaged by my mother, I now felt paralyzed each time I had to render an opinion about what steps to take next—as if decision-making were a muscle that had long since atrophied from disuse. At home, everything I did, everywhere I went, how long I'd be gone, *everything* had been pre-approved, double-checked, and tightly controlled. The multiplicity of rules was sometimes cause for frustration, but it was also a source of great confidence: I'd known what was required of me. I'd known who I was, and where I fit into the world. What did it mean to be the good girl in a world with no rules? I was unmoored. Outside of Westboro's rigid system, fear and uncertainty now consumed me, a physical weight that I felt from the first morning I awoke in my cousin Libby's house and every day thereafter: a boulder sitting on my chest, crushing my lungs, blocking any attempt to see around it. I couldn't breathe. I couldn't move. I was terrified of making a decision that would land my sister and me in some horrific situation. Homeless. Friendless. Penniless.

At the same time, the pressure to make every decision *right now* was staggering. I was keenly aware that Grace and I had a little bit of time and a little bit of money, and that both would be gone in no time at all. I needed to find a way to take care of us. I needed to be *responsible*. I needed a job *immediately*—since I'd graduated from Washburn four years earlier, I'd only worked for the family law firm, which was clearly no longer a possibility. And if the apocalypse wasn't imminent, as Westboro had been proclaiming for years, then I was behind in heeding the counsel of my business professors by nearly a decade already. Two days after leaving Westboro, I panicked to Newbery: "I need to start saving for retirement!" It was a stand-in for my every failure to prepare for this life, and the adrenaline coursing through me was not appeased by Newbery's assurances that I had plenty of time to figure things out.

And beneath the urgency and the loss and the yawning chasm of uncertainty, there was a deeper sort of terror: that no matter what I did, I was spinning my wheels in a futile effort to outpace the wrath of God reserved for *the children of disobedience*. My grip on the steering wheel tightened as I imagined my little black Pontiac spinning off into a ditch, smashing into a concrete divide, crumpling into a mass of metal and broken bones protruding from torn, sizzling flesh resting in pools of blood after a head-on collision with a southbound semi and—

Stop! I ordered myself.

I unclenched my fists again. Sat back. Slowed my breath. Tried to still the tremors in my limbs.

I looked out the window, where no grisly scene awaited. The sun was bright and the fields along the interstate were vast and glistening with frost. Iowa, just after 8 A.M. I glanced over at my sleeping sister in the passenger seat. Though we shared our grief and fear, Grace's disposition could not have been more of a contrast to mine. Where I wanted to cautiously reason and agonize over each decision, she seemed possessed by every emotion that came over her. Whatever she felt in any given moment was a call to action that needed no review and no revision, and she didn't appreciate my offering them. When Grace had first suggested an escape in the days after we left—running away to France was her actual proposal—I rejected the idea. She couldn't possibly be serious, could she? "If we can't have our family," I'd told her, both of us in tears, "then it doesn't matter if we're thirty minutes away from them or three thousand miles. Nothing will bring them back to us." I had argued that running away from that reality wouldn't change anything; it would only waste our ever-dwindling resources. She had just a few weeks left of the semester, anyway. Did she want to waste all the effort she'd already put in? None of these practicalities moved my sister. She was still determined to go, weeping in desperate frustration and despair that I refused. If I truly cared about her, Grace reasoned, then I would go with her.

But after two weeks, I'd started to realize that Grace was right. It *did* matter that we were still so close to home. I'd thought that staying with Libby and her husband would be ideal: Libby had been one of my best friends before she left Westboro three and a half years earlier, and I thought we could pick up right where we left off. And while spending time with her helped me start to find some perspective—not to mention comic relief—it quickly became clear that the thirty miles between Westboro and her home in Lawrence weren't nearly enough. We were commuting to Topeka four days a week for Grace's classes, and though it was a city of 140,000, we seemed to run into our family everywhere. We saw them while driving by pickets on the way to school. At the mall. The university. I was shopping for groceries while Grace was in class one evening, turning into an aisle only to immediately duck back around the corner—there was Margie, reaching for an item on the top shelf at the far end.

When I spoke to Newbery of these incidents, he didn't seem to understand my overpowering physiological *need* to conceal myself from their gaze, and I couldn't explain it. No, they wouldn't yell at me. They wouldn't attack me or otherwise make a scene. They would just pretend that I didn't exist. To say that I hid to avoid judgment and the silent treatment could not convey or justify the depths of that savage instinct to *hide*, but it was the best I could come up with. I couldn't bear to think of the things my siblings would hear from the rest of the church members, who made it a habit to report back whenever they saw ex-members. If Grace and I seemed in good spirits, we would be considered foolish and bestial, not recognizing how vain and worthless our lives now were. If we seemed mournful, we were pathetic, feeling *the sentence of death in ourselves*. In their eyes, we would never be truly happy—and we were delusional if we thought we could be.

And then there were the messages from church members that stopped my heart each time they appeared on my phone's screen. They'd begun back at home, the moment word got to the rest of the church that Grace and I were leaving, but I had assumed they would stop once we were gone. They did not. Gran texted me the morning following our departure: "You need to consider the rebellion of Korah!!!! FLEE the wrath to come!" Jael sent several text messages and emails, as well, and she had changed my name to "Korah" in her phone. In a way, it was nice to know the narrative church members were spinning in my absence. Korah was a biblical figure who publicly challenged the legitimacy of Moses's leadership over the children of Israel. As a result, God made a spectacular display of demonstrating that He had chosen Moses: He caused the earth to open up and swallow Korah, his cohorts, and their families—including their little children. *They, and all that appertained to them, went down alive into the pit, and the earth closed upon them: and they perished from among the congregation.* Afterward, God had sent fire and then a fast-moving plague to kill all who supported Korah. At the end of it all, about fifteen thousand were dead.

On receiving these messages from Gran and Jael, I'd read the story again and was struck by how much my complaints about Westboro's elders sounded like Korah's complaint against Moses: *Ye take too much upon you, seeing all the congregation are holy, every one of them, and the Lord is among them: wherefore then lift ye up yourselves above the congregation of the Lord?* A pang of fear had gripped me, but I'd thought for a moment. Moses had been established as the Lord's chosen leader via direct interaction with God Himself and a series of miracles—among them the parting of the Red Sea, the pillar of cloud that led the Israelites by day, and the pillar of fire that gave them light by night. Westboro's elders had no such evidence to support their claim to unquestionable

authority, and quite the opposite: their legacy was a series of unscriptural edicts and contradictory doctrines. They were not Moses. I was
not Korah. And I would not be intimidated by their decision to paint
me as such. In truth, once the first wave of fear passed, the comparison
even struck me as genuinely funny: in place of a man who'd incited
the revolt of thousands, there was me, perennial nerd and consummate
good girl, leading a rebellion of two alongside my sundress-wearing
sidekick. They gave us—and themselves—far too much credit.

Still, I remembered back to the days just after Josh left. Anger and
indignation had been so much easier to tolerate than grief.

The messages kept coming. One of my aunts called to tell me that
I had destroyed my sister. "It's because of you that Grace has been able
to go down this path to certain destruction. You weren't content to
take your own soul to Hell—you had to drag your sister down with
you." Her voice had sounded cautious at first, but quickly took on a
vicious disgust. I didn't know what to say. There was a good chance
that she was right, and that things would go horribly wrong. I knew
I couldn't take responsibility for Grace's decisions, but if she got hurt,
there was no way I wouldn't blame myself.

Two weeks after our departure, I received a text message from
Margie accusing me of modesty violations and of fabricating reasons to
leave because of my "lust." Since I had been dressing exactly the same
since leaving Westboro, I was confused. We went back and forth for
a little while, and I tried to reiterate some of the actual reasons I left,
but she just couldn't hear me. She could acknowledge no wrongdoing
on the part of the church. This, she insisted, was all my fault. "If your
heart gets broken and you are ashamed," she wrote, "reach out. Otherwise this is done." I had sighed. Clearly, there was no point in continuing the conversation, and I cried to Newbery in bitter frustration.

> NEWBERY: I guess it's important to remember that they are
> trying to deal with this, too. They don't know what to do
> any more than you do, but what they do still have is the
> church and the "certainty" that comes with that. And it's
> all they have to try to find answers and deal with it.
>
> I suppose that's a long way to go to get to an idea that
> is much harder than it sounds, which is: I think you need

to try not to take it personally. The only aunt and cousin I think you *really* need to remember is the one you knew when you were still there. The rest is just coping and probably fear.

I remembered what it was like on that side of this divide, and I knew that Newbery was right. But I was dismayed to realize that even while paying the enormous cost of leaving Westboro, Grace and I were still under the judgmental gaze of its members. How could we possibly move on while living in the shadow of the church?

It was time to go.

Just beyond the WELCOME TO SOUTH DAKOTA sign, the speed limit bumped up to 75 miles an hour. I hit the gas and barreled on.

———

We arrived at our destination at 4:15 P.M., just as the sun was setting over the Black Hills. I'd first seen them on the horizon about an hour earlier, rising ominously from a dense mist toward thick cloud cover that had cast a pall over everything since we'd crossed the Missouri River around midday. Grace read the Wikipedia page aloud: "The hills were so-called because of their dark appearance from a distance, as they were covered in trees." As we drew nearer, I realized it was true—an endless array of pine. Grace looked up from her phone and we stared out at the clusters of trees with every branch and needle covered in a delicate sheet of ice. The fog made it seem like they sprang up and frosted just for our eyes' amusement. "It looks like Narnia," she marveled.

The road through Black Hills National Forest wasn't especially icy, but I steered around the sharp curves with overmuch caution anyway. My eyes kept darting away from the road to a series of small signs reading WHY DIE?—memorials for victims of fatal car crashes, I would learn later—which further elevated my sense of foreboding. The question called to mind a verse my mother referenced often. *Cast away from you all your transgressions, whereby ye have transgressed; and make you a new heart and a new spirit: for why will ye die, O house of Israel?* "Repent!" I could hear my mother say. "*Why will ye die?!*"

Twelve hours on the road had landed Grace and me here in Deadwood. My sister had wanted to go to a beach, but I was afraid to spend that kind of money. I thought we should find a destination that was less expensive and reachable by car, and I'd been drawn to Deadwood for several reasons. Its isolation and beauty. The fact that my brother Sam had been a fan of HBO's television series by the same name. And though there was no chance of running into C.G. on this trip—his home was 400 miles away—some pathetic part of me was heartened at the prospect of sharing his beloved home state for a while. Having just learned about the home-sharing company Airbnb, I'd searched their website for "Deadwood" on a whim, and the very first hit had looked like destiny: the attic room of a huge, Victorian-era house set on a steep hillside in the city's historic Presidential District, a long-term restoration project taken on by its owners, a young couple named Dustin and Laura Floyd. They were preparing to run their home as an inn. I liked the premise of Airbnb, but since I was a bit anxious about the reality of sleeping in the home of strangers, I looked them up on Google before our trip. The website of TDG Communications, a Deadwood marketing firm, listed Dustin as its co-owner and Laura as an administrator. Looking at their silly photos, biographies, and job titles—"benevolent overlord," "administrative goddess"—I figured they were probably safe.

With the nose pointed down the steep incline, I threw my car into park and stepped out into the brisk afternoon, Grace following a second later. We opened the back end and stared past our visible breath for a beat: every inch of space had been filled with backpacks full of clothes, coats, boots, the comforter I'd slept with since sixth grade, Grace-approved foods like chips, bagels, and English muffins, and two hefty boxes full of books. Our heads snapped up as a petite young woman—just a few years older than me, I guessed, early thirties—suddenly appeared on the broad porch, descending the front steps with a warm "Hell-o! You must be Megan and Grace! I'm Laura, I'll show you to your room!" She stepped carefully over the curbside mound of packed snow, paused at the overflowing trunk—"Does all this come inside?"—and grabbed the nearest box to lead the way to the attic.

The three of us maneuvered the contents of my vehicle through the cramped mudroom, past a small room with wood floors, up two flights of stairs that creaked with every step, and into the room I'd seen in the Airbnb photos: L-shaped with scuffed hardwood floors, two large windows overlooking the neighborhood, and steep rooflines that made constant vigilance essential: though twelve feet high at its center, the ceiling sloped precipitously downward until it was just four feet at the room's edges.

Laura gave us a few pointers about the town, told us which way to go if we cared to wander around, and then left us to head back to the office. Grace and I stood in the attic in the midst of all the boxes, silent for a moment, assessing the space, planning. We spent the next couple of hours rearranging the room. We slid the queen-sized bed into the southeast corner, under the lowest part of the ceiling. Beneath the low slope on the west side, the boxes of books and empty suitcases. Clothes in the bureau. Dresses and cardigans on the little rack around the corner, next to a beige-colored door labeled—inexplicably and in sloppy blue marker across the top of the door—JANE'S ATTIC. We speculated as to who this Jane might be—a ghostly old woman haunting the gold miner she widowed? A young woman fleeing an arranged marriage?—while we organized our books and filled the recently remodeled bathroom with bottles of shampoo and conditioner and the rest of our toiletries. Finally, I spread my old comforter over the bed, and we sat down on top of it.

"What now?" Gracie asked.

I looked around. There was still a bit more to unpack, but we'd been at it for two hours already. "Well—" I started.

"Let's go explore!"

Snow was just beginning to fall in thick flurries as we made our way down the hill in the darkness, but once we left the residential section and neared Deadwood's Main Street, the lights seemed almost as bright as daytime. SILVERADO screamed the sign in front of the first casino we came to, row after row of slot machines visible through the front windows. We turned north onto Lower Main to find what looked to have been a thriving downtown at some point—casinos, restaurants, hotels, boutique clothing stores, and souvenir shops—each trying to look as if they still belonged in the Old West.

But like the brick road they lined, each appeared to be nearly deserted.

Many of the souvenir shops were already closed, but we stared through their windows anyway. It still felt almost criminal to simply wander around with no rules. We could take as much time as we

wanted. We could go anywhere we liked. And we needed absolutely
no reason at all. The freedom was heady. We kept going, past Pam's
Purple Door, past the Bullock Hotel, Belle Joli winery, Tin Lizzie's,
and the Gem Saloon. We admired the decorative streetlamps wrapped
in snow-dusted garlands that lined both sides of the street, and followed their alternating red and green bulbs all the way to the end of
the road: the Four Aces.

The entrance opened directly onto a brightly lit gaming floor, with
the musical noise of slot machines and tables for blackjack and three-
card poker. Aside from a large man slumped in front of a slot machine
in the next room, the only people visible were casino employees: a
couple of dealers, the bartender, and a maintenance worker. One of the
dealers gave me an inordinately long stare, but I averted my gaze and
continued on. Grace and I pulled up chairs at the bar and sat down. It
was my first time at a bar—Grace had gone with friends a couple of
times back in Kansas—but I tried to play it cool and pretend I wasn't
freaked out by the whole experience.

On the other side of the counter, a pretty, thirty-something blonde
in a short black skirt, a revealing white button-up, and plenty of eye-
liner turned around and gave us a maternal smile. She'd have to check
our IDs. I told her that Grace wasn't twenty-one and I wasn't drinking,
so there was no need. She looked puzzled but smiled and offered us hot
chocolate. We sipped it through tiny red and white straws and chatted
with her.

"Cora," she said, extending a hand. "So . . . what are you girls
doing here?"

We explained, giving the least amount of information possible:
that we were visiting town for a month, between Grace's fall and
spring semesters. That we didn't really know anything about the area.
And that we had come to read books. Cora's smile was broad. "Books!"
She laughed. She seemed to think we were hilarious, and her voice had
a gentle warmth that made me like her immediately. I forgot to be
guarded.

It started off innocently enough: Why Deadwood? I told Cora that
our eldest brother was a fan of the show on HBO.

"Your eldest brother?" she wondered. "How many siblings do you
have?"

"There are eleven of us total," I answered automatically.

"Eleven! Your family must be religious."

"Baptist," I said.

"What kind of Baptist?"

My eyes widened. How had we gotten here so fast?

"Independent," I dodged.

She nodded sagely. Maybe it was my tone or my expression, or maybe Grace and I were unwittingly giving off a "runaways" vibe, but Cora seemed to intuit that our family's religion and our presence in Deadwood were not entirely unrelated. She began to tell us about her mother, a woman who had created a religion of her own by cobbling together elements of Judaism and fringe Christian denominations.

"My mother was very 'book smart,' and she read a lot about a lot of different religions. She was very strict. She thought she knew better than everybody else. The whole world was wrong, but *she* had figured it all out. Very strict, very controlling."

"What do you mean by 'strict'?" I asked.

Cora described several prohibitions her mother had imposed, including a ban on the celebration of birthdays, Christmas, and other holidays.

"If anything bad happened to me," she said, "it was because I was a sinner. It was because I deserved it. Instead of showing compassion or understanding or trying to help—you know, *being a parent*—my mother said things like that."

I was dumbfounded. Westboro and this woman's mother clearly did not draw from all the same wells, but their attitudes sounded remarkably similar: an unwavering certainty in their righteousness and a categorical disdain for any ideas that did not fit with their own. Although it saddened me to hear, I also felt a surge of recognition that made me oddly hopeful. *Maybe it wasn't just us.* For so long, I had seen Westboro as an anomaly, unique among all the world. I feared no one would understand what that life was like, and it made me feel alone— cast out of our family and forever set apart from the world for all the years we had spent antagonizing others. Hiding from the past seemed like the only answer, and it was another reason we had come to this sleepy tourist town in the frozen Hills.

Grace and I looked at each other, and I knew we were thinking the same thing.

We turned back to Cora and told her everything.

"Next time," she promised at the end of the night, "I'll add a shot of Jack Daniels to your hot chocolate."

———

It was nearing eleven the following morning by the time I finally awoke from a dead sleep. I opened my eyes and waited for them to adjust to the cold light pouring in from the windows just next to the head of the bed. I knew without looking that Grace was still asleep, her breath slow and even. Even under the blankets, I was shivering. I slowly sat up and scratched my sister's head.

"Gracie?" I whispered.

"Emph!" she grunted in protest, pulling the blankets up to her ears.

I persisted. "Shall I go make us breakfast? Half a muffin and coffee?" We still weren't eating much. There was another petulant grunt from beneath the blanket, but Grace opened her eyes and we bargained: I would go on a mission to find the kitchen and return with breakfast, while she did some more unpacking. I picked up a bag of English muffins and a can of Folgers instant coffee and headed downstairs. The kitchen seemed improbably small after the historic grandeur of the other rooms on the first floor—broad spaces with high ceilings, beautiful hardwood floors, and brilliant sunlight streaming in through huge windows that spanned most of the distance from floor to ceiling. When breakfast was ready, I returned to the attic and Grace and I got down to the main purpose of our trip: reading.

Back at the beginning of my communication with C.G.—*Chad*, I chided myself—he had introduced me to the writer David Foster Wallace. I'd begun exploring Wallace's words in whatever forms I could find them—short stories, essays, interviews—and had shared them with Grace. We were particularly enthralled with a scene from one interview, in which Wallace recalled taking a year off from college to drive a school bus. He was unhappy, and there was much he wanted to read that wouldn't be assigned in his classes. "And I read," Wallace said; "pretty much everything I've read was read during that year."

Grace reminded me of the line in the weeks after we left Westboro, and it became an inspiration for our trip. I couldn't think of a more suitable use of our newfound freedom: trying to see the world from the perspectives of others. Following Wallace's example sounded like a grand adventure—an indulgence that would never have been countenanced at Westboro—but more than anything, it seemed like it might help Grace and me find some answers. We would only have one month before she'd have to return to school in Kansas for the spring semester, but it was better than nothing.

In preparation for our reading trip, Grace and I had gathered stacks of books from a few friends, and had also paid a visit to the Lawrence Public Library. While she had wandered off to the fiction section looking for Flannery O'Connor and J. D. Salinger, I'd asked a middle-aged librarian where I might find books on philosophy and religion. I had run my fingers along their spines for a few minutes, reading titles and noting authors: David Hume, Immanuel Kant, C. S. Lewis, Friedrich Nietzsche. After a moment, I'd found myself stepping back and staring up at the stacks, centuries' worth of human thought devoted to understanding God and the world and how to live in it. I had wondered how we at Westboro could have ever believed that we alone had discovered the one true answer to it all. I had flushed with embarrassment at our arrogance, and at my own ignorance. What did I know of these philosophers and their ideas? *Beware lest any man spoil you through philosophy and vain deceit, after the traditions of men, after the rudiments of the world, and not after Christ.* It was a catchall verse that had kept me from ever venturing too far off the beaten path, allowing me to dismiss out of hand any challenges to the most fundamental premises of our beliefs: Did God exist? And was the Bible His infallible Word? I had been taught that these were the questions of fools, but now I felt foolish for all the years I had failed to ask them.

I knew that I would read the Bible on this trip, but at Newbery's suggestion, I had also brought along books by Christopher Hitchens, Sam Harris, and Richard Dawkins: *God Is Not Great, The End of Faith,* and *The God Delusion.* Their presence felt illicit, so I decided to ease into the journey with a short book by Hemingway, whom I had also never read. Lying prone on the hardwood floor with my elbows propped up on a pillow, I picked up Newbery's copy of *The Old Man and the Sea* and began. My phone sat nearby, ready and waiting for me to record any lines I found particularly moving. I needed wisdom and direction, and I intended to cull as much of it as I could from as many places as I could find it.

Dec. 18, 2012—Day 1
THE OLD MAN & THE SEA
Now is no time to think of what you do not have. Think of what you can do with what there is.

———

Despite our best intentions to read uninterrupted for hours on end, Grace and I didn't make it too long before we decided it was time for lunch. Grace sat at the kitchen table and read *Anna Karenina* aloud to me as I assembled peanut butter sandwiches, and then continued as I cleaned up the kitchen after lunch—washing pans, loading and unloading the dishwasher, sweeping the floor. Most of the mess didn't belong to us, but compared to the nightly hurricane that constituted dinner in the Phelps-Roper home, this was nothing.

And in any case, I was always happiest being useful.

A door slammed and we both froze, my eyes snapping up to Grace's. I peeked out the kitchen threshold, past the dining room and the entryway, and saw Laura coming through the front door, followed closely by a tall man with dark sideburns looking smart in a black pea-coat and thick-rimmed glasses. *Damn*, I thought. Too late to hide now. I tiptoed back to the sink.

"I've never seen the kitchen so clean!" the man said. "I'm Dustin. You must be . . ." His finger wavered back and forth between my sister and me. "Megan?" he asked, pointing at me. "And Grace?"

I grabbed a towel to dry my hands and then shook his. He explained that since the offices for TDG, the marketing firm I'd read about, were just down the hill and around the corner, he and Laura often made the ten-minute walk home for lunch. I looked at the clock and made a mental note to stay away from the first floor during any hour that could plausibly be considered lunchtime. With three people now milling about, the kitchen had become uncomfortably full, so I stepped out of the main area and sat down with Grace at the table.

I watched the couple as they raided the refrigerator for leftover pizza and some sort of rice dish, surreptitiously studying them for signs of latent psychopathy.

"So what are you guys up to today? Is there anything specific you're interested in doing while you're here?" Dustin's tone was friendly and helpful, and I sensed that he was in the habit of acting as tour guide.

"Is there anything you'd recommend?" I asked. He rattled off a list of local attractions, most of which I didn't recognize, but he noted that this time of year, many of Deadwood's historic locations were either closed or only functioning on a limited basis.

"And then there's hiking," he continued. "Just up the hill is Mount Moriah Cemetery, where famous Deadwood locals are buried—Wild Bill Hickok, Calamity Jane, and Seth Bullock."

Fifteen minutes later, Grace and I were dressed and out the door. The cemetery gates were only about three blocks up the hill, but we were huffing and puffing almost as soon as we set out. The incline was steep, the temperature was below freezing, and the air up here—nearly a mile above sea level—was far thinner than we were accustomed to. We trekked along a paved path through the cemetery for a time, but layers of snow and ice made it difficult to follow. I looked over my shoulder at the falling sun.

"We're not gonna make it if we keep trying to follow the road," I warned Grace. There were no more gravestones here, so she shrugged and began sidestepping directly up the mountain. Navigating straight up through the trees and around the iciest patches as best we could, we arrived at the top in less than twenty minutes. To the west was a view of pine forests in Deadwood Gulch, and to the east, a vast expanse of the Black Hills with their rounded summits, some covered in snow and others dotted with the standing remains of dead trees. The wind was ferocious. We only had a few minutes before we had to head back—I was convinced we needed a cushion of daylight in case one of us broke several bones tumbling over the rocky edge or down the steep slope—but I sat down on a frozen concrete beam to take in the view anyway. Grace sat across from me and slipped her phone out of her coat pocket.

"The Snail and the Rosebush," she began, "by Hans Christian Andersen."

It was a short tale, maybe half a dozen minutes long, but the wind was whipping away my tears by the end. *"But shouldn't all of us on earth give the best we have to others and offer whatever is in our power?"* the Rosebush asked the Snail.

"What do I have to do with the world?" the Snail derided. *"I spit at the world. It's no good! The world means nothing to me."* My mind called forth images of our most contentious protests, surrounded by scores of counter-protesters who were screaming, chanting, only held back by lines of officers and police barricades. I remembered our intent in those moments, the insistent need to show ourselves unbowed by "these God-haters," our willingness to wound, our desire to cut them down in their arrogance—even when they were preparing to bury their closest loved ones.

Which of those people wouldn't love to hurt me now? An admission of guilt would be blood in the water. They would eat me alive.

It was clear that the Snail's path was the only option now: *"I retire within myself, and there I shall stay."*

My sister came to sit next to me, and we linked arms and wept.

"I don't want to be a snail!" I cried into her shoulder. We could never be more than an object of scorn to the world. What did we have to offer anyone? Our lives were forever tainted and would never amount to anything so good and pure as the Rosebush.

"The sun was warm and the air so refreshing. I drank of the clear dew and the strong rain. I breathed. I lived. A power rose in me from out of the earth; a strength came down from up above; I felt an increasing happiness, always new, always great, so I had to blossom over and over again. That was my life; I couldn't do anything else."

It was just too late for us.

We stood and started back, arriving at the inn at sunset again.

Twenty-four hours.

Dec. 19, 2012—Day 2
THE SUN ALSO RISES
You can't get away from yourself by moving from one place to another.

It was only our second full day up here, but we'd already slipped into the pattern that would define our trip: Sleep late. Eat breakfast. Read.

Eat lunch. Read. Use the late afternoon to explore the Black Hills. Eat dinner. And then read until it was time to sleep again.

Tonight we would do our evening reading at the Four Aces, to keep Cora company on her next shift. I already felt like a regular, and the employees greeted me like one. Cora put mugs of hot chocolate in front of Grace and me, and introduced us to a couple of the dealers working that night, Ryan and Derek. I recognized Ryan as the one who'd stared too long when I came in the last time—and soon discovered that it was because he had recognized me. An amateur filmmaker and fan of the director Kevin Smith, Ryan had followed my years-long Twitter battle with Smith (#SaveMegan).

With eyes wide and mouth agape, I shook my head. How was this possible? I'd traveled twelve hours to this tiny town at the edge of South Dakota to get away from everything and everyone who knew me—only to be spotted on the first night at the first establishment I'd wandered into. What were the odds?

"I need a drink," I told Cora, using a poor imitation of a wink to disguise how unsettled Ryan's revelation had made me. She poured a shot of Jack Daniels' Tennessee Honey into my hot chocolate, which I nearly spewed out the instant it touched my tongue. *Disgusting.* Not wanting to be rude, I sipped the rest of it slowly while we all conversed—and though the flavor didn't improve, I felt my stomach grow warm and my worries fade. As the dealers rotated through their stations and then off the gaming floor, they'd come to the bar to chat. Grace and I would ask them questions about their families and their lives—so foreign to us—and they'd ask about Westboro, what it was like to picket in the face of angry crowds, how our peers at school had treated us. They got a real kick out of the fact that we had made a habit of protesting outside our own high school over our lunch hour, snacking on Lunchables while classmates drove by honking their horns, flipping us off, and throwing the occasional sandwich.

"Do you have any family outside of the church?" Cora asked.

I beamed and told them the happiest moment I'd had since leaving.

Two nights after our departure from Westboro, Libby had driven Grace and me to our brother Josh's house. It had been eight years since he left—several lifetimes, it seemed—and at my request, Libby hadn't alerted him to the fact that Grace and I had left, too. My stomach was in knots during the forty-five-minute drive. I had a terrible feeling that he would be unrecognizable to me, and that I would be to him. I kept thinking of the terrible things I'd said about him when asked by journalists. I'd told them he was a disobedient rebel. I'd told them he was bound for Hell. I'd told them he wasn't my brother anymore. *For whosoever shall do the will of my Father which is in heaven, the same is my brother, and sister, and mother.* I suddenly felt so silly and arrogant for judging him all these years, based only on his behavior as a nineteen-year-old kid and the fact that he wasn't a member of Westboro. Would he forgive me? What kind of person had he become since I'd known him?

It was pitch-dark when we arrived, nearly 9 P.M. Libby found the keypad and entered the code to open the garage door, and I followed her in while Grace stayed outside, waiting to see how Josh would react. All the inside lights were on, and I only needed a glance and a moment to take it all in: the granite countertops and matching kitchen appliances, the hardwood floors, high ceilings, and the inviting scent of maple-vanilla candles. This was the home of someone who'd made something of himself. Libby pointed me down the steps just inside the door, and I proceeded alone, pausing at the bottom of the stairs to look around. It was *classic* Josh. To my right, a framed collection of theater ticket stubs. Still the movie buff. Above the basement door, a wooden plaque that read, "I'm ashamed of what I did for a Klondike Bar." The same sort of saying that had characterized his entire T-shirt collection in high school. And there in front of me was Josh himself, playing a video game with a headset on, his back to me—exactly the same position in which I'd found him so many times in his basement bedroom back at home.

Some things never change.

I held my breath, crossed the room, and sat down on the couch adjacent to the one he was occupying. His head turned, and he froze. Silence. I studied his face for a beat, looking for signs of anger or rejection and finding only incomprehension. I saw that where he had always been slim before, he was thick and muscled now. He had less hair, but his face was the same—the male version of mine.

My head started to spin, and I finally exhaled. In my hands was an envelope full of photos—of our parents and our siblings through all the years Josh had missed. I pulled them out and started to babble, not knowing what to expect.

"Hi!" I squeaked nervously. "I brought these for you. This is Jonah, and this is Gabe, and Noah . . . Luke. Grace took this one of Mom and Dad when we were hiking, and . . ."

He sat still, unmoving, and I rambled on.

Finally, he interrupted: "Hold on a second!" He stood up, took the photos from my hands, set them on the couch, and motioned for me to stand. His embrace had all the intensity of my final ones with Bekah and Mom and Dad, and though this one was "hello" instead of "good-bye," I couldn't stop the tears from spilling over again.

Grace walked in the basement door a minute later.

Josh stepped back from me. "What are you *doing* here?" He sounded truly bewildered. As if he thought it might be a dream.

We stayed up talking until the wee hours of the morning, and if it weren't for the sweeping changes in Josh's life, it would have seemed like we'd never been apart at all. Josh was married now and had a little boy. He'd finished college and gotten a master's degree. He had a great job. He had just bought this house. Motivated, industrious, and hardworking, just like our parents. I was elated for my brother and proud of what he had accomplished without the vast support system we'd grown up with—but I couldn't help feeling very small next to him. There were only seventeen months between our births, and at twenty-eight, he'd already managed to build a wonderful life. I felt a pang of envy and regret that he and Grace had both chosen to leave Westboro so much earlier in their lives. Their decisions had left them more years to live in a world outside of Westboro's conjuring—years I had wasted hurting people in a misguided effort to serve an image of a God that seemed less real all the time.

But I got more years with our family, I reminded myself before bitterness could root itself too deeply. Eight more years of morning coffee with our mother. Of sharing jokes and indie rock music with our dad. Of pulling Noah and Luke around the neighborhood in the little green wagon while they slept. Of French-braiding Bekah's shimmery auburn hair while she read aloud to me. I called forth memories to steel myself against twin but opposing tendencies I felt warring inside me: between regretting the past and romanticizing it. I couldn't allow bitterness to steal the beauty in my family, or love to conceal the destructiveness in it. I wouldn't rewrite history. I would hold the whole messy truth of it to myself all at once.

I wouldn't do to them what we had done to Josh.

"We have more family, actually," I told Cora. "Like my grandparents. We haven't spoken to them yet."

"Why not?" she wondered.

I paused. Growing up, I'd hardly known my dad's parents. Since neither had ever been part of our church community, we didn't see them except for rare visits. My mother had always spoken derisively of them, and I understood from a young age that they were not like us. Nana and Grandpa had married young, and divorced amicably when my father was a baby—a cardinal sin in Westboro's estimation, especially because they had both remarried. Still, their occasional stops had been grudgingly allowed until a few years earlier, not long after Grandpa's final visit. He had stopped by unannounced one summer day, and my mother had used the opportunity to instigate a fight with him: she asked him what he thought of our protests at soldiers' funerals. Grandpa was a career military man, serving in the U.S. Air Force until he retired, so when my mother asked, he told her exactly what he thought of the protests. Seeing the contentious discussion, my nine-year-old brother Noah wandered over: "Who is this guy?!" he demanded. Grandpa had left a few minutes later, and I hadn't spoken to him since. My parents wrote letters to Nana and Grandpa enumerating my grandparents' sins, insisting they wouldn't expose us children to such corrupting influences, and that had been the end of it.

"I don't know exactly," I told Cora. "I just have this . . . bad feeling." She nodded, but she clearly didn't understand.

The truth was that I didn't understand, either, and the fact that I lacked a good answer—a sound explanation for this "bad feeling"—bothered me. My grandmother had shown me nothing but kindness, but I couldn't seem to stop judging her according to the church's rubric. I had already crossed the lines between "Us" and "Them" several times—for Josh, Newbery, Chad, Libby, even Cora and Ryan here in the casino—but somehow, those lines remained firmly in place.

It was an obvious point, but it suddenly struck me that this Us/Them mindset was deeply ingrained and resistant to change. Unless

I wanted to be forever ruled by a nebulous fear of outsiders, it wasn't enough for me just to *cross* that line a few times; I needed to decide whether the line should be moved, or changed, or erased entirely. It couldn't be a simple matter of a blanket rejection of my former beliefs, either, which would be no less silly and irrational than unquestioning acceptance of them. Instead, I would need to look at the evidence. I'd need to carefully examine each of these thought patterns, holdovers from Westboro that would have to be challenged and reconsidered— over and over again—if there was any hope for lasting change. *Prove all things; hold fast that which is good.*

I thought about the last time we'd heard from Nana—a birthday card she'd sent to Grace back in October. I had felt so sad for her, ignored by our family for years on end. *Happy birthday, Grace,* she'd written. *I'll bet you are growing up beautiful. Wish I could hear from some-one. I love you.* As little as I'd seen Nana, she hadn't missed sending us birthday cards in all my years. Like my mother, I had seen her efforts as a pitiful substitute for having a real presence in our lives, but now the gesture seemed like determined persistence—an effort to maintain an open door despite my parents' attempts to seal all doors shut. Nana had been trying to show that she loved us, even though she couldn't be around us.

"I think I want to call Nana *now,*" I said to Grace. She nodded. What was there to stop me from picking up the phone that instant? I got her phone number from Josh and began to pace an empty room filled with slot machines, tuning out their jingles as the phone began to ring.

"Hello?"

"Hi, Nana . . . this is Megan."

"Hello!" she said. "Megan who?"

I winced. The moment I clarified that I was her granddaughter, Nana started to cry—and all the harder when I explained that Grace had left, too. "I have been waiting for you grandchildren for years," she said. "*Decades.* Megan. I *never* thought it would be you."

"I didn't, either," I told her truthfully.

Listening to my grandmother describe her years of struggle and sadness, I began to see the lasting effects of Westboro's treatment of outsiders. Nana's pain didn't come from a one-time decision to keep her at arm's length and out of our lives, but from a continuing and active rejection—from watching the years of her life tick by without the love of her family. Nana had been living this nightmare for more than *thirty years*. The pain was ongoing. I wondered how I would ever bear it.

———

Dec. 20, 2012—Day 3
THE SUN ALSO RISES
Wonderful how one loses track of the days up here in the mountains.

Time slowed to a crawl in Deadwood. The hours stretched out end-lessly before me, and on the good days, I couldn't get enough. After year upon year of constant churning and contention, I began to relish the quiet. I would take the day's reading to the fluffy green couch by the huge window in the living room—a single pane, so it was a view unbroken—but I'd often end up spending more time staring out the window than at the page, watching the snow blanket my car and the neighborhood and the pine forests farther up the hill. When Grace was ready for chocolate or an adventure, I would happily in-dulge. I loved seeing where her whims would take us. Donning thrift store wedding dresses for an impromptu photo shoot at Deadwood Dick's Antiques. Watching students put the finishing touches on the life-sized log cabin they were building in shop class during a drop-in tour of the local high school. Wading through knee-high drifts of immaculate snow along a creek in Spearfish Canyon, where the echoing snarls of a pack of dogs—another possible instrument of God's wrath?—suddenly broke the silence and sent us hightailing it back to the car. Taking care of my sister gave me purpose. I knew I couldn't give her what she truly wanted—the return of our beloved family—but after all we had lost, I wanted to offer consolation how-ever I could.

"No!" Grace objected playfully one evening. We'd been reading by lamplight in the attic, and she had just hauled her huge old, clunky, barely functioning typewriter across the room, setting it down eleven inches from my face. After several minutes of poking and grumbling and paper-loading and reloading and random *ding*s later, I moved toward the door to find a quieter space. "You can't leave me! You'll be reading to the sound of my typewriter! It will be so poetic. *In Deadwood.*"

"Everything is poetic in Deadwood," I told her, laughing, but settled back down to read.

"I'm writing that down," she declared. She continued noisily pecking away for a few moments and then apologized. "I want to write these thoughts as I have them," she said by way of explanation.

I considered. "I like to think about my thoughts before I have them."

She laughed again. "I'm writing *that* down, too!" Her delight was contagious.

But it wasn't enough. The bad days—the ones where Grace would refuse to speak to me, behaving as though she didn't see me, couldn't hear me—began to multiply. The smallest of disagreements could grow into a days-long episode of the silent treatment, and I struggled to understand why my sister was so upset with me. If I didn't immediately get on board with her ideas—like the indefinite trip to France— she would insist that I was impossibly selfish and didn't care about her. If I offered an explanation for my disagreements, then I was simply "justifying myself" and not listening to her.

And then there was Chad. He had reappeared a few days before I left Westboro, and we'd been in touch ever so cautiously—and only via text message—ever since. He explained his sudden and protracted absence in a way that both relieved my hurt and made my heart ache: he'd been fevered and immobile for weeks, after he'd managed to contract both mononucleosis and West Nile virus simultaneously. He had almost died. Our communication had been as tentative as ever, due in part to a new anxiety he harbored: that I might suddenly show up on his doorstep unannounced. As unpracticed as I was in the art of "normal" relationships, I was under no illusions that such a move would be a good idea. He telegraphed his reticence just as clearly as he had his care. There was that small part of me that delighted in the idea of our being in the same state, but South Dakota was vast. In Deadwood, I was nearly as far from Chad's home as I had been back in Kansas. And when I told him about our plans to run away and read books, I didn't tell him where we were going.

I wasn't going to make a fool of myself.

By the time I arrived in Deadwood, Chad and I were back to texting nearly every day, though still cautiously. He was curious about what I was doing and thinking, wondering how I was adjusting to life on the outside. His queries seemed like a test sometimes, and at the heart of each stood a single question: Did I really belong outside of Westboro's fences? When he finally asked me where we had chosen for our reading quest, I told him the truth with studied nonchalance. "Enjoy Dead-wood," he answered. "I'll be out there sometime after Christmas. I'll try to look you up. Until then." My whole body hummed with excitement, but when Grace caught me grinning stupidly at my phone, she was angry. She never had to ask when it was Chad I was messaging, and she seemed to have an uncanny ability to intuit when I was just *thinking* of him. She didn't like that I wanted to share so many things with him, and told me that his influence had bothered her for a long time.

"I can't help but think he poisoned a part of you," she wrote. She suspected that he was the cause of my initial doubts.

Reading Grace's message, I was overcome by a powerful sense of denial. *No, no, no.* We were never supposed to be influenced by outsid-ers, and that idea had been a constant refrain at Westboro since I was small. "These people have nothing to offer us!" we would say, a senti-ment often accompanied by a dismissive sneer. God instructed us to stand fast and hold the line against evildoers. *Behold, I have made thy face strong against their faces, and thy forehead strong against their foreheads. As an adamant harder than flint have I made thy forehead: fear them not, neither be dismayed at their looks, though they be a rebellious house.* I was revolted by the thought that I had let an outsider affect me. It made me feel weak and vulnerable. Corrupted. I responded to Grace's as-sertion with a slew of words about the church's cruelty and doctrinal errors—but the more I tried to frame the words to insist that Chad's arguments had not influenced me, the clearer it became that my sister was right, at least in part.

MEGAN: And Gracie—assuming for a second that he *did* poison a part of me, I can only see one possibility. I can see one thing that I lost (though I believe this process started way before Chad). If the thing he poisoned was my ability to go along with something even if I disagreed with it—if he killed my ability to ignore and turn away from my conscience—then I'm glad he poisoned it.

GRACE: I will never like him.

Although I tried to respond to my sister's moods with gentleness and restraint, reason and logic, my efforts often failed spectacularly. A tsunami of rage, pain, confusion, and despair would engulf us both as we exploded at each other, storming off to far-flung corners of the inn with venom coursing through us. It was fast becoming clear that we had no idea how to navigate relationships outside the church's black-and-white, all-or-nothing paradigm. I'd thought that going through this process with a most beloved sister might make things easier— and it did, in some ways—but leaving together had also created a situation I hadn't foreseen. With two of us, the mental, emotional, and logistical struggles of starting life again, almost from scratch, were concentrated and compounded. We had never learned how to "agree to disagree," because to church members, such a concept was blasphemous. *Can two walk together, except they be agreed? What communion hath light with darkness?* At Westboro, every decision had moral implications. Every question had a single correct answer. Miscommunication required blame, and mistakes required punishment. My sister and I knew how to cajole, issue ultimatums, attribute ill motives, and assign moral failure to the other party in a dispute, but we couldn't compromise and we couldn't move forward without a resolution as to which of us was in the wrong. Without an absolute authority who could resolve the problem and declare one side as just and righteous, we floundered.

"Are you . . . okay?"

Curled up on the couch in the parlor, I glanced up to see Laura's tiny frame in the doorway, barely visible in the dwindling light coming in from the west window. She and Dustin had been out of town for several days, visiting her family for Christmas, and her presence here on Christmas Eve surprised me. *Why are they home already?* I hadn't even heard her come in. I swiped at my swollen eyes and tried to reassure her that I was fine, but I choked on another sob instead. She sat down and tentatively put an arm around my shoulder. I briefly debated an attempt to preserve my dignity and walk away, but the last remains of my life were falling apart. What did I have to lose?

"She won't talk to me!" I wailed. "I don't know what to do!"

I wasn't sure what I expected Laura to say. I just knew that I couldn't stand another second of this solitary confinement. I needed my mother—but in her absence, I needed *anyone*.

Laura shushed me and rubbed comforting circles on my back while I calmed down.

"Do you want to have dinner with Dustin and me?" she asked.

I followed Laura into the kitchen, watching as she and Dustin maneuvered around the small space, chopping herbs and vegetables for some sort of soup. I had assumed they found it burdensome to have two guests puttering around their house, but they both seemed perfectly at ease with an emotional stranger recovering from a crying jag at their kitchen table. Dustin explained that they loved to travel and to meet new people, but since full-time jobs now made such excursions difficult, hosting guests was the best alternative. Laura waxed eloquent describing their experiences studying abroad—she in Belgium and the Netherlands, he at Oxford—and it was obvious that she missed the freedom and adventure.

When I'd regained full possession of my composure, Laura tactfully probed the cause of my distress. I was evasive, but explained that my sister's lack of communication wasn't really her fault. That we had just moved out of our lifelong home, and that our family wasn't speaking to us anymore.

"Can I ask why?" Laura said gently.

I paused. Talking with Cora and Ryan at the bar was one thing, but Grace and I were living with these people. What if I told the truth and their response was outrage and anger? I knew such a response would be justified, but I didn't want to risk it.

"We don't agree with their religion," I hedged.

They both nodded, and an inscrutable look passed between them.

As we loaded the dishwasher after dinner, Laura offered me another room—the old library on the first floor—to take some of the pressure off Grace and me.

"For free?" I blurted. "Thank you!"

She laughed. "No problem. Goodnight, Megan."

———

A split second before I stepped into the kitchen the following morning, I realized the date and felt a surge of panic.

What am I going to say when they say, "Merry Christmas"?!

After all the years of picketing Christmas services, of singing our version of "Santa Claus Is Coming to Town" ("Santa Claus Will Take You to Hell"), of listening to my mother read to us of the holiday's pagan roots, and of reciting from the book of Jeremiah to passersby— *For the customs of the people are vain: for one cutteth a tree out of the forest, the work of the hands of the workman, with the axe. They deck it with silver and with gold; they fasten it with nails and with hammers, that it move not . . . they are altogether brutish and foolish: the stock is a doctrine of vanities . . .* After all these years, my abhorrence of Christmas was visceral, and the thought of trying to frame the words "Merry Christmas" made me physically ill. I could ignore the shop clerks and Salvation Army bell ringers, of course, but I was a guest here.

"Good morning!" Dustin said brightly. I'm sure my face projected "deer in headlights," but he was standing at the counter working the contents of a mixing bowl. "Waffles," he explained. "Laura will be down in a few minutes." He wrinkled his nose and lowered his voice: "She's not a morning person, but my waffles should do the trick."

When Laura trudged in a minute later, there was no sign of the chipper, friendly host from the evening before. She was still in pajamas, eyes half-closed, mouth half-open, and literally dragging her feet. She pulled a chair from the table and dragged it to the open heat register that I'd discovered on my first morning here, so that the warm air blew up her pajama pants. Her mannerisms and short stature put me in mind of a small child, and I couldn't stop myself from laughing out loud. Dustin joined me.

"Dustin makes the best waffles," she moaned with a sigh. "That's the *only* reason I'm not in bed."

"It'll be an easy day, anyway," Dustin assured her, and then to me: "We're just gonna watch *Lord of the Rings* movies all day. It's an annual marathon. You're welcome to join us."

Laura was right about the waffles—copious amounts of real butter were the key, Dustin confided—but before I joined the movie marathon,

I decided to test the waters with Grace. I returned to the attic to grab a change of clothes, my toothbrush, and a blanket, and though my sister was sitting in bed awake, she said nothing. She didn't look up, studiously staring down at her phone. No rapprochement in sight. I made my way back down to the living room, wrapped myself in the blanket—all three of us had the same idea; the house was freezing— and I settled in on the smaller couch.

Only the extended versions of the films would suffice for this pair of self-professed nerds, so *The Fellowship of the Ring* ran for nearly four hours. We had to keep pausing the action so they could explain more about this world of elves, dwarfs, wizards, and hobbits, but they didn't seem to mind. As the credits began to roll, I remembered the holiday and looked around. Not only had there been no "Merry Christmas," there was no tree, no red and green lights, no decorations, nothing.

Curious.

When I asked why, Dustin told me that they were Jehovah's Witnesses and thus didn't observe holidays that weren't sanctioned by the Bible. That was why they had returned home on Christmas Eve: they'd been visiting Laura's parents and couldn't celebrate with them without running afoul of God and conscience.

My relief was palpable. "Oh!" I said. "We've never celebrated Christmas, either!"

"Really?" he asked. "What religion is it again?"

"Baptist," I said.

"Don't Baptists celebrate Christmas?" Laura asked.

"Not . . . our church."

Dustin's brow furrowed, and they both nodded. "Well," he said, "should we pause for lunch?"

What I *actually* wanted was to spend the rest of the day firing questions at them. What did they believe? And why? How had they chosen to become Jehovah's Witnesses? If they took instruction from the Bible, why had Laura's beautiful dark curls been chopped? What about the passage that clearly requires long hair for women and short hair for men? *Doth not even nature itself teach you, that, if a man have long hair, it is a shame unto him? But if a woman have long hair, it is a glory to her: for her hair is given her for a covering.*

I managed to suppress my curiosity at first, but as the day wore on and we became more at ease with each other, I couldn't help bringing the conversation back to religion. I tried to assume the role of objective observer, but I found it impossible to discuss the Floyds' beliefs without contrasting them to my former tradition—and since Westboro's beliefs and practices were so unusual and well-known, it didn't take them long to guess which church I might be describing. As with Cora and the dealers at the Four Aces, I was surprised again at how understanding of my past Dustin and Laura seemed to be. Instead of anger or judgment, it was fast friendship that resulted from our opening up to one another. For the next several days, we spent every spare moment we could find together, talking about belief during their lunch hour, chopping vegetables for dinner, and sitting around the living room afterward with Bibles and Web browsers at the ready.

When communications with Grace thawed again—always a mysterious but welcome process—she joined the discussion, as well. It would have been easy to spend all our days talking about theology, but Laura suggested we take our conversation on the road so that we wouldn't sit at the inn and miss the beauty of the Hills. At Mount Rushmore National Memorial, Laura pointed out an old educational video featuring the fathers of both of our hosts—Dustin's had been the first employee of the Mount Rushmore Society, and Laura's had been the superintendent here for nearly two decades, later moving to Yellowstone National Park.

"I was born in Yellowstone when my dad was an employee there," she said. "He's the superintendent now. That's where we went to visit my parents last week."

Laura explained that her decision to become a Jehovah's Witness in college had put a strain on her relationship with her parents and siblings. She'd been raised Presbyterian and was inspired to convert by Dustin, a longtime friend and love interest who had grown up in the faith. Like members of Westboro, Witnesses are instructed to date and marry only those who share their beliefs—but Laura hadn't blindly converted for her future husband. Instead, she had carefully studied with Witnesses for four years before deciding to seek baptism and membership in the organization. Although her parents had responded in different ways, both were hurt by her decision. Her father was stoic, but her mother's pain manifested in occasional angry lamentations about the things Laura would be missing: participating in non-Witness religious ceremonies like weddings and baptisms, and celebrations of holidays and birthdays—important milestones in the life of their family. Laura's beliefs now spurned the traditions that brought her family together, and inherently judged non-Witnesses as wrongdoers.

"I became something 'Outside' in my family," Laura told me later. "Being present at family gatherings that centered around holidays felt like being a vegan at a meat feast. No one can figure out exactly why this person is here, and are they really just going to stand over the meatballs and judge us?"

In the eyes of her family, Laura was behaving irrationally. Canvassing neighborhoods to knock on the doors of strangers to explain to them the importance of joining an organization whose members were convinced that Armageddon was imminent and that Satan had been loosed upon the earth in October of 1914, running amok throughout the world ever since? It made no sense. This was not the life her parents had wanted for her.

Laura's predicament sounded uncannily like my father's, and I was surprised by how many similarities there were between the doctrines of Westboro and the Witnesses—but right then, staring out the window at the sixty-foot-high carvings of George Washington and company, what held my attention were the *differences* between the two groups. In contrast to Westboro's version of Hell—eternal torment, an idea that had become detestable to me—Witnesses believe that Hell is simply death. When I quoted Bible verses that seemed to contradict this, Dustin and Laura brought forth other verses to support their position. *For the living know that they will die, but the dead know nothing at all . . . there is no work nor planning nor knowledge nor wisdom in the Grave, where you are going.* Their understanding of the verses I presented was fundamentally different from the one I had been raised with, and I was slack-jawed to realize that there was more than one way to read the text—that from one passage, multiple meanings could be deduced without contradicting the language in the original.

That *interpretation* was a phenomenon with real implications for believers.

At Westboro, we had denied that interpretation allowed for any disagreements on doctrines. *Knowing this first, that no prophecy of the scripture is of any private interpretation.* For any question or issue, there was a single correct understanding, and it was ours. Legitimate disagreement with Westboro's theology could not exist within this framework, and though I had come to reject some of the church's precepts, I immediately fell back into that paradigm—that there was only one way—because I hadn't yet seen another that made sense to me. I was still assuming that anyone contradicting "the clear meaning of Scripture" was either deliberately mangling the truth or deluded by God into believing a lie.

And yet, here were two people whose kindness, intelligence, generosity, and good intentions were all self-evident. They weren't evil, stupid, or delusional. They just saw things differently than I had been taught to, and they could articulate the logic and reasoning behind their thinking.

My head was spinning as the four of us fought the cold wind and made our way back to the Floyds' car. Grace and I looked across the backseat at each other, amazement on both of our faces, my thoughts reflected in her features: *How was this possible?* If there truly *was* more than one legitimate way to understand the world, then there was nothing inherently wrong with people who believed differently than we did. We could cease presuming most people were evil and ill-intentioned.

The hope that sprang from this realization would become the new foundation of my life, but along with that hope came still more confusion:

If there was more than one possible answer, how did anyone manage to decide between them?

———

Dec. 30, 2012—Day 13
THE GOD DELUSION
The journalist Andrew Mueller is of the opinion that pledging yourself to any particular religion "is no more or less weird than choosing to believe that the world is rhombus-shaped, and borne through the cosmos in the pincers of two enormous green lobsters called Esmerelda and Keith."

CHAD: I can tell you that I already know you'll talk too fast.
You did leave a pretty long YouTube fast-talking trail.

I did think the screen liked your face. That's a fact.

The shit you said was crazy. You think I discount that
because of the screen liking your face. I don't.

I need to know that it wasn't necessarily you. You know?

MEGAN: Where to begin?

CHAD: I don't believe Obama is the literal antichrist.

I don't believe gays marrying will trigger the end of days.
Etc. etc.

MEGAN: I don't believe either of those things, either. I didn't
think there was even enough biblical evidence to support
them.

Start with: I believed the Bible was It. That it was right
no matter what I would have come up with myself, even if
I thought something it said was Wrong, even if it made me
Angry, even if it hurt other people.

CHAD: Okay. Not tonight. And know that I think in spite of all
of that, your family has so many great qualities . . . and obviously did such a great job of raising, educating you, etc.

Learning about the Floyds' belief system was eye-opening to me.
In many ways, it seemed to be exactly what I had wanted from my
family—an improvement on several of our most objectionable doctrines. Where we had been deliberately provocative and even cruel, for
instance, Witnesses strove for gentleness: in contrast to our boisterous
funeral pickets, they knocked on doors to preach their gospel, meekly
walking away when requested. And yet, in spite of that fact, I still
found myself unsatisfied. My questions had become deeper since I left
Topeka. In all my conversations with Dustin and Laura, I had refrained
from asking the question that now weighed so heavily on my mind:
Why did they believe that the Bible was the capital-T Truth in the
first place?

I wasn't looking to be persuaded from the position I had held
throughout my conscious life. I had dearly loved the Scriptures from
the time I was a child listening to my mother read from them each
night, her reverence clear in every word. When I quoted from the King

James Version to journalists or curious passersby on the picket line, their eyes would often glaze over at the seventeenth-century prose— but the language and the imagery were as familiar and beautiful to me as my own mother's voice, and comforting in their familiarity. *How sweet are thy words unto my taste! yea, sweeter than honey to my mouth!* The Bible's words became mine, and at all hours and in all circumstances, my mind would call them forth for guidance, courage, inspiration. I read them, studied them, memorized them, recited them, and defended them daily.

Though I had turned away from it while we were still at Westboro, the question I had posed to Grace months earlier wouldn't be denied any longer: "What if the God of the Bible isn't the God of creation? We don't believe that the Koran has the truth about God. Is it just because we were told forever that this is How Things Are?"

At home, my siblings and I had learned a principle: Even if God's actions or instructions in the Bible *seemed* evil to our finite minds, all that He did was—by definition—perfect and just. *For my thoughts are not your thoughts, neither are your ways my ways, saith the Lord. For as the heavens are higher than the earth, so are my ways higher than your ways, and my thoughts than your thoughts.* God's Word was the standard by which all men were measured, and His actions were righteous simply by virtue of the fact that He had taken them. All that was in the Bible was unquestionably Good.

For me, this belief was becoming more and more difficult to sustain.

Fortunately, the Bible's truth and reliability was the subject of the first Sunday meeting I attended at Rapid City's Kingdom Hall, as Jehovah's Witnesses call their meeting places. I hadn't been inside a place of worship in nearly two months, and in all my years, I had been inside non-Westboro churches on only the rarest of occasions. The foreignness of this place was both an intense curiosity and a physical revulsion, and I had to fight to suppress the latter. The thoughts that kept me from bolting from the building were becoming something of a mantra: *What am I feeling? Why am I feeling it? Are my feelings justified by evidence, or a matter of instinct?*

Laura guided us to sit in the middle section of the hall, and I looked around, trying to collect myself by focusing on specific details.

The room had a capacity of about two hundred, though fewer than half the seats were filled. Rows of upholstered chairs instead of pews. Industrial beige carpet and a raised platform with a small lectern for the speaker. "You" and "your" instead of "thee" and "thou" to address God. During the prayer, husbands in suits wrapped their arms around wives in long skirts. The women left their hair uncovered, giving me a sense of our collective nakedness among the congregation. When I asked Laura later about the lack of head coverings, she directed me to the very same passage that Westboro used to *require* them—which, I was shocked to realize, was not in keeping with the plain language used there. *But every woman that prayeth or prophesieth with her head uncovered dishonoureth her head,* the passage read, and then clarified that *her hair is given her for a covering.* In spite of this language, Westboro required a second head covering—and took other churches' refusal to do so as dispositive evidence that the whole congregation was rebellious and damned by God.

In Laura's Bible, the text was even clearer: *For her hair is given to her instead of a covering.*

That Jehovah's Witnesses used an entirely different version of the Scriptures—the New World Translation—brought up yet another layer of doubt. I knew that translations of the Bible often varied widely in their language—and thus their meaning—but Westboro had declared the King James to be the only acceptable text. All others were tainted by human hands and desires. The arbitrariness of this claim now seemed apparent to me—a judgment my grandfather had made long ago on the basis of his conscience, but then denied all others the right to do likewise. At Westboro, when outsiders reminded us of the many contradictions among the various versions of the Bible and questioned our use of the KJV, I instinctively avoided answering their positions directly. "Because Gramps said so" would seem not to be a very convincing argument.

No better than "The Bible is true because my wicked heart says so," I thought, remembering the paradox that had caused me to doubt the Bible's infallibility in the first place.

I had hoped that Brother Alt's sermon would shed some light on this question, but the longer I listened, the more fragile his case seemed. Perhaps because the speaker was not my beloved mother or grandfather or relative, I listened to his sermon more critically than I ever had at Westboro.

He began with a quote wherein the Bible describes the Bible's goodness. *All Scripture is inspired of God and beneficial for teaching, for reproving, for setting things straight, for disciplining in righteousness, so that the man of God may be fully competent, completely equipped for every good work.*

In my head echoed the dry words of the BBC's Louis Theroux, who refuted this sort of circular logic in his second documentary about Westboro: "Well, the Bible *would* say that, wouldn't it?"

Brother Alt continued. "Some people say, 'Experience is the best teacher.' No. The Bible is the best teacher."

I surreptitiously glanced around at the faces scattered throughout the hall, rapt and nodding. His words rang hollow in my ears—as if simply asserting such a thing could make it true—but I knew that only months earlier, I would have accepted this idea without doubts, as this congregation now seemed to.

"Human advice leaves something to be desired, but not so with the Bible," he said. "It provides the best guidance in the world." I couldn't dispute that the Scriptures were filled with practical advice, meditations on human nature, and beautiful sentiments that I could never imagine rejecting.

Love your enemies.

Better is a little with righteousness than great revenues without right.

He that answereth a matter before he heareth it, it is a folly and shame unto him.

Hatred stirreth up strifes: but love covereth all sins.

But what of the tale of the Levite and his dismembered concubine? And God's commandment to put disobedient children to death? His threat to punish idolaters by causing them to eat the flesh of their sons, of their daughters, and of their friends? I listened to Brother Alt extol the virtues of the Scriptures without qualification, and I felt resistance growing inside me. As I had for weeks now, I kept coming back to the image of the Almighty that my mother had first explained to me as a child holding a Barbie in the backseat of our old Camry: the divine Potter of Romans 9, fashioning a tiny group to join Him in Heaven, while sentencing the teeming billions to pass the eons of eternity in exquisite, ever-increasing torment for sins He caused them to commit—simply because it pleased Him to torture them.

Could there be any clearer portrait of evil?

I simply could not believe that this was good in any sense of the word. More important, I simply *did* not believe it—however fearful I was to declare it plainly, even in my own mind.

Regardless of what the Bible said.

At the conclusion of the sermon, Laura introduced Grace and me to several cheerful women who welcomed us with warmth and genuine interest, and then she led us to the cabinets filled with Witness publications. There were dozens of stacks of books and Bible tracts, but she found what she was looking for—a small yellow book with "What Does the Bible *Really* Teach?" emblazoned on the cover—and offered to go through it with us back at the inn. I nodded. "Please."

I didn't want to offend my new friends by launching into a critique of Brother Alt's talk, so I was vague and quiet on the forty-five-minute drive through the darkness back to Deadwood. With Grace sprawled across the backseat, her hair strewn across my lap as I scratched her head, I pondered my doubts and tried to make sense of what it all meant.

> **MEGAN:** Chad. Is the Bible just another book? One with beautiful language and compelling stories—but not divine? Like reading David Foster Wallace's speech at Kenyon College and being moved (to feeling, to action) via words like "on fire with the same force that lit the stars"—but not thinking he's God or speaks for God or that every word he says has to be obeyed?

But as he'd done so many times since I left Westboro, Chad declined to share his thoughts on the question with me. We could speak of music and movies, tech and television, but when it came to matters of belief, he would change the subject instead of offering an opinion. I found it frustrating, but I understood why he did it. I hadn't been so malleable since I was a child, and he was taking great pains to avoid unduly influencing me. He wanted to know where my *own* heart and thoughts would lead me. If I was going to grow out of the mental and emotional boundaries that had so long characterized my existence—*the bounds of my habitation*—I would need to forge my own path.

———

I awoke before dawn one morning in early January, my left hand still protectively covering my phone beneath the pillow. Like most nights, I had fallen asleep texting Chad. And like most mornings, I would begin my day stalking my family on Twitter.

Within days of my departure from Westboro, several members of the church had proactively blocked me from viewing their posts on the platform. I had created a fake account in response, one whose sole use would be following—but never engaging—every account associated with the church. I recognized Twitter as the only real window into my family's lives and daily activities. They might be holding signs in every photo, but where else could I see my parents and siblings? How else could I know what they were up to?

Not even *I* thought this was a particularly healthy habit for me to cultivate—like Emily in *Our Town*, reliving the days of her former existence—and in the beginning, I had tried to limit the time I spent staring into the past at my old life. Now, I didn't even make the attempt. I understood that it would be pathetic and sad to spend my days watching other people live via social media, a waste of the new life and freedom I now had. Still, whenever I encountered resistance from Grace, Newbery, Libby, even Dustin and Laura, I justified the time I spent with a new hope taking root inside me:

What if someone could get through to them?

While it was tempting to despair that Westboro would ever change, I couldn't forget the obvious counterpoint: that *I* had changed. I had been zealous, dedicated, and absolutely convinced of our cause. True, I had spent my final months at the church trying without success to change their hearts and minds—but if *I* could be convinced, it stood to reason that others could be, as well. Part of my motive was undeniably selfish: I was desperate to have my loved ones back in my life, to lose the howling pain that held my insides in a vise grip. But it was becoming clear that this wasn't the only reason we should try to persuade church members away from their views.

Like the rest of the country, I had watched in horror at the news coverage of the December shooting at Sandy Hook Elementary School. I knew what my family would say, but I was still saddened and dismayed to watch the scene play out the way it had so many times before: an eruption of tweets and news releases pouring salt into the gaping wounds of the victims' families, celebrating the mass murder of first-graders as the condign wrath of God, and vowing to protest the memorials. PRAY FOR MORE DEAD KIDS, the sign read. My relief at not participating was tempered by distress at the number of times I had done exactly the same—and to more families than I could guess. I couldn't undo anything I'd done, but didn't I have a responsibility to do *something*? If Grace and I could find a way to convince our family to change their minds, or even to moderate their positions, maybe we could help save other families some of this added pain.

Scrolling through my family's tweets that morning, though, I understood that Twitter was a double-edged sword. #WhereIsMegan-PhelpsRoper was the hashtag, speculation by Westboro detractors who noted my unusual absence from the platform. Twitter connected one especially hard-core critic with a Topekan, who was dispatched to drive by my home in search of my car, and by church protests to see if I could be spotted on the picket line. I panicked reading their exchanges and their taunts to my mother, bile continuing to rise in my throat as I found a Facebook message from a Topeka reporter—cleverly worded such that if I didn't provide a response, she could assume that I had left Westboro.

I pounced on Grace the moment she woke up, trying not to let myself become overwhelmed by my panic as I read the messages aloud. It felt like being hunted. Forced to publicly reckon with a past I was still trying to understand, a present I was wholly unprepared to navigate, and a future that remained a terrifying abyss. Clearly, we were going to have to say something—but what?

Grace led the way out of the attic and down the hidden stairway to the kitchen, where we found Dustin and Laura eating breakfast. They would help us figure this out.

"Why do we owe *anyone* an explanation for *anything*? Why do they get to care?!" Grace exploded in the middle of the discussion, angry at our having been put in this position. I couldn't blame her, exactly, but the question felt shortsighted to me.

"The way we did things at home . . ." I started. "We put *everything* out there. We lived our whole lives in front of cameras and reporters. We spent our days preaching a message that hurt so many people, and all of that is public—*so* public—and we spent years working hard to make it that way. Twitter, YouTube, Facebook, all those interviews and news articles . . . all those things are still out there. Maybe we don't 'owe' people anything . . . but I feel like we do."

"And right now," Dustin pointed out, "that's who you guys are to the world. You are 'God Hates Fags.' If you don't think that's true anymore, you'll want to do something to change that."

Laura looked pensive and nodded. "I understand how you feel, Grace. I think I'd feel the same way in your position . . . but it's a little more complicated than that."

"Okay," I said, after a tense silence. "I'll try to write something, and we can look at it together later."

I picked up my phone and wandered out to the living room, tucking myself into the green couch by the big window and staring, unseeing, at the pine forests up the hill.

Where would I even begin? Should I try to explain why I had done and said the things I had while I was at Westboro? Should I unequivocally apologize for everything? What exactly did I feel sorry for?

When I saw Laura shuffling across the hardwood floor in her stocking feet, I turned sideways, pushing myself up to sit on the arm of the sofa while she took the seat next to me. It hadn't taken long for Grace and me to invite her into our circle of shoulder massages and head scratches, and I was comforted by the remnants of our happy life back home. Laura sat quietly as my mind leafed through the pages of my memory, searching, but I wasn't sure what for. I narrated the scenes to her aloud. Those sweltering early days at Gage Park, surrounded by loved ones in fanny packs, my tiny fists wrapped around the edges of a sign I couldn't read. How upset I'd been at age twelve after Matthew Shepard's death, not because of his murder, but because it wasn't my turn to travel to picket his funeral. I remembered the day Josh left— I'd been eighteen for a few months at that point, so I could have left the church then. Technically, I'd had that choice.

"I'm not sure where you're going with this," Laura said.

"I guess I'm looking for a line," I told her. "Am I responsible for what I did at Westboro after I turned eighteen—and my parents, everything before?" I didn't wait for an answer. "But turning eighteen didn't magically wipe out all the years before it. I might have had the legal choice to leave, but how could I possibly have done it? Every part of my life hinged on the belief that leaving would only bring me Hell and destruction—and that staying was good and righteous. I just couldn't leave until I saw differently. How could I?"

As I reasoned aloud, another thought occurred to me: Wasn't the same true of my mom? The indoctrination, the physical enforcement, the absolute unwillingness to tolerate dissent of any kind—all of these had been hallmarks of my mother's upbringing, too. The fact that she was now in her fifties didn't suddenly give her the freedom to throw off the shackles of those beliefs. If anything, it just meant that she'd had more years to marinate in them. She could no more decide to deny those ideas than she could spontaneously decide not to believe in the existence of gravity.

"Who do you think is responsible, then?" Laura asked. "Your grandfather?"

I shook my head and continued to pull my fingers through her hair. "I don't know. He didn't invent these ideas, either." I told her about the sermon that Gramps gave after the September 11 attacks, how amazed I'd been to see that the doctrines we preached had once been mainstream. In high school, one of my English textbooks had contained "Sinners in the Hands of an Angry God," a famous fire-and-brimstone sermon by the influential American theologian Jonathan Edwards. The sermon sounded so much like my grandfather that it was startling, and the beliefs it espoused were by no means fringe at the time it was preached. Edwards himself was even president of the college that would later become known as Princeton University—not a reviled man, but honored and respected.

"So here's a question for you, Megan." Laura's voice was gentle. "Does it really matter where that line of responsibility lies? Would knowing that change anything about where you go from here?"

"It really is a moot point, isn't it?" I said after a minute. She was right. Ultimately, it didn't matter how much any single one of us was responsible for any particular wrong we had wrought in the world. It was good that we hadn't intended to do evil, but our intentions didn't erase the harm we'd done. The fact was that harm *was* done, and what mattered now was finding a way to address it.

"I guess I just want to say that I'm truly not looking to avoid taking responsibility for my actions," I clarified. "That isn't really the point of the question. I think the point is that . . . I just have a hard time blaming my family. I don't think they're bad people. I think they're good people who have been trapped by bad ideas . . . There just has to be a way out."

———

He finally called me on the phone late one snowy evening.

I'd already known that I loved his words and his humor and his biting wit, but that night I fell in love with his voice: soft and sonorous with just a hint of country twang. I paced the creaky wood floors of the inn's old library as Chad and I talked for nearly an hour, my fingers twisting in my curls, daydreaming of the time when his would do the same. Other than to have my family back, I can't recall ever wanting anything in my life as much as I wanted to meet him, to see him with my real eyes for really real in real life.

It seemed that he didn't want the same, though, despite his words to the contrary: he had already twice reneged on his commitment to come see me in Deadwood. Back in December, he hadn't told me that he had canceled his plans to visit the Hills after Christmas. He just became withdrawn. Slow to respond. I got the message.

MEGAN: You're so careful with me, Chad. Oh, so careful. Are you always so cautious?

CHAD: I'm not cautious. I'm Scandinavian. I'm shy and loud. I like the intimacy of large parties.

Meg. I'm almost 40. You're not.

MEGAN: I've face-planted so many more times than you.

I talk too fast.

I used to picket soldiers' funerals.

CHAD: When I smile, the sides of my eyes wrinkle. I smile often. When I was 26, that didn't happen.

I'll see you out there somehow, before you leave.

In spite of myself, I fell for his promise. My heart soared at the prospect of finally laying eyes on my constant companion, this friend who also happened to be—quite literally—the man of my dreams. And then, as the day of my departure from Deadwood neared, mid-January, it happened again. I knew that Chad had more than a little anxiety about our situation, but my feelings for him far outweighed my own doubts and caused me to dismiss the ones he described so elliptically. Some of his worries were of the more average kind: whether we would be attracted to one another in person, whether our age difference would prove insurmountable. But there were far more significant ones, too. Though it felt like years to me, I'd only lived outside of Westboro for two months at that point—certainly not enough time to have developed an entirely new worldview and identity. He didn't know who I was becoming or what I believed, and neither did I. He also suspected that I might still be a member of the church, sent to try to lure him to Topeka. I'd heard that this was a tactic sometimes used by other fringe groups to boost membership, but it was so utterly unthinkable at Westboro that I laughed out loud at this scenario. At the time, I just couldn't conceive that the weight of these anxieties was enough to justify all the hesitation and mixed signals.

> **MEGAN:** I literally feel insane.
>
> I had hoped you would come, but I thought this would happen.
>
> In the future, you should be careful. Especially when you know you're being misunderstood. You'll save a heart (or hearts) a lot of pain.
>
> **CHAD:** Seems a little dramatic and precious for a guy that was trying to get the nerve to ask her to dance.
>
> It's a common plot line, and the movie rarely ends with it.

I felt pathetic for trying to convince him, for wanting so badly something that he so clearly did not. Did I have so little self-respect that I couldn't just take the hint? I decided to spend my final days in South Dakota with Daisy, Gatsby, and their doomed romance—a nod to our beginnings and apropos for our demise.

And still—*still*—I couldn't let it go.

Jan. 11, 2013—Day 25
The Great Gatsby
Reserving judgments is a matter of infinite hope.

———

"You know . . . you guys don't actually have to leave if you don't want to."

My knife froze mid-chop, and I stared up at Laura, who was busy transferring a loaf of homemade sourdough into a hot cast-iron pan. Dinnertime at the inn.

"Yeah," Dustin agreed. "You can stay with us for as long as you need or as long as it's helpful."

Grace and I looked at each other with wide eyes. *"Really?"* she asked.

"Oh, my God!" I gasped, and we all laughed. The prospect overwhelmed me with gratitude. We were nearing the end of our time in Deadwood, and the thought of returning to Kansas filled me with dread. I loved my brother Josh and his family, and I wanted to spend time with Libby—but they lived at the epicenter of trauma. How could I leave this place and return to that? The inn was the first place I had felt safe, tucked in among the expanse of the Black Hills. The landscape was so muted and lovely, and it made me feel small in the very best way. It gave me hope. I knew that Grace didn't feel the same way, that I'd have to work hard to convince her—but at least now there was a chance we could stay.

I wondered what the Floyds were thinking to offer such generosity to two girls they had only just met—but in that moment, I was afraid to ask for fear they might reconsider. Years later, as Dustin and Laura and I reminisced about the earliest days of our friendship, Laura would answer that question by sharing a few of her journal entries with me.

I so much want to help. I know Megan really loves it out here, and seems to be enjoying the time away. Grace is on less comfortable footing, I think. She doesn't like the snow (it's been doing that a lot), she's homesick, and she seems to be—I actually don't know how I was going to finish that sentence. I've been trying to draw her out with bribes of fresh-baked bread and access to all the local libraries. More than anything, I suspect the most useful thing I can do is be a friend.

We went out into the Hills for the Grand Tour yesterday and they started in with questions about what we believe. We talked about free will and hell and birth control and gay marriage and a dozen things in between. I am quite amazed about how many basic beliefs we have in common, which "regular" churches do according to tradition rather than biblical guidelines (not celebrating holidays, staying out of politics, the desire to warn other people that their course may be wrong, etc.). But where we choose a path based on showing love in a kind, humble and patient way, the WBC is, well . . . accused of being a hate group.

They also took the opportunity of our outing to revel a bit in certain new-found freedoms. They talked about getting haircuts and bought clip-on earrings (for a test-drive before committing to actual holes), and were flaunting flashy colors of nail polish. Yesterday evening they went out looking for a New Year's party to crash and today Megan was trying to get a buzz (off 7up and brandy) in order to write a tipsy letter. It's kind of fun to see them trying to find their feet in this new life of theirs. And I'm pleased to say that we're probably the mildest possible influences for such an exploration. I'd also like to say that I *really* like them, and am so delighted that we've had this opportunity to get to know them, and hopefully help in some way.

Reading Laura's account of those times, I laughed remembering how childlike we could be, that roller coaster of trepidation and wonder, guilt and exuberance, despair at our loss and delight at the smallest of freedoms. I marveled again at my good fortune, at how a random booking on Airbnb had brought my sister and me to such warmhearted people to help us navigate the squalls of our new reality. At how quickly our friendship helped me understand that it was possible to love someone—to be close to someone—even while seeing the world in a wildly different way. *Can two walk together, except they be agreed?* The answer to this rhetorical question—"Of course not!"—had always been obvious and obviously true, but it seemed like such a simplistic notion to me now. The idea that agreement was a prerequisite for friendship. That comity required conformity. My friendship with Dustin and Laura had so quickly helped me arrive at the opposite conclusion, and it seemed as obvious to me now as the original once had.

Can two walk together, even if they disagree?

Of course we could.

Not exactly revolutionary, but I couldn't help feeling that it was.

9. Lift Up Thy Voice

Head Full of Doubt / Road Full of Promise
"There's no fresh start in today's world. Any twelve-year-old with a cell phone could find out what you did. Everything we do is collated and quantified. Everything sticks."

Don't act surprised that I'm quoting Batman. At WBC, reciting lines from pop culture is par for the course. And why not? The sentiments they express are readily identifiable by the masses—and shifting their meaning is as easy as giving them new context. So put Selina Kyle's words in a different framework:

In a city in a state in the center of a country lives a group of people who believe they are the center of the universe; they know Right and Wrong, and they are Right. They work hard and go to school and get married and have kids who they take to church and teach that continually protesting the lives, deaths, and daily activities of The World is the only genuine statement of compassion that a God-loving human can sincerely make. As parents, they are attentive and engaged, and the children learn their lessons well.

This is my framework.

Until very recently, this is what I lived, breathed, studied, believed, preached—loudly, daily, and for nearly 27 years.

I never thought it would change. I never wanted it to.

Then suddenly: it did.

And I left.

Where do you go from there?

I don't know, exactly. My sister Grace is with me, though. We're trying to figure it out together.

There are some things we do know.

We know that we've done and said things that hurt people. Inflicting pain on others wasn't the goal, but it was one of the outcomes. We wish it weren't so, and regret that hurt.

We know that we dearly love our family. They now consider us betrayers, and we are cut off from their lives, but we know they are well-intentioned. We will never not love them.

We know that we can't undo our whole lives. We can't even say we'd want to if we could; we are who we are because of all the experiences that brought us to this point. What we can do is try to find a better way to live from here on. That's our focus.

Up until now, our names have been synonymous with "God Hates Fags." Any twelve-year-old with a cell phone could find out what we did. We hope Ms. Kyle was right about the other part, too, though—that everything sticks—and that the changes we make in our lives will speak for themselves.

Megan and Grace

February 6, 2013

As I flew back to Rapid City from New York, my eyes traced the final version of the "statement" again and again, until I was on the verge of vomiting. I knew that the only people who might care about these paragraphs were my family and a handful of curious Twitter followers, but I was still terrified of how they would be received. Public apologies in the age of social media could be brutal, every word parsed to ensure that no unacceptable sentiment remained in the offending party—and anything less than full repudiation of one's "sins" would exacerbate the public flogging. Twitter mobs could tear a person's reputation to shreds, demanding that they lose their job over an errant tweet or a joke that didn't land—transgressions that were far less egregious than the dedicated campaign of condemnation in which I had been a willing participant for many years.

My apology was not a blanket condemnation of Westboro, a desperate plea for forgiveness, or a complete recanting of all my previous words and deeds. As I'd stood weeping and packing the day I left the church, Jael had insisted that these were my only options—that the world would make my life a living Hell otherwise. But even though they might have seemed like better strategies, I could not bring myself to employ them. This apology would not be for show. I would not begin this new life guided by expedience over truth. Regardless of the response, I could only be honest and hope for the best.

I had put agonizing thought into writing the words that would be published the following morning, to be sure they conveyed exactly what I felt, meant, and believed in that moment. It seemed to me that part of the enormous disconnection between Westboro and the rest of the world resulted from how we communicated. We had long invited confusion and hostility with language and methods that were deliberately grievous, provocative, and recondite. "Westboro is responsible for their own PR," a friend told me one day, articulating a sentiment I had found so frustrating after I joined Twitter: that the church's refusal to consider how our words and actions would be construed by our targets had caused much unnecessary pain for everyone involved. Why were we endlessly translating our signs and behaviors so that outsiders could understand them? Why didn't we just *begin* our efforts by speaking with clarity, gentleness, reasonableness? *Except ye utter by the tongue words easy to be understood, how shall it be known what is spoken? for ye shall speak into the air.*

Honesty and good intentions weren't worth much, I decided, if they were lost in translation.

To ensure that mine wouldn't be, I had turned to a group of family members and new friends. *In the multitude of counsellers there is safety.* Among these were two writers I had met while they'd been visiting Westboro for research, and with whom I had maintained friendly communication via Twitter after their departures. Daniel Shannon and Jeff Chu were both incredibly kind, both gay, and both living in New York. I spoke with them by phone from the inn's living room, but by chance, I had the opportunity to visit them in person—another occasion to

push back at the Us/Them divide. As one of very few ex-members of
Westboro who had chosen to be open about her experiences, my cousin
Libby had been invited to New York to be interviewed on the *Today
Show* and Anderson Cooper's *Anderson Live* at the end of January. She
asked me to accompany her for moral support, but when the producers
pressed me to join her for the interviews, I insisted that it was impossible. I could not imagine standing in front of an audience—not now,
not ever.

Away from the studios, I arranged for us to meet Daniel for dinner in Manhattan, and then Jeff and his husband, Tristan, for coffee
in Brooklyn the following morning. We spoke of Daniel's atheism and
Jeff's Christianity, and how strange it all felt, this transition from picketing gays in Topeka to brunching together in New York. Like so much
of this new world, it was head-spinning. Watching Jeff and Tristan interact in the warm light of the diner, I was surprised to realize that I
had no bad feelings about their relationship. They reminded me a bit
of my parents, teasing and doting on each other. "Jeffy," Tristan called
him. The situation felt awkward only because it was new and foreign,
and the only trace of negativity in me was a sense of betrayal: that my
mother would be disappointed to know that I no longer felt that disgust she'd been describing to reporters all my life. "When you think of
these fags, there's something that just rises up inside you and says"—
and here she would bellow—"*yuck!* You all know it!" But I felt no such
thing—and I doubted she would have if not for her own upbringing.

When I shared my epiphany about interpretation with Jeff, he
said, "That's one thing I have never understood about your family.
They're all lawyers, right? The U.S. Constitution was written some two
hundred years ago in essentially modern English, and there's so much
disagreement about how the U.S. Supreme Court should interpret and
apply those words today. The Bible was written thousands of years ago
in languages no one speaks anymore . . . and somehow, Westboro alone
has figured out its one true meaning?" Articulated that way, the arrogance of our position seemed even more incomprehensible. In court,
Margie's job was to present and defend her interpretation of the facts
and the law before a judge, who would hear all sides before making
a final decision, which was subject to review by higher courts. But
when it came to the purported Word of God, in all its complexity,

we considered our judgment to be so reliable as to merit absolute confidence, so unquestionable that we could insist that all of humankind follow it. I shook my head and inwardly cringed. Coming face-to-face with my arrogance, aggressive in its misplaced certainty, was a special sort of shame.

When my flight landed in Rapid City, I picked up some essentials at Walmart—peanut butter, chocolate, apples, and English muffins— and then pointed my car to Deadwood, my little sister, and our new friends. Laura had convinced us to audition for a play at the local theater, and so—less than twenty-four hours before our scheduled return to Kansas in mid-January—Grace had agreed to stay in South Dakota. The spring semester had been set to begin the very next day, and we had scrambled to remove her from all of her Topeka classes, exchanging them for online coursework that would allow us some distance from Westboro. I would interview for a job working with Dustin at TDG—as a public relations assistant, ironically, not so different from work I'd done for Westboro—and Grace and I would stay in Deadwood at least until the play's final performance. I was elated, and the promise I received from Chad made me feel all the more hopeful.

CHAD: You'll be back in SD. I'll figure out the math and approach the chalkboard. I promise.

After unloading the groceries, I found Grace in the attic and told her the plan: the statement would go up the following morning on a new blogging platform called Medium, along with a short article Jeff had written while I was in New York. "Your statement actually creates more questions than it answers," he had told me. "If you don't explain a bit more about why you left, it will leave people to speculate and fill in the blanks on their own."

I watched as my sister read over both documents. She seemed so calm about it all. Poised. *Graceful*, I thought, and laughed out loud.

Grace looked up. Something in her expression reminded me of the years before she started kindergarten, tooling around in a black romper covered in red flowers, a look of knowing defiance that seemed incongruous on a face so young. A spark of fearlessness.

Her bright hazel eyes narrowed slightly, and she nodded.

"Yeah?" I asked.

"Let's do this."

CHAD: I'm just happy for you today. I'm sure it's a weight lifted. If it's not, it should be. Recognize it thusly.

MEGAN: It is. I have a hard time believing nice things people say anyway, so on this scale, it's all just unbelievable.

Both in tone and in magnitude, the response to what Jeff and I had posted was nothing like I had expected. Messages of encouragement and well-wishing flooded my Twitter account, and I was floored by how rare were the people who chose to denounce Grace and me. To tell us that we could never be forgiven. People from across the country and all over the world offered my sister and me friendship, places to sleep, and invitations to church by the hundreds. Dozens of newspapers and blogs around the world picked up the story, and even Gawker—notorious for its lack of scruples—had kind things to say.

> . . . good for them for escaping what is essentially a cult and de-
> fying its wrath by going public about it. As far as the deprogram-
> ming process goes, Megan says, "I don't know what I believe,"
> but she claims that she wants to determine how she can be "an
> influence for good." And she has the rest of her life to atone.
> Happy coming out day, girls.

Particularly moving were the messages from those with whom I had sparred on Twitter over the years—people I had come to know and like, people who had seen me regularly sling around condescension, condemnation, and words like "fag" and "whore." Chad Darnell was one such person, a gay man living in Los Angeles. Our exchanges had been full of Bible verses, friendly sarcasm, and sincerity—but as with all outsiders, I had been suspicious of his kindness and concern. His response to my post about leaving Westboro was an open letter, which read in part:

> Dear Megan:
> Hey, girl, hey.

When I woke up to messages from family and friends that
you had left the church, I literally burst into tears. I sat in bed
for 20 minutes reading your letter with ugly tears (like bad
Oprah crying) streaming down my face and I couldn't stop.

I am so proud of you.

I am so happy for you.

I (we) never felt hate in our hearts toward YOU. Sure, we
didn't like you that much, but the action of you physically removing yourself from that situation is a strength that most humans
will never know. That was your family and your main source of
interaction with people. We get it. Trust me, we ALL get it.

Megan, it would be the great honor of my church, my
people to have you as a guest. We just want you to come and
breathe and feel what a community trying to make the world
a better place should be. We feel a special bond to you after
all your tweeting over the years.

And know that we all, everyone at our church, forgive
you. And we wish you support and kindness and love.

Love,

Chad (and everyone at Hollywood United Methodist
Church)

With each new kindness, I understood with ever greater clarity
the depths of my ignorance about the world. Clearly, the people writing these words were not the demons I had been warned about. They
didn't hate Grace and me, and they didn't expect us to hate our family.
They understood that the same people who taught us to curse Westboro's enemies were the ones who had kissed our cheeks and tucked us
in at night. Though we had shown these people hostility and contempt
in their most vulnerable moments, they extended generosity and compassion to us in ours. They empathized with us in our pain and wanted
good things for our future. Dustin and Laura, Newbery and C.G., Cora
the bartender and Ryan the dealer—I had seen them as exceptions, but
it was starting to occur to me that there might be a lot more goodness
in the world than I had believed. I'd been so sure that it was filled with
hateful, selfish, vindictive people, and I had never found so much hope
in being proved wrong.

For their part, Westboro members responded exactly as I expected—
which didn't stop my heart from racing or my insides from twisting in
anguish. It was everything they had said about ex-members before,
but I couldn't grasp that they were saying such things about *me*. How
could they? Knowing everything that had happened, how could my
parents? The church issued a statement with one assumption at its heart:
that the church was blameless in the departure of any member, because
there could be no legitimate reason to leave Westboro. I read the words
of an elder in several newspapers with growing bitterness, the same
self-serving position we had always assumed when church members
departed. "She just decided that she didn't want to obey God," Steve
said. "They wanted to serve themselves." Years would pass and the
lies would continue unabated. Steve seemed to have no compunction
about publicly denying every fact that revealed the church as flawed,
hypocritical. He denied the takeover by the elders, the petty back-
biting among church members, the merciless shunning of my mother.
He pretended their cruel treatment of her—removing my mother from
the work she had done for decades as a way of shaming and isolating
her—wasn't punishment but *kindness*. "We lifted her burden," he said.
It was an especially embittering fabrication because it was exactly what
they *should* have done—what I'd wished so often that they *had* done.

And then, amid the deluge of words, this paragraph:

Shirley Phelps-Roper, the mother of the sisters, is doing OK
in the wake of her daughters leaving the church, Drain said.
On Wednesday, she was at a local facility welcoming the
birth that morning of a grandson, Jason Brent.

Jason Brent. Sam's son. A nephew I might never know.

Sitting on the green couch by the inn's living room window, I
watched a whitetail deer cross Lincoln Avenue and disappear around
the side of the house. My efforts at remaining calm were proving un-
successful, and I sobbed tears of desperation—not because outsiders
might believe Steve's dissembling, but because church members would.
Just as I had done with Nate and Josh and Libby, they would accept
these narratives about Grace and me. We would be painted as evil, and
they would be disposed to listen. I had tried to preempt this process

back at home, to thwart it in as many ways as I could, even turning my final tweet as a Westboro member into a message to my sister Bekah. An angry person on Twitter had told her that "nobody loves you," and she had retorted, "That's not true! @MeganPhelps loves me. ;)" My response remained there for months, and I had refused to post anything else afterward. It was a reference to a line from a movie we had watched together, delivered forcefully by Jack Nicholson—a standing reminder to her in my absence.

"You're goddamn right I do!"—A Few Good Men

They had to do it, though. Demonizing Grace and me was the only way to protect their image of Westboro as not just benign but wholly good. They couldn't allow themselves to truly contemplate the idea that Westboro might be wrong about the ideals to which they had dedicated their lives. They needed to believe in the righteousness of their cause just as much as we needed them to see its destructiveness.

What were they telling my siblings right now? That I had traded them in because I wanted the approval and love and attention of outsiders—that I wanted to *enjoy the pleasures of sin for a season*, because I loved the world more. Had I chosen the love of the world over the love of my family? My mind rebelled at the thought, at the crippling guilt. I would never have willingly made such an exchange. This had never been a choice between strangers and family, between the world's love and its hatred. It wasn't the desire for an easy life that led me to leave. Losing them was the price of honesty. A shredded heart for a quiet conscience.

—

There was silence on the other end of the line for a beat.

"*What?*"

I sat down at the kitchen table at the inn, watching Luna stalk across the hardwood floor. She was one of the Floyds' two black cats, a stray they'd taken in not long before Grace and I arrived. Animals made me anxious, because we'd never had pets in our home—"We had brothers and allergies, instead," I always joked—but Luna was beautiful, her fur thick and lustrous, her eyes a piercing yellow. She suddenly turned and scampered up the stairs, spooked, and I switched my phone to the other ear. "Yeah," I said. "You've definitely got part of the blame for my leaving."

It had been a few days since Jeff and I had published our posts online, and I was catching up with another of my new friends and counselors. David Abitbol was an Orthodox Jew living in Jerusalem, and the two of us were discussing a question that had been on my mind frequently in the months since it had first occurred to me to leave the church: How had this happened? How had my perspective changed so much in such a short amount of time, from an obedient follower who instinctively suppressed doubts to a malcontent who just couldn't leave well enough alone? I had spent endless hours racking my brain for clues, tracking the changes in my perspective over time, and I found myself returning again and again to Twitter and to my complicated friendship with David—the source of my first conscious disagreement with one of Westboro's doctrines. I had reflexively suppressed it, but it had come rushing back the day that I first considered leaving Westboro, painting in that cold basement.

David and I had met on Twitter in 2009, almost immediately after I had brought Westboro's message to the platform. He ran a popular Jewish blog called "Jewlicious" and was active on social media, so the Jewish Telegraphic Agency had listed him second in their ranking of the "100 Most Influential Jewish Twitterers." He had become one of my first targets. Our initial exchanges were plagued by unbridled antagonism—I told David that Jewish customs were "dead, rote rituals," while he maintained that my grandfather was a closet case—but it didn't take long for him to tone it down, and for me to follow his lead.

DAVID (@Jewlicious): Ultimate frisbee in the park today against Christian team. Told an Israeli, "Dude, it's okay to hit them, because they HAVE to turn the other cheek . . ."

MEGAN (@meganphelps): You give them too much credit! They don't follow any other teachings of Jesus; what makes you think they'd follow that one? =)

DAVID: Aw c'mon, Megan! These were nice Christians! Just because they don't go picketing all over the place with signs that say "God Hates Fags . . ."

MEGAN: I'm a tad skeptical of their niceness; after all,
what's nice about encouraging people on their way
to Hell?
   Plus, I'm a little suspicious of anyone who plays ultimate
frisbee. =D
DAVID: You know, for an evil something something, you sure
do crack me up . . .

When David started asking me questions about our picket signs,
it gave me a kind of permission to ask him questions about Jewish
theology. In those days, the only thing I knew about Jews for sure
was that they had killed Jesus and were thus cursed by God. . . . *Jews:
Who both killed the Lord Jesus, and their own prophets, and have persecuted
us; and they please not God, and are contrary to all men.* But I didn't know
what Jews actually *believed.* I wanted to understand so that I would
be better prepared to argue against those beliefs, to show them from
the Bible that Jewish ideas were wrong. I tried to read books to help
me—including *The Complete Idiot's Guide to Understanding Judaism*—
but I found greater clarity in speaking with a flesh-and-blood person.
Thanks to Twitter, the distance between Kansas and Israel was no
obstacle.

At first, I had used passages from the New Testament to argue
against David's doctrinal positions. When he said he didn't believe
in the divinity of New Testament books, I started limiting my references to the Old Testament. "That's not actually what those verses
say," he would tell me. "Your translation is off. You would know
that if you spoke Hebrew!" In response, I bought all three levels of
coursework from Rosetta Stone and signed up for webinars on biblical Hebrew so that I could learn the language. David started sending
me tips, teaching me new words, and saying *laila tov*—good night—
when he signed off. The dynamic between us was strange—never
charged in the way that my friendship with Chad would be later,
but still conflicting. David was an enemy of Christ. There was no
confusion about the fact that we were at odds with each other, and I
was certain that his understanding of the Bible was wrong—but as
with C.G. and so many others on Twitter, I found myself liking him
anyway.

My conversations with David had continued for more than a year, during which time I twice protested events at which he was speaking—first at the Jewlicious Festival in California, and then at a conference in Louisiana. David came out to talk with me both times, and though I continued to warn him that he was on the path to Hell, our banter had an ease to it that was unusual on the picket line. In New Orleans, we even exchanged gifts. He brought me a Middle Eastern dessert from the market near his home in Jerusalem, and I brought him some of my favorite peppermint chocolate. He flipped the bar over and started teaching me about the kosher symbols on the packaging, while I listened earnestly and held a GOD HATES JEWS sign.

The temporary end of my communication with David came shortly after the picket in New Orleans, following a debate about Westboro's DEATH PENALTY FOR FAGS sign. He had pointed out that our sign contradicted Jesus's own instruction about the death penalty—*He that is without sin among you, let him first cast a stone at her*—but he had also connected it to an issue that was far more personal. "Didn't your mom have your oldest brother out of wedlock?" David had asked me. "That's another sin that deserves the death penalty, isn't it?" Until that moment, I had never thought through that fact that if my mother had been killed for her sin, she wouldn't have had the opportunity to repent and be forgiven.

That without mercy, my beloved family would not exist.

Pacing around the inn's dining room table, I finished explaining to David why I had suddenly stopped speaking to him two years earlier.

"I was terrified. The points you made about the DEATH PENALTY FOR FAGS sign—that was the first time I consciously rejected one of the church's doctrines. It was the first time I believed that I could be right about something, and that the rest of the church could be wrong. It gave me some little bit of confidence in my own thoughts, and helped me not to just blindly trust the elders. It might seem like such a small point, but it was huge for me—a loose thread of contradiction in our tightly woven arguments. I doubt I would have ever had the confidence to challenge other Westboro doctrines without that."

I suddenly remembered that even my cousin Jael had realized the significant role that David had played in my departure from Westboro.

I read him the text message she had sent me the day after I left, specifically alluding to both David ("Jewlicious") and C.G. ("FKA").

> I think over some years you turned aside to try to persuade
> Satan through clever argument on Twitter, etc. Speaking to
> Jewlicious, FKA, & others—you let Satan nibble on your ear
> and flatter your vanity—during long and continual conver-
> sations. Whether that was with one or many Satan-inspired
> minions, it has caused you to dig for doctrinal fallacy—when
> you know better.

I had rejected my cousin's accusations the instant I read them.
Being influenced by outsiders was a moral failing, and I couldn't
bring myself to acknowledge that I had allowed it to happen—and
on *Twitter*, no less. But as I considered Jael's assertions, I stopped
seeing my change of mind as a sign of weakness or vulnerability.
At the root of my shame was the assumption that I had nothing to
learn from people like David and C.G.—a premise that had so clearly
proved false. Bit by bit, my shame was being replaced by profound
gratitude to Twitter for its commitment to being "the free speech
wing of the free speech party." Instead of booting me from the platform for "hate speech," as many had demanded, it had put me in
conversation with people and ideas that effectively challenged beliefs that had been hammered into me since I was a child—and that
conversation had been far more illuminating than decades' worth
of rage, isolation, and efforts to shame and silence. It struck me as
ironic that this very idea had been repeatedly referenced by church
members when they spoke of the First Amendment, a quote from
1920s-era Supreme Court Justice Louis Brandeis: "If there be time
to expose through discussion the falsehood and fallacies, to avert the
evil by the processes of education, the remedy to be applied is more
speech, not enforced silence."

"Listen," David said, after listening to all this, "you have to come
to Jewlicious next month. You should meet some of the people you
protested here three years ago. You can come and see what Judaism is
really about."

I chose my words carefully. "Uh, I don't . . . think that's a good idea." In fact, it specifically went against the plan that Grace and I had concocted, *to wit*, disappear into the ether forever.

"I'm sure it's a good idea," David countered. "And listen, I know you're afraid to talk about this stuff. I know the wounds are still fresh and that we were 'the enemy' and all of that . . . but I think this will help you, and I know it will help others. It could bring a lot of healing to a lot of people. If you can bring yourself to do it, you absolutely should."

I told him I didn't think I could do it.

"If it would make you feel better, we'll do it on Saturday. It'll be Shabbat, so there won't be any recording—no photos or videos. Just a conversation. Just you and us."

Everything inside me screamed *no*. Enemy territory. Betraying my family. Making myself vulnerable to people I had hurt, and who had hurt me. Who had every reason to hate me. How could I possibly?

I closed my eyes and the line went silent again.

"Megan?" David asked.

"Let me talk to Grace."

———

Three weeks later, my sister and I found ourselves in Los Angeles at the Museum of Tolerance, a modern, multilevel complex whose purpose was to encourage visitors to challenge their prejudices and assumptions. I couldn't help feeling a bit wounded by David's suggestion that we visit—wasn't I already doing so much to challenge my prejudices?—but I recognized in my resistance more of Westboro's teachings: our derision of the whole concept of "tolerance." Ideas that contradicted our own were inherently morally bankrupt. Why, in the name of God, should we tolerate them?

Standing just outside the entrance to the first exhibit with David and Grace, I listened as the docent expounded on the museum and its history. She was a stately woman, midsixties, I guessed, with silver hair cropped short. The purpose of this museum wasn't just to tell the stories of human rights atrocities, she explained, but to remind us to *act* when we saw things going awry. To encourage us to be more than passive bystanders. I had a sinking feeling listening to her descriptions of the exhibits. There was going to be something about Westboro in here.

Sure enough, immediately after passing through the entrance, I spotted a photo on the wall. "Hey, look," I said to David. "There's Bekah and Gran." It was a photo of my sister and grandmother protesting during the trial of one of Matthew Shepard's killers. Bekah had always been tiny as a girl, and in the photo she looked much younger than her twelve years.

David laughed and mocked me. "'There's Gran!' Well, this is why we're here . . ." The three of us spoke for a few minutes about the impact that Westboro had had on the world, the number of people who had been jarred by our message. *Their* message, I reminded myself. I had to stop saying *we* and *our* and *us*.

As the three of us spoke, another docent led a group of young people in matching hunter-green sweat suits over to the photo of Bekah and Gran, a security guard trailing behind them. The guide told the story of Matthew Shepard, a gay college student who was brutally murdered by two young men he met at a small-town bar, and the protests and counterprotests at his funeral. We listened from a few paces back, and then David said quietly, "That's their grandmother."

I felt panicky.

"Excuse me?" the woman said.

"They grew up in that church that protests gays. They left a few months ago."

Fifteen confused faces stared over at Grace and me. "*You* hated gay people?" one girl asked.

"I didn't hate them . . ." I trailed off. "I thought that God hated them. I thought that the Bible said so. I thought it was my duty to God to tell people that."

The questions came one after another—about Westboro's doctrines and beliefs, about what it had been like growing up there, about our family, and then finally about why we had left. What had made us change.

I pointed at David. "He helped."

David held up his hands as if in self-defense. "I was just trying to get her to see how misguided her ideas were—how hurtful she was being to other people."

When the kids finally fell silent, the docent stood wide-eyed for a moment, and then thanked us for sharing our experiences. "I'm sure it must have been so painful to leave your family, but this is an example for us, too. We *all* need to stand up. Our families might not be like yours, but when we see people being hateful or bullying others, we need to speak up."

Back in the lobby at the end of our tour, David and Grace and I stood reflecting as groups of young students milled about.

"See?" he said. "That wasn't so bad, was it?"

"It made me anxious," I said. "And ashamed. It's so hard to frame the words to admit that what I so passionately believed for so long was wrong and destructive in many ways. And I can't help but feel like I'm betraying my family every time I open my mouth about any of it . . . But it could have been a lot worse. They were very kind."

I had a brief moment of hope, thinking that maybe the Jewlicious Festival that weekend might be a similar experience—but then I flashed back to the furor that had taken place three years earlier. Each one of us picketers had been separated and surrounded by angry mobs. Counterprotesters had dressed up as Jesus and the Easter bunny, screaming and chanting and hitting us with their signs while Long Beach police officers looked on and laughed. Two old women sporting sunglasses and sneers had found their way through the boisterous crowd and planted themselves directly behind me, each whispering lurid descriptions of sex into my ears—not as Gramps had done from the pulpit, referencing gays, but with me at the center of their sick fantasies. I was repulsed, wanted to bolt, but I couldn't move because of the throng. I strained to lift my signs up above the melee and sang at the top of my lungs just to keep the words of the old women out of my ears.

The festival, I feared, would be a different experience entirely.

—

The ninth annual Jewlicious Festival was to take place in Long Beach, California, aboard the RMS Queen Mary, an ocean liner from the 1930s now retired and permanently docked in Queensway Bay. It was billed as a gathering of fifteen hundred Jewish students and young adults, who would come together for a three-day celebration of Jewish culture. I spent the first two days roaming from one conversation to the next with an endless stream of questions about Jewish history,

food, music, and theology, but soon ran headlong into the original cat-
alyst for the trip.

After lunch on Saturday, David led Grace and me into a grand
banquet room for our public discussion. It had been relatively easy to
endure the rejection of outsiders while I was at Westboro, surrounded
by people who took the heat right alongside me—and who likewise
believed that we were speaking *God's* words, not our own. *For I have
not spoken of myself; but the Father which sent me, he gave me a commandment, what I should say, and what I should speak.* But this—standing on
my own two feet, accountable for my own thoughts and ideas, which
were still in constant flux—this was panic-inducing. David took in my
blank stare and shallow breath. "I'll be right there with you," he reassured me. "It'll be okay."

We took our seats at a cloth-covered table at the front of the room,
which had been filled to capacity with rows of chairs lined up like a
firing squad. Once those were taken, more people filled in the space at
the edges of the room, crowding at the back before the doors were finally
closed. The group was about 150 strong, crammed in close, waiting.

"Well!" David called out. "Welcome! Can you all hear me okay?"
No amplification equipment on Shabbat, either. There were murmurs
from the back. All good.

The room was impeccably silent as David directed the conversation. He returned to the earliest days of our relationship as fren-
emies on Twitter, offered probing questions about Westboro and its
doctrines—especially as they related to Jewish people—and, finally,
asked me to explain why we had left. I stared assiduously down at
the white tablecloth as I spoke, at the beads of condensation dripping
down the sides of my glass of ice water, at David's face as he tried to
gently coax the conversation forward. I did not dare to look across the
table, which felt to me like a shield. The first row of chairs sat just on
the other side of it, the closest faces only a few feet away.

Grace said little until David asked about leaving our family. I tried
to be vague so as to avoid openly weeping, but she spoke up suddenly
and passionately, until it felt like we were both drowning in it again.

"We'll answer some questions in a minute," David said, as Grace
and I collected ourselves, "but the last thing I wanted to share is a
revelation I had this week during my conversations with Megan and

Grace. To be honest: I don't know if I could do what they did. If I had been raised the way that they were raised, I would've been out there holding signs with Grandpa Phelps, too. If I was brought up in their family, would I have the strength of character and the moral fortitude to leave my family? To leave everything I've ever known?" He shook his head. "I want to say that I would have, but I don't know."

When I finally looked across the table, my eye was drawn instantly to a woman a few rows back. I recognized her as one of the counter-protesters from three years earlier. Long dark hair. Sharp brown eyes. She had been part of the group that had surrounded me, grabbing for my signs, pushing and pressing in on me. It had been her face, twisted in disgust, that had been screaming into mine while those two old women whispered in my ears. I felt my skin crawl, my stomach clench-ing as fear and betrayal surfaced again. Some of these people had *at-tacked* my family. What was I *doing* here?

But the woman's face wasn't vengeful now. It was splotchy with tears. As David began to call on audience members with questions, I was moved to find similar expressions on faces all over the room. Not angry. Mournful. They framed their questions with kindness. They offered forgiveness. Again and again, they expressed the hope that if *we* could change, then others could, too. Many would find Grace and me later, embrace after embrace, and tell us their stories of Westboro. Students with LGBT friends driven to self-harm by an atmosphere of intolerance we had fed. A twenty-something whose parents had forced him from his home when he'd come out as gay—"I know what it feels like to lose your family," he said as he wrapped me in a bear hug. "You're not alone." A U.S. Marine who had witnessed Westboro's pres-ence at the funeral of his friend. It had been over a year, he told me, and still he had so much rage. He couldn't turn on a dime and let it all go, but it helped him to understand. He believed he could find peace now.

Most shocking of all would be the handful of apologies. Some had accosted me on Twitter, others outside the festival three years earlier. "I didn't know," they said. "I was angry. Next time, I'll try to find a better way."

"Just a few more questions, guys," David said. "They're gonna need this room for the next session soon."

"What's the most important thing you've learned since you've been here?" one girl asked. "And what do you hope will happen to the church?"

I had spent the week parsing Bible verses with David and Rabbi Yonah Bookstein, who ran the festival with his wife, Rachel, and I couldn't help diving into the verse I had most fixated on. "One of the most mind-blowing things is how they understand the verse that says, 'Love thy neighbor.'" I quoted the verses. *Thou shalt not hate thy brother in thine heart: thou shalt in any wise rebuke thy neighbour, and not suffer sin upon him. Thou shalt not avenge, nor bear any grudge against the children of thy people, but thou shalt love thy neighbour as thyself.*

"At home," I continued, "we always equated *love* with *rebuke*, because of that passage. As long as we believed our words to be truthful, we were free to rebuke the rest of the world at any time, in any place, and in any way that we wanted. We could be harsh, and crude, and insulting, and it didn't matter, because everyone else was Hell-bound anyway. Those verses justified almost everything we did—including picketing funerals. But David told us about that passage from a Jewish perspective."

"From our view," David said, "a rebuke is supposed to happen privately, kindly, and with people you have reason to believe will hear you. If you're attacking someone you know won't listen—if you're trying to correct them harshly, in a way that will provoke them to anger instead of encouraging them to change their ways—then *you're* the one who is committing a sin."

"I feel so stupid saying this," I said, "but we really believed that it was irrelevant how we spoke to people. 'Gospel preaching is not hateful!' we always said. 'Truth equals love!' But now it seems so painfully obvious: of *course* it matters how we talk to people. Truth and love are not synonyms. The New Testament even says it plainly. *Speak the truth in love.* The Apostle Paul said, *To the weak became I as weak* and that we should *weep with them that weep.* I don't know how we missed that for so long."

"Your other question about what we hope will happen to the church . . ." Grace paused. "We want them all to leave. People have been speculating for a long time about what would happen if Gramps dies—"

"You mean *when* Gramps dies?" David asked.

"He doesn't believe he's going to die," Grace said. "He thinks Jesus will return while he's still alive. People think the church will fall apart if Gramps dies . . . but if the church ever *did* fall apart and our family still believed the church's doctrines—that would be awful. We're not sure how the church could come to an end without destroying the lives of everyone inside."

"We're still hopeful, though," I said. "We think our best chance is that someone will be able to get through to the people in the church. What we really hope is that we can find a way to do for our family what David helped do for me."

———

Two days later, having been unofficially adopted by both David and the Bookstein family, I returned to Deadwood alone. I loved the new members of our southern California family, but part of me was wounded that Grace had chosen to stay in Los Angeles with Rabbi Yonah and Rachel and the kids. I remembered that Libby had felt the same way when I'd chosen to stay in Deadwood. "I feel like you're choosing strangers over family," she had accused me during a phone call, her voice breaking. *Don't you understand?* I'd thought. *It's not a decision meant to hurt you. I just can't be there.* When it came to Grace, I wouldn't keep repeating the pattern we'd learned at Westboro—the tendency to moralize every decision as good or evil, the wielding of guilt and the withholding of affection to control the people I loved. Sometimes, a person just needed to do what was right for them.

I tried to focus on the good that might come of my sister's absence. Maybe it would lift some of the pressure off our relationship. Maybe we needed a little space to grow on our own, rather than trying to live as a unit. Because we shared a bank account and the car I'd bought a few years earlier, our sisterhood sometimes felt more like a marriage, and the confusion was a source of strife between us. Sometimes it seemed that Grace wanted me to be a big sister, sometimes a substitute parent. She resented needing me for anything and was desperate for independence, but she relied on me for practical skills she hadn't yet developed. My need to take care of and protect her was so strong that I was having a hard time distinguishing between us, always speaking in terms of "we" and "us" and "ours." Sometimes it felt like we were the same person.

"No," Laura said emphatically when I told her this, "the two of you are *so* different." I was bewildered by this declaration, honestly believing the exact reverse. "I think this will be good for both of you."

And it was. Even though I felt awkward and anxious without Grace by my side, even though I would never have chosen to be apart from her, I realized that it was nice to have some space to myself. I started spending time with my coworkers at TDG—long conversations about politics and human nature with Jack, fierce games of volleyball with Brittany and Amanda and the boys. I was heartened when a man claiming to be a member of Anonymous called the office to threaten me, and one of my coworkers responded by lambasting him, standing up for me and telling the man that I was a good person. I also became closer with Dustin and Laura, who would remain two of my closest friends long after I left Deadwood, long after they left the Jehovah's Witnesses and joined me in the wandering path of doubt and skepticism and confusion and wonder and awe at how different the world was than we had believed. When we compared stories of our unraveling faith, I was struck by the similarities. In the same way I had been perplexed by the arbitrariness of the different modesty standards among Westboro families—*How could the standards of God differ from house to house?*—Dustin had been confounded by the Witness prohibition on movies with an "R" rating. In the United States, that meant *The Matrix* was forbidden—but when he saw the film on the shelf of a Witness in the U.K., an elder explained that the rating system in that country was different. For both Dustin and me, one of the earliest sources of doubt had been incredibly trivial matters that highlighted internal inconsistency and a deeper issue—a dawning awareness of human perception coloring and altering apparently divine laws. In the stories of others departing similar high-control groups, I would notice this pattern again and again: an "unshakable faith" first called into question by the group's failure to live up to its own standards.

And then I finally—*finally*—met Chad.

He had declared he'd come to the play and then failed to show, and I had nearly decided that he was a lost cause. That he didn't really want to meet me. That it was all just some sort of imaginary friendship for him. That this whole thing really *was* an episode of *Catfish*. Three times in as many months he had told me he'd be in Deadwood and would see me, and three times he had failed to appear. I'd spent those months making excuses for his behavior, rationalizing and justifying his neglect: "What respectable person *would* want anything to do with someone with a past like mine? Whatever the reason, a girl who'd tormented grieving families at funerals and liberally tossed around epithets like 'fag' isn't the one to bring home to Mom."

Still, I was wholly unable to grasp why he refused to just *tell* me that. I must have seemed insane to him, expressing my undying love in one breath and begging him to please just let me off the hook in the next, to just admit that this wasn't going anywhere so that I could move on with my miserable life. I was in the throes of obsession and despair that I suppose is typical of an unrequited first love, so *I* certainly wasn't going to act the part of the sane, rational, self-respecting one. After the third misfire, though, I could not ignore what was painfully, devastatingly apparent: his dereliction was no accident.

> **MEGAN:** Chad? Tell me sometime. I can be patient. I just don't want to chase something that doesn't want to be caught. I'm almost convinced that's what I'm doing.

To my great amazement and relief, he finally materialized the weekend after the Jewlicious Festival. I had been cut off from my family for more than four months by then, and had been slammed repeatedly into the outermost threshold of my capacity for heartbreak and rejection. Just at the point when I thought I would lose my mind from hurt, shame, and rage—at myself, mostly, for having believed his sweet words when I knew in the smallest parts of myself that I didn't deserve to have someone care about me like that, that I didn't deserve any good thing in this life—Chad texted from a casino in town and said that I should come meet him there.

It was 10:30 P.M., and I was livid. In the back of my mind was a niggling worry about what he'd think of me, whether he'd be disappointed, but I had no mental energy to process it. Instead, my circuits were overloaded with humiliation and anger: we had obviously arrived at the portion of the program where the catfisher pretends to finally

follow through with a meeting and then stands up his foolish victim
for the last time. I was incensed at the thought, and I *absolutely was not
going to take another moment of this sham* if it turned out to be another
evasion. I had every intention of following through with the threat I
issued in response to Chad's invitation.

> **MEGAN:** If I leave my comfy bed and come there and don't
> see you, I'm so never talking to either one of us again!

I changed out of my pajamas and made my way through the crowds
dressed for St. Patrick's Day—it was March 16, the night Deadwood
was having its holiday pub crawl. The casino was packed with people
alive with alcohol, roaring with laughter in outlandish green costumes,
and I had no idea how to find him. He must have been watching the
door, because after a few moments, he stood up at one of the blackjack tables with a sheepish look, almost apologetic. I recognized him
instantly from across the room—too tall, too blond, and too like his
photo to be anyone else—and my anger evaporated. I slipped through
the throng, following him to a less populated corner of the room where
we sat down at adjacent slot machines and began to talk.

The chaos surrounding us dissolved as I watched him in the garish
lights of the casino floor. I couldn't take in anything but him. Some
remote corner of my mind noted that his gray pullover and lean, mus-
cular frame made him look like a college frat boy, but it was his face
that held my gaze: the blue eyes, the half smile, the blond curls that
fell over his forehead. I noticed these things, but most of my attention
was spent in a struggle to assimilate the reality of his existence. That
he was, in fact, corporeal. He didn't say it, but I surmised that he *was*
still afraid of me—of our age difference, afraid I'd meet him just this
once and then bail, afraid that *I* would reject *him*. Preposterous. For
two hours we tried to feel each other out, both of us quiet and cautious, laughing and talking about everything except what we really
wanted to. Just like our days of Words With Friends chats, our conversation was entirely chaste, decorous—"appropriate," as my family
would say. I did manage to ask for a hug at one point. It was clear from
his body language that he thought this a strange request—he kept
glancing anxiously over his shoulder to the table where his friends were

still playing blackjack—but he got up to oblige me. He stood nearly a foot taller than me and he didn't bend down, so my face was pressed awkwardly into his chest. I didn't mind. I inhaled slowly and closed my eyes.

It wasn't the embrace I'd dreamed about back in Topeka so many hopeless months before—the city was wrong, and the season, his hands weren't in my hair and it was midnight instead of noontime—but it was a damn good start. I said a simple goodbye, left him to his cards, and headed back out into the night.

—

The rest of the year felt like sprinting in slow motion, urgent and constant movement that made the hours pass like deep breaths. The odometer hadn't quite reached five thousand miles the day my Pontiac pulled out of its spot on the Phelps-Roper driveway for the last time, and by the time November 11 rolled around again, more than forty thousand miles of cornfields, mountains, Midwestern thunderstorms, and Canadian countryside had raced past my windows. Grace rejoined me in Deadwood after five weeks in Los Angeles, only to leave again a few weeks later, our orbits converging and diverging as we tried to understand who we were and what it might mean to live a good life outside of Westboro's paradigm. Every tenuous connection we'd made to the world while at the church suddenly became a lifeline, pulling us along from place to place, and into communities of people we'd learned to despise—from Bible studies with Christians in icy Des Moines, to Yiddish classes and volunteer work at the Jewish Federation in Montreal; from walking a former Westboro member down the aisle at her wedding in Connecticut, to supporting my former Twitter enemy Chad Darnell at the screening of his new film at the Kansas City LGBT Film Festival.

Month after month, my sister and I continued to drift around the country, never spending more than a few days or a few weeks at a time in any one place. We supported ourselves on the money we'd saved at Westboro, with Grace's excess scholarship funds from her university, with an insurance settlement for damage done to my car by a wicked hailstorm in the Black Hills, and with part-time jobs we found—Grace working as an assistant at a daycare center, while I worked remotely for TDG and did freelance administrative work I found online.

But more than anything, the sustaining force behind this period of wandering was our family and friends, friends of friends, even friends of friends of friends, people who opened their homes to us and helped us learn to see the world from many perspectives.

In the midst of my travels and several weeks after our St. Patrick's Day adventure in Deadwood, Chad called to ask me out on my first date ever. We met for dinner in Omaha the following week, and caught an opening-weekend showing of—what else?—*The Great Gatsby*. It was a cool evening and everything was foreign to me, each sensation making it difficult for me to find my breath: the warmth of his big hand as it enveloped mine; the drumbeat of my pulse when he wrapped his arm around my waist; the way my whole body seemed to melt at being kissed for the first time. I knew I never wanted to say goodbye, but we did, and I cried after he left. He went home to South Dakota, and I returned to California to visit the Booksteins.

Two weeks later, I drove twenty-two hours straight from Los Angeles to Deadwood to see him. He made the six-hour drive to meet me that weekend, and we met up nearly every weekend of my first summer away from home. We explored the wild of the Black Hills all season long, my elation tempered only by the knowledge that my parents would be dismayed by the path I had chosen. Instead of becoming habituated to Chad's visits, I found each one more improbable than the last. As I came to know him, it became clear that just about every part of his existence made our relationship so unlikely that it should have been impossible. He had painstakingly built for himself a successful life and career, arranging it all to be as simple and quiet and predictable as possible. Understanding how intensely he valued privacy, the lengths to which he went to eschew attention, how little of himself he tended to reveal to others, I couldn't help but marvel that he had ever shared anything with me while I was still at Westboro. He marveled, too, with that particular smile he'd get—awe mixed with disbelief— when he couldn't seem to grasp the reality of us. "Why are you *here*?" he'd balk, searching my face as if an answer might be discovered in the blue of an iris or the curve of a cheekbone. *"How?"*

That question became my obsession, too, and the further I ventured from the constraints of Westboro's belief system, the more I found myself looking back across what seemed to be an ever-widening gulf, wondering how others might be able to traverse it. I remembered how much sense the church's beliefs had made to me while I was a member, and became fixated on trying to pinpoint exactly where Westboro's error lay—and most important, how to communicate my changing perspective to my family in a way that they could hear, and wouldn't just dismiss out of hand. I read through their tweets and sermons compulsively, challenging myself to articulate both sides of the argument: why Westboro held each of their positions, and why I no longer did. In some cases, the distance between us felt too vast to even make an attempt at persuasion—rushing directly into casting doubt on a literal interpretation of the Bible, for instance, would certainly go nowhere. Instead, I let my arguments be guided by the pattern that had worked with me, with Dustin and Laura, and with others whose stories I was coming to learn: the discovery of internal inconsistency and hypocrisy as an important first step in seeing outside of group dogma.

Though my arguments largely went unanswered, I made them to Westboro members via interviews, on Twitter, and through private messages. Coming up against their wall of certainty was often a frustrating and painful exercise, and not just because of the callousness and condescension that so often filled their rhetoric. At Westboro, any admission that we might be wrong about any doctrine was accompanied by intense shame and fear. If we reversed course on any issue, we did so quietly, never admitting publicly to our mistakes. From our point of view, acknowledging error and ignorance was anathema, because doing so would cast doubt on our message. While I engaged church members as an outsider, I started to understand that doubt was the *point*—that it was the most basic shift in how I experienced the world. Doubt was nothing more than epistemological humility: a deep and practical awareness that outside our sphere of knowledge there existed information and experiences that might show our position to be in error. Doubt causes us to hold a strong position a bit more loosely, such that an acknowledgment of ignorance or error doesn't crush our sense of self or leave us totally unmoored if our position proves untenable. Certainty is the opposite: it hampers inquiry and hinders growth. It teaches us to ignore evidence that contradicts our ideas, and encourages us to defend our position at all costs, even as it reveals itself as indefensible. Certainty sees compromise as weak, hypocritical, evil, suppressing empathy and allowing us to justify inflicting horrible pain on others.

Doubt wasn't the sin, I came to believe. It was the arrogance of certainty that poisoned Westboro at its foundations.

Whenever friends and family expressed concern about my continued focus on the church and the past, I would gently dismiss them—but inwardly, I began to wonder if my identity would be forever tied to Westboro. Would I ever be truly free of it? Should I be doing more to try to extract myself from anything related to them?

For several reasons, I ultimately answered these questions with an emphatic *no*. First, when I stopped to consider the idea, I realized that I didn't *want* to be free of them—and that it didn't seem possible anyway, not without rewriting or erasing most of my history. Attempting to do so would have been inauthentic, the denial of a truth that David had been quick to recognize and point out: that the church had made me who I was, including many of the best parts of me. "You left out of principle," David had told Grace and me, "pretty much the same principles you were raised with. And your departure was both a rejection and an affirmation of everything you were taught. *You are your parents' children*." Weeping, I had asked him how he could possibly say such a thing. We were betrayers. "In a way," he said, "leaving Westboro Baptist Church was the most Westboro Baptist Church thing you could have done. They're the ones who taught you to stand up for what you believe in, no matter what it cost you. *They* taught you that. They just never imagined you'd be standing up to them."

I also fundamentally disagreed with the characterization that I was "focused on the past." Though I occasionally found myself litigating old grievances, my examinations of the past felt urgent precisely because this was a *present* and *future* issue. My family remained stuck in a pattern of thinking and behavior that inflicted unnecessary harm on themselves and on the communities they continued to target every single day. As someone who had contributed to that harm for so long, I felt an obligation to those communities to work to dismantle it from the outside. As the longtime recipient of so much love, attention, and care from my family, for me to simply abandon them seemed like the height of ingratitude, a failure to reflect the kind of person my parents raised me to be: strong in the face of difficulties, willing to do hard things and make sacrifices for those I love. And as someone who had learned to see Westboro's ideology from both sides of the divide, I couldn't help feeling that it would be an abdication of responsibility and the waste of a gift to turn my back on a problem into which I may have some useful insight. I didn't want to become the embodiment of the example from the book of James: *For if any be a hearer of the word, and not a doer, he is like unto a man beholding his natural face in a glass: For he beholdeth himself, and goeth his way, and straightway forgetteth what manner of man he was.* To have been transformed by the gentle, persistent entreaties of strangers—and then to walk away and forget that example, to refuse to extend that same courtesy and grace to others? Brutish.

But perhaps the most important reason I couldn't just leave it all behind was the lesson that began to crystallize in my mind from my very first night in Deadwood, talking with Cora at the bar inside the Four Aces Casino:

Westboro is not unique.

The church's garish signs lend themselves to this view of its members as crazed doomsayers, cartoonish villains who celebrate the calamities of others with fiendish glee. But the truth is that the church's radical, recalcitrant position is the result of very common, very *human* forces—everything from fear, family, guilt, and shame, to cognitive dissonance and confirmation bias. These are forces whose power affects us all, consciously and subconsciously, to one degree or another at every stage of our lives. And when these forces are coupled with group dynamics and a belief system that caters to so many of our most basic needs as human beings—a sense of meaning, of identity, of purpose, of reward, of goodness, of community—they provide group members with an astonishing level of motivation to cohere and conform, no matter the cost.

Others with stories like mine have shown me repeatedly that the root of Westboro's ideology—the idea that our beliefs were *"the* one true way"—is not by any means limited to Westboro members. In truth, that idea is common, widespread, and on display everywhere humans gather, from religious circles to political ones. It gives a comforting sense of certainty, freeing the believer from existential angst and providing a sense of stability—a foundation on which to build a life. But the costs of that certainty can be enormous and difficult to identify. Ultimately, the same quality that makes Westboro so easy to dismiss—its extremism—is also what helps highlight the destructive nature of viewing the world in black and white, the danger of becoming calcified in a position and impervious to change.

Though their ideologies manifested in vastly different ways, it was fundamentalist religious groups, from Jehovah's Witnesses to members of the Islamic State, that first permitted me to recognize the patterns of my upbringing. But as I watch the human tribal instinct play out in the era of Donald Trump, the echoes of Westboro are undeniable: the division of the world into *Us* and *Them*; the vilification of compromise; the knee-jerk expulsion of insiders who violate group orthodoxy; and the demonization of outsiders and the inability to substantively engage with their ideas, because we simply cannot step outside of our own. In this environment, there is a growing insistence that opposing views must be silenced, whether by the powers of government, the self-regulation of social media companies, or the self-censorship of individuals. At the heart of this insistence lie several false assumptions, including a sentiment that Westboro members would readily recognize: *We have nothing to learn from these people.* This sentiment was troubling to witness even among our tiny fringe movement, and I was relieved to abandon it when I left the church—but watching it spread among a vast and growing populace has been altogether more alarming, filling me with a growing sense of unease.

Another assumption gaining particular traction is that refusing to grant mainstream platforms to hated ideas will halt their spread. While the desire to shield people from these ideas is well-intentioned and completely understandable, I can't help but see it as a fundamentally flawed strategy, one that ignores the practicalities of human nature. The fact is that people come to embrace these ideas in a multitude of ways: some argue themselves into destructive beliefs; others come to them as I did, taught by parents and loved ones; still others find them in books, films, and the annals of history. Especially in the age of the Internet, it seems clear that we cannot reasonably expect to permanently halt the spread of an idea, whether good or bad. What we *can* do, however, is foster a culture in which we have the language to articulate and defend sound arguments as to why certain ideas are harmful, the precise ways in which they're flawed, and the suffering they have caused in the past.

Although private companies like Twitter and Facebook are clearly free to set the terms of use for their platforms, the principles enshrined in the First Amendment are no less relevant to social media than they are in public spaces: that open discourse and dialectic is the most effective enabler of the evolution of individuals and societies. That the answer to bad ideas is to publicly reason against them, to advocate for and propagate better ones. And that it is dangerous to vest any central authority with broad powers to limit the bounds of acceptable discussion—because these powers lend themselves to authoritarian abuse, the creation of echo chambers, and the marginalization of ideas that are true but unpopular. In short, the principles underlying the freedom of speech recognize that *all* of us are susceptible to cognitive deficiencies and groupthink, and that an open marketplace of ideas is our best defense against them. And though my life's trajectory has led me to strongly believe in these principles, I continue to actively seek out, examine, and seriously consider the arguments of those who oppose them. To my mind, this is the essence of *epistemological humility*—not a lack of belief or principle or faith, not the refusal to take a position or the abdication of responsibility to stand against injustice, but a constant examination of one's worldview, a commitment to honestly grappling with criticisms of it.

Along with so many others, I now watch the increasing hostility and hysteria of our modern political discourse and wonder how we, as a society, might change course. I consider the impending arrival of the baby girl I will shortly bring into the world with Chad—now, impossibly, my husband—and wonder how we'll teach her to avoid falling into these destructive patterns in her own life. And though my experiences at Westboro would have been sufficient on their own to fix these questions in my mind, nothing has made me pursue them with greater urgency than witnessing the devastating end of my beloved Gramps.

———

One year after my appearance at the Jewlicious Festival, I was back with David in Los Angeles for another. My phone rang, and the voice on the other end of the line was my brother Zach, recently departed from Westboro. The tears running down my face were a mixture of happiness at having my brother back, and grief at the thought of my parents and siblings facing yet another void in the Phelps-Roper family. Another empty room in the home we'd shared for so long. I asked my brother the eternal question—Why?—and listened as he described a disillusionment that was achingly familiar to me.

But I had another question.

"Zach, what's going on with Gramps? I've been checking the church website for months, and he hasn't been giving any sermons. Is he okay?"

My brother's voice dropped almost to a whisper. "Well . . . he . . . uh . . ." Zach stammered. "He's in hospice."

My heart stopped. My grandfather had believed that he was never going to die. That Jesus would return and bring him to Glory before that could ever happen. He'd said it so often that it seemed a foregone conclusion even then, even though I scarcely believed in God anymore.

". . . and he was voted out of the church."

Neither of us said anything for a few minutes as I sobbed at the image of my grandfather sick and dying and alone in a hospice bed. At the unparalleled cruelty of my family, which had somehow grown even worse since my departure, consuming even Gramps himself. *But if ye bite and devour one another, take heed that ye be not consumed one of another.* I had been pacing the sidewalk in front of the Booksteins' home, walking across the elaborate chalk paintings that Grace and I had done with their children. The same sorts of drawings we'd done with my siblings, cousins, nieces, and nephew back in Topeka. I sank to the ground, pants covered in chalk, face covered with tears, ignoring the stares from groups of twelve-year-old Jewish girls walking by in their long skirts and opaque tights. And again, I put the question to my brother. *Why?*

I disconnected the call a few minutes later and returned to the Booksteins' Shabbat table, sitting across from David.

"What's wrong?" he asked immediately. I shook my head, unable to speak.

"Would it make you happy if something bad happened to my Gramps?" I finally managed to choke out. I hoped the answer was no. I thought it would be. I knew that my Gramps had taught us to celebrate the tragedies of our enemies—that many would see this outcome as his just comeuppance—but that very idea was one of the reasons I had left Westboro. I couldn't bear the thought of anyone celebrating this. Especially a good friend.

"Of course not!" David insisted. "Why would I be happy?" When I told him what had happened, he said he would pray for my Gramps. And when he returned home to Jerusalem the following week, he would go to the Wailing Wall and put a note in it asking God to help my Gramps. "I hope and pray he gets well."

Instead of returning to my new home with Chad in South Dakota, I flew to Kansas with Grace, terrified that Gramps would pass before we had a chance to see him. Zach had given us the name of the hospice, and I knew that our best chance at seeing our grandfather would be to show up unannounced. As in the months before I left Westboro, I hated the sneaking around. The church would not want us to see him, and my fear of defying them was still almost paralyzing—but we were his grandchildren. *We* were his family, too. The miles from Kansas City to Topeka passed in the snowy darkness of midnight, Grace sleeping in the passenger seat as I made my case, my inner monologue growing more outraged by the second. The people charged with my grandfather's care had cast him out of their family—out of his own church—after all these years. They had isolated him in his most vulnerable hours after a lifetime surrounded by his wife, children, grandchildren, and great-grandchildren. They were using his last days to punish and cajole him into "repentance." And after all of that, they would surely prevent us from seeing him—the only people willing to sit by his side, to offer a comforting presence to a dying man, largely abandoned by those he had loved and trusted—all so that they could maintain control of a narrative in their minds and in the media. I could already hear them talking dismissively among themselves: *We don't owe these people anything.* They didn't answer to anyone, least of all us.

Pulsing through me was an unmitigated disgust for my family, frightening in its intensity. Had Gramps still been a member of the church, there would have been another member keeping vigil at his bedside at all hours of the day and night—talking with him, reading with him, singing with him. I gripped the steering wheel so hard my nails bit into my palms, weeping bitterly at the thought of the church sentencing him to live out his final days alone, confused, and afraid. Not even I would have envisioned them sinking to such depths of cruelty.

I found Zach the following afternoon and spent an hour reading text messages on his phone, following the progression of my grandfather's illness—and his status within the church—from day to day. In the beginning, my family's words were full of tenderness and praise. "We should all be very thankful," my uncle wrote, "that we have a faithful pastor who genuinely cares for our souls and has—at great personal lifelong sacrifice—fed us with the manna of God's word without dilution." I read on through the weeks and months as the tenderness disappeared, replaced by a cold and clinical distance. After my grandfather was stripped of his role as pastor and of church membership, most other members ended all contact with him, as required. And when his health deteriorated further, one of his daughters was designated to handle his care and send daily updates to a select group of trusted church members—my brother Zach among them—while the rest were kept largely in the dark. They couldn't desert him *entirely* to Topeka's medical establishment, lest word of his illness and abandonment find its way into the newspapers that had been closely watching for signs of his demise for at least a dozen years.

My aunt's messages stopped the day that Zach left, of course, but they were enough. More than a month of daily reports while Gramps had been in professional care. In addition to his many physical problems, the messages spoke of "cognitive decline," "dementia," and failing organs that sometimes led to a state of "delirium." When his body began to improve, a doctor warned that my grandfather would likely not show improvement in his cognition unless he was motivated to, suggesting that the presence of more familiar and comforting voices would help—but Westboro continued its campaign of isolation. My grandfather's mental condition would be on his death certificate two weeks later, as well, not the cause of death—respiratory failure, pneumonia—but a "significant condition contributing to death": encephalopathy. Disease of the brain, as Google explained, manifested by an altered mental state. Zach described some of the symptoms that ultimately contributed to my grandfather's exclusion from the church, and it was abundantly clear that some of his actions were so strange and out of character that he could not possibly have been in his right mind in those moments.

With other symptoms, though, it seemed that his actions weren't ravings but genuine changes in his perspective, particularly as it related to the church. According to Zach, my grandfather had come to see his congregation as cruel and unmerciful. I remembered my despair at coming to the same conclusion when I was painting in that dank basement: *as if we were finally doing to ourselves what we had been doing to others.* I believed Zach's assessment, because in the months before I left Westboro, my grandfather had been one of the few men in the church who was encouraging more kindness, gentleness, and compassion. *Only by pride cometh contention*, the verse said, and after the new elders took over, Gramps had quoted and paraphrased it often. "If there is no pride, there will be no contention," he intoned. "Where there is great humility, there will be no contention." As if he were trying to reform the beast he had created.

But it was too late. He had spent decades inculcating us with an ideology that valued fear and control over mercy and grace. He was the one who had taught church members to have unshakable faith in their own perspective, to believe their judgment was as *God's* judgment, with de facto status as infallible. Not even my grandfather could stop the course he had set in motion. *Though we, or an angel from heaven, preach any other gospel unto you than that which we have preached unto you, let him be accursed.* Gramps was the heretic now. His illness was proof not of his age, but that God had condemned him. To church members, dementia was the *result* of my grandfather's strange behavior, rather than its cause. *If he were a man of God,* the argument went, *then he wouldn't have this illness.*

I thought of the blind man of John 9. *And his disciples asked him, saying, Master, who did sin, this man, or his parents, that he was born blind? Jesus answered, Neither hath this man sinned, nor his parents: but that the works of God should be made manifest in him.* The story—along with the entire book of Job—showed clearly that not all illness was punishment for sin.

Westboro knew better, though.

Shortly before he was removed from church membership, as Zach told me, our grandfather had stepped out the front door of the church to address the young people running the Equality House across the street. A nonprofit called Planting Peace had bought the house in 2012 and painted it in the colors of the rainbow, the global symbol of the LGBT rights movement. It was a perpetual monument standing in opposition to the church and its message of judgment and damnation. "You're good people," Gramps called out to them from across the street, before he was hustled back inside by Westboro members. At the church meeting where he was excommunicated, the elders gave this incident as the clearest evidence of my grandfather's heresy—*casting his lot in with the Sodomites*—and judged that he was lucid when it occurred.

Given all the harm Gramps had sown during his life, I knew that many would find an end-of-life change of heart to be too little, too late. That if they could witness his devastating end, some would rejoice in it the same way that he had done to others for so many years. They would see my family's cruel treatment of him as righteous recompense for a man who beat his wife and children into submission, who used his considerable resources to attack and antagonize the world without compunction. I could already hear their arguments, and though I wanted to defend him—"But his decades of civil rights work!"— I had no real rebuttal. Still, I couldn't stop the overwhelming sense of hope that washed over me. My own change of heart and mind had already made me optimistic about the same potential in others—and now with evidence that even someone like Gramps could experience this kind of change, the idea of completely writing *anyone* off seemed senseless.

After I hugged Zach and handed his phone back to him, I picked Grace up from school and pointed my car to the Midland Hospice House. I drove past Gage Park and the corner where we had first taken our signs to the streets, past the pond where my father had taken us to feed the ducks when we were kids, and pulled my car into the most remote section of the hospice parking lot—just in case my aunt showed up. Grace and I stepped out and looked at each other across the hood of the car, assessing. What was out of place? Our earrings, we decided. We removed them while debating whether Grace should put her hair up. "It doesn't look cut!" she insisted. We didn't want to upset him.

The woman who greeted us at the front door looked suspicious when I asked for Fred Phelps. "And you are . . . ?"

"His granddaughters," I said firmly.

She looked doubtful. "Let me check with his nurse."

The nurse rounded the corner a moment later. "You're the one who called from California?" she asked. I was. The nurse gave me a sad little half smile, nodded, and led us down the hall to the door of his room. "This is him."

I put my hand on the doorknob and paused. "Is he . . . lucid?" I asked.

"Yeah. At times, he is. At times, he is."

I nodded and stepped carefully into my grandfather's room. The waning light of dusk drifted in through the window over his bed, brightened by the warm glow of a few lamps scattered around the room. The television was on, as so often it had been in his bedroom back home, but he wasn't paying attention to it. Grace stood just outside the door, waiting to see how he would respond. Would he be happy to see us? Or was he of a mind to rejoin the church, viewing our visit as a hindrance to that goal? Was the disdain he felt the day I left still seething? My heart clenched at the thought. His last words to me still reverberated often in my thoughts, that bitter, biting tone. *I thought we had a jewel this time.* The last thing I wanted was to dredge up bad memories for him. If he showed any sign of being upset at our presence, we would leave immediately.

But there were no such signs. The head of his bed was elevated, and when I approached, he looked over at me with recognition and welcome. I couldn't understand almost anything he tried to say at first—he was so weak, his mouth so dry, his voice so far from the booming proclamations he had delivered from the pulpit all those years. But his eyes seemed aware, and he laughed at me when I tried to interpret his words. I gave him water when he pointed to his glass, and told him that Grace had come to see him, too. She came in a minute later.

We sat next to him on his bed, me by his side, she near his feet. We realized quickly that he was in and out of lucidity. In his mind, he seemed to be preaching in front of a congregation. He asked me to pass out the hymnals. He wanted to sing. I knew the song as soon as he started quoting the lyrics: *When peace like a river attendeth my way /*

when sorrows like sea billows roll. I searched YouTube and pressed play. "It Is Well With My Soul." A friend would tell me later that it was a popular funeral hymn. The three of us sang along with the music, Gramps oblivious to the tears pouring down our faces. He prayed to God in thanks for the church and for His help. I held his hand while he started to preach a wedding sermon.

A little time, and he seemed to be in a different place mentally.

"Brothers and sisters," he said gravely, "I hope you believe that I'm doing my best, and that I'll continue to do more with pleasure and privilege. I'm not a threat." He looked at me. I told him that I believed him, and squeezed his hand tight. I imagined him at the center of one of those godforsaken disciplinary meetings. I hated their self-righteousness. I hated their sociopathic lack of empathy. Whatever God there might be, He was not in that place.

Gramps didn't seem to understand where he was until I told him about Libby. She had just given birth to her first child, a son. Paxton, meaning "peace." I showed him a photo, and he seemed to snap back to the present immediately. "Was he born yesterday?" he asked.

"Two days ago," I said. I told him we would all come back to see him tomorrow.

He said, "I remember her as a sweet little baby. Just a little baby. And now she's a mother." He asked how old she was now.

He looked at Grace and said, "Mama." He was asking about Gran. I told him that Gran loves him very much. His eyes found mine instantly and he said, "She said that?" I nodded and said yes. I'd heard her say it many times.

"Such a beautiful woman," he said. "I can never get over how beautiful Gran is. She's in all you grandchildren and great-grandchildren. So beautiful." He looked at Grace. "You look so young." He told her she looked tired. "You need to find a place to lie down."

He thanked us for coming to see him. He asked if we'd come back and said that he wouldn't hold it against us if we did, joking like his old self. I kissed his forehead, and he looked at me and said that we were wonderful grandchildren. Just wonderful. That we always were.

"Special," he said. "So special." I hugged him for a long time and cried with my cheek pressed against his chest. He lifted his hand and held my face while I did. And when I stood up, he motioned me down as if to kiss me. I put my cheek to his lips, and he kissed it several times quickly, the way he always had. "Muah, muah, muah, muah, muah." I did it back.

He looked at Grace and said, "Sugar, I just want you to know that I love you." She told him she loved him, too.

We kissed and hugged him again, and he kissed our cheeks, and we promised to come back tomorrow to see him, all of us unaware that the church would uncover our visit the next day and instruct the hospice to keep us—and every other visitor—away from him. He was drifting off to sleep as we left.

The sun was gone when my sister and I left the hospice, my car automatically steering its way back home. Driving around the block was always the last thing we did before leaving town. For over a year, we had been reaching out to our family here. To share with them the experiences that opened our minds. To remind them of passages we had so long ignored while we were together. To convince them that there were other ways. We knew the messages were unwelcome—not unlike Westboro's decades of protests—but we sent them anyway and would for years to come. We did not use the bombast of our grandfather or the florid insults of our mother, but the still, small voice I had learned from Chad, from David, from the sassy start-up employee in Chicago, and the hilarious Australian guy, people who learned the lesson that Margie had tried to teach me as a child. *A soft tongue breaketh the bone.* In the years that followed, I watched in amazement as the signs I most often argued against—PRAY FOR MORE DEAD SOLDIERS; PRAY FOR MORE DEAD KIDS; FAGS CAN'T REPENT—began to disappear from their repertoire, replaced by messages like CHRIST OUR STRENGTH and BE RECONCILED TO GOD. It was all the encouragement I needed to go on. Grace and I use tweets and letters and postcards to reach them, cupcake deliveries and birthday presents.

And just once, we used a sign.

For four years, it sat at the corner of 12th and Cambridge, right in the midst of our old neighborhood. A brand-new bus bench I had noticed on a similar drive just a few months after we left. It had been blank back then, except for a phone number to call if you wanted to buy the ad space. Grace and I had spent over a month trying to figure out what to put on it. What would we say to our loved ones living in the surrounding houses? What was the most important thing to tell them? To anyone driving past, the bench's message looked like a nonsense saying written in chalk paint, surrounded by brightly colored drawings that belonged in the pages of a children's book. To our family, it was a reminder. "Goldbugs forever," it read in Grace's loopy handwriting. A mistaken iPhone autocorrect for "good night" that became a saying among the siblings.

"Goldbugs, bro." "Goldbugs, sis."

A sweet way of saying *Good night. I love you.*

The drawings were for the children who couldn't read yet. The ones Grace had always drawn for them. The little sailboat on its choppy waters. The fat, floating bubble man stretching his arms out toward a heart. The jolly baby with a lollipop, a shirt too small to cover his belly, and a bib that read simply FOOD. The interconnected symbols of the sun, the flower, and the swirl. Grace, Bekah, and me, back together as we should be.

And on the back of the bench, a line from a story my sister read to us after Bible study one evening. Another Hans Christian Andersen.

There is always a clinging to the land of one's birth.

Gramps is gone now, buried unceremoniously in an unmarked grave under the Kansas sun. Yet his church remains. I'm just around the corner from it, right outside my old front door. Gran lives here now, with my mom and my dad and my brothers and my sister. Their hearts beat just inside. I can't knock, and I don't pray anymore, but I can wish that it all would end. That the walls they built to keep me out would vanish. I want to tell them that the world isn't evil. That it's full and complicated and beautiful and good, filled with unknown truths and unbroken hopes, and that it's waiting just for them. That I'm waiting just for them. I want to tell them that I love them.

I'll just have to find another way.

Acknowledgments

This book began as an essay, written as a gift for my dearest C.G. Chad, I wouldn't have undertaken this project without your unwavering belief in me, your honest and tactful criticism, and your willingness to walk with me through the difficulties. I love your mind, and can't believe I get to have you as my first reader.

My friend and mentor Eric McHenry played an instrumental role in bringing this book to life. Eric, when I first asked you to edit that essay back in 2014, my only goal was to write something beautiful for the man I loved—but with your endless encouragement, it became something more. I have no idea where I'd be if you hadn't been so willing to share your writerly wisdom, to read so many of my ugly first drafts, to connect me with a wonderful editor who became *my* wonderful editor, and to write on my behalf to literary agents. Given how reluctant I was to write about my life, I have every reason to believe that this book wouldn't exist without you. I am forever in your debt!

And now, to contain my loquacity and in homage to my favorite social media platform, tweet-length expressions of gratitude:

To my brilliant editor, Alex Star—You gave me the book's structure the day we met, and expertly molded the text each time you touched it.

Mel Flashman, literary agent extraordinaire—I couldn't have asked for an advocate more enthusiastic and equipped (in all ways!) than you.

Richard Arcus, Elizabeth Masters, Ana McLaughlin, Laura McKerrell – I am astounded by your excellence and passion for the project. Thank you.

Adrian Chen—I've never known a more thorough reporter. The depths of our conversations made my thinking and writing infinitely clearer.

Willing Davidson—The title you gave Adrian's profile in *The New Yorker* was truly inspired. Thank you for sharing it with this book.

Keith Newbery—We wouldn't have lasted nearly as long without you. Existential heroines forever. (P.S. Everyone follow @TchrQuotes!)

David Abitbol—Your guidance and friendship have shaped so much of the life I've made. You helped me find my voice, and I owe you much.

Laura Floyd—Darling! The attention with which you read is astounding, and this book benefited enormously from your keen eye. I adore you!

Dustin Floyd—From Yellowstone to NY to Israel, discussing ideas with you and Laura has clarified much for me. Thanks for going the distance.

Louis Theroux—Your thoughts and questions on early drafts were insightful and important to the life of this book. I appreciate every word.

Andy Mills—You're an extraordinary friend and teller of stories, and I'm grateful for the time we spend discussing ours. You are invaluable.

Dana Meinch—Thank you for teaching me how to be a good human, to set boundaries, to question assumptions, and to remember who's on my team.

Rabbi Yonah, Rachel, Moshe, Tzofiya, Shlomo, and Nafi Bookstein—Your kindness and generosity of spirit are unsurpassed! An example to all.

Mike Savatovsky, Sarah Atkins, M., N., H.—Our month in MTL taught me intentionality and the magic of taking action—and chances. All my love.

Dortha, Mark, and Nate Phelps—Thank you for answering my questions about long-ago events. Dortha, you were so generous, and I am grateful.

Steve Fry and the *Topeka Capital Journal*—For opening the archives and shedding light on the early days, thank you very kindly.

To my early readers—Tom Kenat, Mike Savatovsky, Brittan Heller, Karrie Fjelland, too many to name, but you know who you are: Thank you!

And finally, to the family who have been my everything:

Josh Phelps-Roper—Going through this process with you has helped me heal in ways I didn't know I needed. You are a rock, dear brother.

Zach Phelps-Roper—Your comments on this text were full of wisdom and comedic relief. You and your sweet disposition are a light to me.

Grace Phelps-Roper—I still aspire to the "wondrous things" you wrote of so long ago. Thank you for sharing your adventurous spirit with me.

Nana Toews and Grandpa Fundis—I now know whence my dad got much of his goodness. Thank you for the love and thought you've given this book.

Stephanie, Gabe, Asher, and Emmie Roper—Your presence in my life has been unparalleled joy & lightened the dark times. I love you dearly!

Sølvi Lynne Fjelland—You are the most precious gift, sweet dolly. The embodiment of joy. What a delight it is to be your mom.

Kurt, Karrie, Halle, Kate, and Jasper Fjelland—Halsnøy, the Hills, rocket ships, and princess cake. Oh, how I've loved joining this family!

Marlin and Joyce Fjelland—I couldn't be more grateful for your wild enthusiasm and love. Thank you for raising my beloved so wonderfully.

Sam, Bekah, Isaiah, Gabe, Jonah, Noah, and Luke—Our years together were a treasure, and I ever wish for more. I am lucky to be your sister.

To my beloved Gran—Having your name is a constant reminder of the gentle wisdom & patience you inhabit, & to which I aspire. I love you so.

To my padre—There isn't a day I don't think of the wonderful father you've been to me. Your absence is felt always.

And to my madre—Who could ever ask for the sacrifices you made for me? I will never have a greater teacher than you.

A NOTE ABOUT THE AUTHOR

Megan Phelps-Roper is a writer and an activist. Formerly a member of the Westboro Baptist Church, she left the church in November 2012 and is now an educator on topics related to extremism and communication across ideological divides. She lives in South Dakota with her husband, Chad, and daughter, Sølvi Lynne.